WAR AND SOCIETY IN RENAISSANCE EUROPE 1450–1620

J. R. HALE

McGill-Queen's University Press
Montreal & Kingston · London · Buffalo

© J.R. Hale 1985, 1998

ISBN 0-7735-1765-0

Legal deposit first quarter 1998
Bibliothèque nationale du Québec

First published in 1985 by Fontana Paperbacks.
This edition published simultaneously in the European Union by
Sutton Publishing Limited.

McGill-Queen's University Press acknowledges the support of the
Canada Council for the Arts for its publishing program.

Canadian Cataloguing in Publication Data

Hale, J.R. (John Rigby), 1923–
War and Society in Renaissance Europe, 1450–1620
(Fontana history of war and European society series)
Rev. ed.
Includes bibliographical references and index.
ISBN 0-7735-1765-0
1. Sociology, Military–Europe. 2. Europe–History, Military.
3. Renaissance. I. Title. II. Series.
U43.E95H35 1998   306.2'7'094'09031   C97-901202-5

Cover illustration: *The Capture of Parma, c. 1570,* by Tintoretto (Jacopo
Robusti). Alte Pinakothek, Munich/Bridgeman Art Library, London

Printed in Great Britain by
The Guernsey Press Company Limited,
Guernsey, Channel Islands.

Contents

Editor's Preface

The re-issue of a series of books after fifteen years' exploitation of its field invites justification and prompts reflection. The justification – other than what lies in the qualities of the books themselves – is simply that no comparable series has appeared to replace it. Our purpose was to sum up what had so far been achieved in the rather new study of 'war and society' and to make it available as an attractive accompaniment to the Fontana and other general series on the history of Europe and its empires. That we were right to sense a need for such enlargement of view on the military side, has been amply confirmed by the army of historians and history-minded social scientists who have continued active in the field, and whose relevant contributions will be duly noted in our revised reading lists. Some of them, especially in the United States, march under the banner of 'the new military history'; which however boils down to much the same thing as was meant by the 'war and society' pioneers, a generation ago. The more recent writers evidently having shared with the earlier ones the aim of distinguishing their historical operations from those of the 'old' military history, it seems worth while to reconsider what I wrote about the series' purposes and principles, fifteen years or so ago.

The 'war and society' movement took shape in the 1960s, to make good what had come to be felt as something missing in the traditional style of histories of wars and warfare. Although the latter had paid much attention to what armed forces did to one another in war, they normally showed little interest in how those armed forces related to the societies from which they were drawn and in what war itself – the experience of it while it was going on, the perhaps huge net effect of it once it was over – did to the societies which engaged in it. The years 1935–1945 were crucial to the new perception. Each of the Second World War's major participants experienced social mobilization on a scale of totality historically unprecedented. Even before it was over, official histories of it were being planned to do justice to everything that happened away from the firing lines as well as on them; and those who survived it tended to feel sure that it must have caused great social changes. Particular inquiries into this latter possibility were what brought to the forefront of the movement the historian who more than anyone else launched 'war and society' as a viable and (to the limited extent that any area of historical studies can be so) self-sufficient branch of historical studies. Arthur Marwick effected this notable step forward when his history department at the Open University produced in 1973 its famous third-year course 'War and Society', in which pretty well every apposite part of the field came into view. About five thousand students took this course during its six years' lifetime, the teaching units expressly produced for it acquired a wide circulation, and some of them remain among the best things so far written. (Nor is that the end of the story; over six thousand students have, by the time of writing, taken its successor 'War, Peace and Social Change'.)

This new approach to war history's popularity was no doubt partly because it offered to those who disliked war (numerous indeed after the Second World War, and subsequently under the shadow of nuclear weapons) a way of studying war without what seemed to them its rebarbative and retrogressive aspects. From certain morally committed standpoints the new approach might appear to be positively progressive. After all, it was happening during the same years as the movement within the social sciences to learn more about the causes of war – and thus a hoped-for preventability of war – than had been made apparent in the well-established genres of political and diplomatic history. From the traditional point of view, these were the very novelties and connections which invited criticism. Practitioners of military history proper, continuing to work within the parameters of the tradition, pointed out that the new fashion, too enthusiastically followed, failed to do justice to certain inescapable historical facts: for instance, that war was about the use of force, that force normally made itself felt as armed violence, and that books about war without the battles which usually brought it to a close were not to be taken seriously. That such books, ignoring what they did not like to recognize, did surface on the further edges of the field, cannot be denied. Our series, however, seeks to avoid such imbalance. Far from rejecting, we gladly acknowledge the parallel labours of those (one of the most distinguished of them, a contributor to this series) who prefer still to be known by the honourable title of military historian. Their campaigns and commanders, their armies and battles and the ways in which they were fought are all to be found here, in proportionate relation to the societies which supported them and which would in the natural course of events be affected by them. All that is missing is, inevitably, space to dwell as much on any of the many relevant aspects as keen inquirers may wish; and for them, our up-dated reading lists will show the way forward.

There are some passions for military history and war studies which the 'war and society' approach will never satisfy. Believing that the place of war in the world is best studied with as much detachment and objectivity as can be managed, it avoids the nationalistic and hyper-patriotic attitudes which were the norm in military history writing (one might just as well say, in national history writing) before the early twentieth century, and which continue to colour many of its popular productions. Nor can 'war and society' history appeal to men who find excitement and stimulus in tales of violence and in the contemplation of instruments of violence: all those guns and knives, etc. which fill a certain class of magazines and picture books, and which (along perhaps with innocent interests in military uniforms and model soldiers) are evidently what many 'militaria' fans alone are interested in. In the face of those interests, and in obvious contrast with them, our war and society approach is no doubt better suited to the interests of the peace-minded than the military enthusiast. There is no reason why it should not prove interesting to military persons – indeed, one volume in the series has seemed interesting enough to the Spanish Ministry of Defence to have been translated into their language – but it will not long hold the attention of the militaristic.

The attractiveness of the kind of war studies which this series has helped to popularize is no doubt partly because it matches the very common civilian feeling that war and soldiering – ancient, admirable and 'normal' though they may seem to be – are worth more critical inquiry than military men and their numerous admirers used to seem to like, and the not uncommon realization by thoughtful people that war and peace, after all, are two sides of the same medal. Ideal as a title would be 'peace, war and society'. That alone comprehends the two poles of moral and historical interest between which 'war and society' studies oscillate. Why do wars happen at all?, is a question much more likely to be in the mind of a historian now than it was before the Second World War. Like the post-war boom in 'conflict analysis and peace research', it is related to the preoccupations of the generation born under that shadow of the mushroom-shaped cloud.

But it is nothing new, that the more reflective of our humankind should ponder upon the idea of war itself. War and the imagination of it are the ultimate link between armed forces and society. Human society, politically organized, becomes a State; and States have traditionally distinguished themselves from other States, to put it bluntly, by their abilities to defend their borders and, should they be of the expanding sort, to extend them. Whether there is something congenital in the natures of men (I say 'men' deliberately, because women may be different) and States which impels them towards competitiveness and conflict, is an enormous field of inquiry which has for long engaged the attention of some of the most thoughtful and caring of our kind. The idea of war may, to many living now, have become repulsive, unnatural and essentially destructive. The historian has to note that this marks a big change from the past. War appeared in quite a different light through the greater part of history. It was the normal accompaniment of State-making and almost inevitably the means by which States gathered empires around them. Societies which benefited from these processes thought nothing wrong in them; societies which lost out, bemoaned only the failure of their fights to defend themselves. Win or lose, the literatures and traditional ethics and (if they had them) written histories of societies throughout all history before the twentieth century accepted war as a fact of international life and admired the heroes who were good at it. War may not wholly begin in the minds of men (a lot of it begins simply in material need or greed, and in the gross appetites attached thereto) but a good case can be made for saying that it begins there more than anywhere else. The idea of war therefore, the place of war in what the French and many of the rest of us call *mentalité*, is of itself a matter of giant historical importance: how at particular epochs and in particular societies the idea of war is diffused, articulated, coloured and connected. Only by way of that matrix of ideas about God and man, nature and society, can come full understanding of the causes of wars that have happened, and of the armed forces which have for the most part conducted them.

Ideas, then, we consider to matter at least as much as the social and economic history of war and of readiness for war; they form the, so to speak, cultural and material envelope within which exist the armed forces whose existence and activities lie at the centre of our common interest, and about which something more must be said. Armed forces are a very special sort of social organization. They can be more nearly 'complete societies' than any other of the 'secular' associations and interest groups which structure society within States so far as governments permit. Their internal life is by nature peculiarly structured, tough and ritualistic; their business – discipline, force, violence, war – makes them exceptionally formidable; by definition they subscribe to codes of behaviour – honour, loyalty, obedience, etc. – which emphasize their solidarity and reinforce their apparent differences from the societies beside and around them. It is not difficult to understand why so much that has been written about them (not least, by 'old' military historians) has treated them as if they were absolutely different and apart.

But of course they are by no means wholly so. Except in cases where an armed force or a coalition of armed forces succeeds in totally militarizing society, or where a 'war-minded' ideology possesses a whole society to the extent that every citizen is as much a soldier as any other, there are bound to remain differences and distinctions between armed forces on the one hand, and the societies from which they spring on the other. And yet, while there are differences and distinctions, there must also be relationships and interactions. So they can and to some extent must be studied 'on their own', because in their own right they tend to be so remarkable and influential; but in other respects their history, nature, and influence demands that they be studied in their relationship with the world they belong to. We try, within the limits of our enterprise, to acknowledge both demands.

War, to sum up, is a unique human interest and activity, with its own character, its own self-images, its own mystiques, its own forms or organization and, to crown all, a prime place in determining the standards of national societies and their political viability as States. Such is our case for picking out of the whole seamless web of history the scarlet warps of war, for putting the more social and cultural of them under a magnifying microscope, and for writing about them in a way which the general historical reader, who is not normally a 'military buff', will appreciate. This was brilliantly done in miniature by Michael Howard in his *War in European History* (1976), a few years before this series began to appear. At that time, there was not much of similarly relevant character that had to be pointed out besides his book, the pioneer classics by Alfred Vagts (*A History of Militarism, Civilian and Military*, 1937) and Preston and Wise (*Men in Arms: A History of Warfare and its Interrelationships with Western Society*, 1956), and such specialized periodicals as the American periodical *Armed Forces and Society* and the *War and Society Newsletter*, since 1975 an English-language annual supplement to the celebrated German periodical *Militärgeschichtliche Mitteilungen*, and an ideal way to scan everything that is published year by year. A good deal has come out since then (besides the Open University material already mentioned) and this general preface may appropriately close by highlighting some of the most useful items.

Conspicuous among the war-and-warfare publications of the past twenty years are some of encyclopaedic type, worth mentioning because they should be available in most libraries and because within their broad spans of coverage, particular war-and-society interests may find satisfaction. The most impressive is the improved English-language version of what was begun by the most eminent French historian in the field; it now appears as the *Dictionary of Military History and the Art of War*, edited by André Corvisier, revised and expanded by John Childs, translated by Christopher Turner (1994). Still international, but slighter and more conventional is Charles Townshend (ed.), *The Oxford Illustrated History of Warfare: the triumph of the west* (1995); of national interest merely are David Chandler (ed.), *The Oxford Illustrated History of the British Army* (1994) and John Pimlott (ed.), *The Guinness History of the British Army* (1993). Another feature of the past twenty years or so is the appearance of several periodicals dedicated to the history of war in its broader sense: probably most appropriate are the Australian *War and Society* and the British *War in History* and the *Imperial War Museum Review*.

Of the writing of long-span histories of war and/or warfare, especially by retired generals, there is no end; the only ones known to me as doing justice to the war-and-society aspects of the subject are, in their different ways, William H. McNeill, *The Pursuit of Power. Technology, Armed Forces and Society since AD 1000* (1983) and John Keegan, *A History of Warfare* (1993). Readers with an understandable curiosity as to how the outbreaks and conclusions of wars have been conditioned by the practices, customs and laws of the society of States, a.k.a. international society, within which they were all contained, will find instruction in F.H. Hinsley, *Power and the Pursuit of Peace* (1963), Kalevi J. Holsti, *Peace and War: Armed Conflicts and International Order, 1648–1989* (1991), and (though the title hardly suggests it) Martin Wight, *International Theory: The Three Traditions* (1991, ed. G. Wight and B. Porter). Two ambitious works of sociological inspiration with pockets of the suggestively relevant in them are: Michael Mann, *The Sources of Social Power* (2 v., 1986 and 1993), and David Evan Luard, *War in International Society* (1987). And it is good, at the last moment before going to press, to be able to mention Peter Paret's very instructive and finely illustrated book *Imagined Battles. Reflections of War in European Art* (1997), which begins in the Renaissance and comes right up to the present.

Geoffrey Best
Oxford, 1997

Author's Preface

Professor Lawrence Stone gave me the time to draft much of this book by inviting me to spend a semester at the Davis Center, Princeton University. Professor Geoffrey Parker most generously helped in the correction and reorganizing of that draft. Another greatly appreciated invitation to Princeton, to the Institute for Advanced Study, has enabled me to benefit from the advice of Professor John Elliott while correcting the proofs. The faults that remain are stubbornly mine. So is the responsibility for two maimings of the subject; I lack the lauguages which would give a sense of involvement with the countries north and east of Germany, and, I fear, the interest to deal adequately with naval affairs. I thank Professor Geoffrey Best not only for asking me to write for his series, but for showing a patience and understanding far beyond the normal call of an editor's duty. As notes have had to be kept to a minimum, I concentrate on identifying quotations. This means that conclusions arrived at by others have been exploited without specific acknowledgement. I can only hope that the bibliography will be seen as an expression of respect and gratitude towards the many authors on whose work I have built.

POSTSCRIPT

Since Sir John Hale completed this book over twelve years ago, Renaissance war studies have forged on with great vigour (see Addenda to the bibliography), but little has emerged which substantially revises the arguments it contains. Moreover, some of the principal works which elaborate on or extend what he then wrote are by himself. Perhaps the most important of these is his *Artists and Warfare in the Renaissance* (1990), which explores a subject the scope of which was too big to discuss in the present book and which had never been properly considered elsewhere, though it has already provoked a sequel (see Addenda, entry under Paret). Profusely illustrated, Hale's *Artists and Warfare* contrasts the 'culturally and pictorially mediated images of war' by Italian artists with the realistic, meant-to-shock, moralistic work of northern artists, which highlighted the vices and brutality of soldiers rather than condemned war itself. Hale's *The Civilization of Europe in the Renaissance* (1994) also stands out in the list, since he included on its vast canvas numerous further reflections on human conflict, discord and military organisation, or the want of it, during the same span of time which the present book covers.

Meanwhile, the volume of the subsequent literature has owned much to the very impact of what Hale had already written. This debt is acknowledged by Geoffrey Parker in the new (1996) edition of his own widely successful study *The Military Revolution: Military Innovation and the Rise of the West*: 'pride of place must go to the work of Sir John Hale, especially *Renaissance War Studies* and *War and Society*' (p. 246). Parker's book, first published in 1988, itself did much to generate new literature in the form of disputacious rejoinders and revisions, provoking the so-called 'military revolution debate' which turned very largely on chronological definitions (see entries under Black, DeVries, Hall, Rogers, etc.); Parker has also provided a twenty-page 'Afterword' as well as a bibliographical note. Perhaps it should be pointed out that Hale had deftly and presciently avoided the pitfall of using that highly charged word 'revolution', with its many connotations including a short time-span, by entitling his fifth chapter 'The Military Reformation'. Here the reader will find all the key topics: increasingly effective use of gunpowder, the prevalence of siege warfare and development of artillery fortresses, a huge increase in size of armies and in the complexity of logistics. In addition, the subject is enlivened by the author's characteristic range of vision, his particular skills of condensing deep knowledge and devising unexpected questions, penetrating observations and verbal imagery. For example, the notion of sixteenth-century armies as 'walking cities' (pp. 90–100), the reflection that the armies of Henri II of France 'contained more stomachs than Milan or almost than London' vividly summarise the implications of feeding, clothing, equipping, paying, and of medically and sexually servicing these mobile mixed societies.

Other bibliographical addenda to which attention needs to be drawn are, first, two studies relating to naval warfare (their authors' names both begin with the letter 'G') about which in his Introduction Hale confessed he 'lacked the interest' – he might well have added 'the space' – 'to deal with adequately', but contextually these books are important in relation to siegecraft, gunpowder and bombardment. Secondly, it should be noted that the English translation of Philippe Contamine's *La guerre au moyen âge* has been included, not only to make this major work more accessible but also because it contains some updating on the French edition of 1980 and a comprehensive bibliography. Thirdly, attention may be drawn to the festschrift edited by three of Sir John Hale's former students (including the present writer) to celebrate his seventieth birthday in 1993. For it not only includes a number of essays with specific bearing on 'War and Society in Renaissance Europe' but testifies with admiration to Hale's stature as a leading exponent of the new school of war history, not the sort written by 'military men and war-enthusiasts', as described by Geoffrey Best in his Introduction.

Although the severe illness which Sir John suffered in 1992 has unfortunately prevented him from writing more, it has not, happily, stopped him from reading, travelling and still participating with his habitual gusto in the world of Renaissance studies. Having been asked to add this brief new Introduction on his behalf and to compile the further bibliography, I should like to thank him and Sheila Hale for their trust and longstanding friendship, and also to thank Geoffrey Best, Michael Mallett and Simon Pepper for help and advice. The text of the book, apart from the correction of a few misprints, is unchanged.

David Chambers
The Warburg Institute, London, October 1997

1

Why there were wars

The period covered by this book opens in 1453 with two sieges that resolved, for the time being, conflicts that had each lasted for a century: in the west, the recapture of Bordeaux marked the end of the Hundred Years War between England and France; in the east, the fall of Constantinople to the Ottomans marked the consolidation of the Turks' rule in Greece and the Balkans that had begun when they first crossed the Bosphorus in 1352. It closes with international relations so taut with mutual suspicion from Spain to Poland and from Sweden to Italy, that in 1618 a riot in Bohemia could release tensions that delivered the centre of Europe over to the unprecedented horrors of the Thirty Years War.

And meanwhile? The 'society' in the title is readily justified. There were more people within it because of an overall increase in population across the century and a half. And thanks to economic growth (again, overall), changes in the machinery of government, and the consequences of the redirections of religious impulses and organizations prompted by the Reformation, there was a richer mixture than formerly of occupation, status, manners and self-awareness. But also, even if no single conflict dragged on so long as did the Hundred Years War, and no multinational one caused so much suffering as the Thirty Years War was to do, 'war' played a role between 1453 and 1618 which, if thought away, radically maims our understanding of the social experiences of these years.

Before 1494, wars in western Europe were chiefly a matter of violent housekeeping. The English on-and-off Wars of the Roses (1455–85) decided who were to be the supreme landlords of the realm: Henry VII and his successors. In France, Louis XI had first to fight a general league of nobles who resented his efforts to break down the feudal regionalism they represented, and then to reattach the outlying duchies of Brittany and Burgundy to French control by force of arms in 1482 and 1491. It was in the same spirit of setting a national house in order that in 1482, three years after the marriage of Isabella and Ferdinand had united the crowns of Castile and Aragon, a ten-year series of crusading campaigns finally evicted Spain's Moors from the southern kingdom of Granada, where they had assumed squatters' rights since the thirteenth century. And in similar vein the Swiss confederation of cantons, after fighting off attacks from an expansionist Burgundy in the 1470s, won, at the battle of Dornach in 1499 against their national overlord, the Emperor Maximilian of Germany, independence and the image of being an entity of fixed importance in the diplomatic and military calculations of the future.

This simplified formula of wars as part of a process of territorial self-definition within roughly traditional frontiers and approximately national languages, breaks down elsewhere. In spite of the border which a cartographer can draw around the area which opinion in the mid-fifteenth century accepted as within the Holy Roman Empire, that is the chiefly Germanic zone between France and Hungary, and Denmark and northern Italy, he cannot colour in the multitude of cities, princely enclaves and militant ecclesiastical territories that saw themselves as actually or potentially independent, without giving the reader an impression that he is suffering from a disease of the retina. The Habsburg emperors' hereditary lands in the south east (roughly modern Austria and Slovenia) provided an insufficient base from which to exert a real, rather than theoretical control, and this remained true when the marriage in 1477 of Frederick III's son Maximilian to Mary of Burgundy added the itself highly volatile mixture of Franche-Comté, Luxembourg and the Netherlands to the Habsburg domains. Yet at the same time the emperor was the fount of an honours and patronage system that led ambitious princes and cities to curry favour with him. He could, on occasion, raise an effective army, and he provided a rallying point and court of appeal for those who felt themselves outmanoeuvred in terms of purely local politics. The result was a constant flickering of minor wars between prosperous cities and rural potentates, between secular and ecclesiastical authorities, and between the princes of the greater territorial units – Brandenburg, Bavaria, the Palatinate – and their more recalcitrant subjects and most vulnerable neighbours; 'minor' wars, but often conducted in the spirit of the Margrave Albert Achilles of Brandenburg's remark that arson gave glory to war in the same way that the Magnificat illuminated Vespers.

Radically different was the situation south of the Alps. Here, too, 1453 was an important date, for to end a long war between

Milan and Venice it saw negotiations that were – by the Peace of Lodi of the following year – extended to a non-aggression pact agreed by the other dominant territories within Italy: Florence, the Papacy and the kingdom of Naples. They agreed because all five powers had already reached the affordable limits of expansion and were anxious to rationalize resources they had already got. Jammed as they were within the dangling length of the peninsula, there were tensions and, indeed, two wars (Florence v. Naples and the Papacy, 1478–80; Venice v. the Papacy over Ferrara, 1482–4), but Italy was the most peaceable area in the west until, in 1494, a series of wars began so unprecedented in cost, manpower and international entanglements that they constitute, at least from those points of view, a new era.

From an invasion by Louis XI's successor Charles VIII in that year which led to his conquest of Naples, a series of campaigns waged in Italy by *his* successors, Louis XII and Francis I, by Ferdinand and his successor as king of Aragon and Castile Charles V, by Maximilian and by the Swiss, left Milan and Naples by 1530 subject to Spain and no other state except Venice unaltered in its form of government, unscarred by battle losses or unshaken from its tradition of independence. Even Venice had been for a while stripped of its mainland possessions by a coalition comprising France, Spain, Maximilian, the Pope and the neighbouring rulers of Mantua and Ferrara. Florence had been transformed, through one military crisis after another, from a free republic into a duchy under Imperial tutelage. Rome itself had been brutally sacked. 'Peace and war, war and peace / These two rule the world today,' wrote an anonymous versifier in the course of the thirty-six-year Wars of Italy.

That the lament was to have a broader significance for the rest of the period, however, was due to factors that coincided with the wars but arose outside the peninsula.

In 1519 Charles V, king of Spain from 1516, succeeded Maximilian as emperor. Already master of Naples, this gave him a heightened interest in Genoa and Milan as a port of entry and land bridge between his Spanish and German lands, and as a base for communications and troop movements northwards to his possessions in Burgundy and the Netherlands. But save between 1512 and 1515, when they had been forced out by the Swiss, this area had been occupied by the French for twenty years. To prevent France's land frontiers from being ringed by the territories of a rival power, a conquest which had been a luxury now became a

15

strategic necessity. Dynastic competition was heightened by personal rivalry; in 1519 Charles was nineteen, Francis I twenty-five. Francis, moreover, had been a contestant for the Imperial title, which was elective. So the wars in Italy became increasingly polarized between Habsburg forces and allies and those of the French royal house of Valois and their supporters, a peak of personal vengefulness being reached when Francis, having lost Milan in 1523, was taken prisoner trying to regain it in 1525 and shipped to Spain for a year's captivity.

Created under such pressures, the rivalry expanded north of the Alps after 1530, causing, or at least conditioning, before the international peace settlement of Cateau-Cambrésis in 1559, wars in Savoy, Piedmont and Provence, north-eastern France, Luxembourg and Lorraine, drawing England to new French adventures with Imperial support (while France riposted by sending troops to Scotland), and, sensationally, directly involving the Turks in western politics through an alliance with Francis. It was a telling indication of the new desperation that afflicted international relations when Toulon in 1543–4 became a Moslem naval base, complete with mosque and slave market.

The Ottoman pressure, in a new phase of aggression, was a second factor affecting the incidence of wars. In 1516–17 the Turks conquered Syria and Egypt, in 1522 they captured Rhodes. Thenceforward, throughout the period, this Mediterranean presence led to naval wars against the Turks themselves (most notably the Christian victory of Lepanto in 1571 which was, however, balanced by the loss of Cyprus), and to expeditions, drastically costly in cash and lives, against the headquarters – Tunis, Algiers, Oran – of their Moslem protectorates along the north African coast, and a constant alert against coastal raiders and sea piracy from the Canary islands to the Adriatic. In south-east Europe they occupied Belgrade in 1521, Buda in 1526, and in 1529 besieged Vienna before accepting that the lines of communication from their Asian recruiting centres were too long to permit the conquest of Habsburg Austria. Nonetheless, Ottoman control of practically the whole of eastern Europe south of Lithuania and up to a contested line between the Gulf of Kvarner, south of Trieste, to the no-man's-land mountainous zone south of Cracow, meant that border warfare was endemic. And as late as 1593–1606 it modulated into one of the period's 'long' wars, and a savagely inconclusive one.

The third factor that sharpened weapons during that extraordinary political generation 1494–1530 was Protestantism.

Luther's famous gesture of 1517, when he denounced, in a placard nailed to a church door in Wittenberg, the Roman Catholic teaching about indulgences (and, by implication, about so much more), touched a nerve of spiritual uneasiness and patriotic and social resentment that produced with surprising speed, given foot- and hoof-pace communications and patchy literacy, the liberated sense of purpose that psychiatrists search for and agitators batten on. During the Thirty-six Years War the Reformation played no part in Italy save for the vindictiveness shown by the Lutheran contingents of the Imperial army that sacked Rome in 1527. But from 1531 those German princes and cities which had embraced – for reasons not always directly concerned with religious conviction – Lutheranism formed themselves into the mutual defence League of Schmalkalden. This was a challenge to Imperial authority which, in spite of some of the Leaguers taking the obvious course of invoking Valois military aid, Charles tried to deal with by concessions and religious mini-summits, until in 1546 he turned to all-out war instead. In the most thoughtful heroic image of the century, Titian portrayed him as the crusading victor over his heretic subjects at the battle of Mühlberg. It was not until 1555, however, that he could finally disband his army, following a reluctant agreement to the Peace of Augsburg whereby princes were permitted to follow, and to encourage their subjects to follow, either the Lutheran or the Catholic faith. This meant, in effect, that Imperial authority was lifted from the great sprawl of territories between the Habsburg personal domains. From 1555 Germany resembled the Italy of 1454–94, a mosaic of small states pursuing their independent and on the whole peaceful courses until violently broken in on by the forces of the Thirty Years War.

The next three 'long' wars of major significance all erupted during the decade 1562–72. The so-called Nordic (but more accurately Baltic) Seven Years War of 1563–70 arose from Sweden's counter to a thrust by Ivan IV (The Terrible) from Muscovy into Estonia. Denmark, backed by its clumsy satellite Norway, saw this as a bid by the kingdom of Sweden–Finland to close the Gulf of Finland to its shipping. It was a war of savage coastal raids and of semi-piratical naval engagements, all made the more rancid by a long history of dynastic and trading rivalries. But it was not, as were the other conflicts, complicated by religious issues.

From 1562 to 1598 France was shaken by civil wars. Though the military peaks of battles and sieges were intermittent, spaced by uneasy truces and hasty accommodations, the war virus settled in every crack that had occurred as successive monarchs from Louis XI had tried to constrict the scattered estates of France into one structure. The great provincial satraps had not always seen the advantage of becoming agents as well as advisers of the crown. Prosperous cities had seen part of their wealth diverted into political ventures not of their own choosing. Above all, Protestant worship, in its Calvinistic form, had become congenial to the point of necessity to hundreds of thousands of men and women, many of high station, who resented its illegality within the realm of their Most Christian Kings.

It was not long after the death in 1559 of Francis's successor Henry II from a lance thrust in a tournament and the accession of the fifteen-year-old Francis II under the tutelage of the unpopular foreign queen mother, Catherine de Medici, that the country fissured along these cracks into territorial and clientage power blocks each seeking to control the crown. With Francis's death in the following year and the succession passing to a ten-year-old Charles IX, under Catherine's regency, the continuing weakness at the centre allowed the competitors to broaden the bases of their support and, increasingly, to define themselves in religious terms, rigidly Catholic or Huguenot or, at calculated times, to demand or offer toleration. With feelings about the monarchy, regional loyalties, economic rivalries and religious sentiments all exacerbated, civil war became almost a state of mind; and it took a monarch – Henry IV – of exceptional mental balance, military flair, charm and flexibility of conscience to restore peace and, more slowly, law and order.

Meanwhile, from 1567 to 1609 Spain was involved in the Netherlands, the most northerly and richest of the Habsburg–Burgundian possessions, in countering, with increasingly massive armies, a revolt in the provinces later to be known collectively as the Dutch Republic, or Holland, that turned into a patriotic and Protestant war of liberation. This was the conflict, with its amphibious operations, long-drawn-out sieges, occasional pitched battles and endless multinational debate about military methods, that led contemporaries to refer to the Netherlands as 'the school of war'. And 1609 was marked merely by agreement to a twelve-year truce.

This is not the place, indeed this is not the book, in which to elaborate the phases of this or the other wars so far mentioned. The intention in these pages is simply to remind the reader of those long-term conflicts which in themselves justify looking at the period in terms of wars and their consequences. For of course there were others: the war of 1552–5 between France on the one hand and Spain and Florence on the other to determine the status of Siena; another bruising trial of strength between Sweden and Denmark in 1611–13; the war of 1613–18 which took place in the tiny cockpit of Monferrat but whose outcome was weighed with fascinated attention by observers upon whose pockets and lives the Thirty Years War was to fall. And we will encounter more.

For the mainstream conflicts all had a vortex effect, drawing in, as allies or jackals, others than the main contestants. England is a case in point. Apart from the wars of Henry VIII and Edward VI in Scotland, and Elizabeth's dragging campaigns to impose obedience on the Irish, which were domestic issues (though France helped the Scots and Spain the Irish), Henry VIII's invasions of France in 1512, 1523 and 1544 sailed in on the back of Habsburg support, and Elizabeth's French expeditions of 1562–3, 1589 and 1591–7, like the forces she sent to the Netherlands from 1585 and to Portuguese and Spanish ports in 1589 and 1596, all reflected a growing fear of the territorial might and intransigent, Papacy-backed Catholicism of Charles V's successor Philip II. And if this was the reaction of a separate, almost invasion-proof (in spite of occasional scares like the Armada year, 1588) island, it is readily understandable how landlocked states found it difficult to turn their backs on conflicts which, in terms of immediate war aims, had nothing to do with them.

In the course of a wide European tour, Baron Leo of Rozmital in Bohemia approached, in 1466, the great Spanish pilgrim cathedral of St James of Compostela, eager to pay his devotions to the relics of the true cross and the crown of thorns which it contained. But it so happened that his entry was delayed. Four hundred crossbowmen were pouring fire into the windows, from which they were answered in kind, their commander, the local magnate, being shot in the throat as he was pressing his siege against the family of the archbishop, whom he had thrown into prison. Neither of the men in Rozmital's entourage who chronicled his journey evinced any surprise at this hold-up.

Such feuding-feudal episodes were characteristic of an age in which governments were essaying good housekeeping while understaffed and underpowered. In 1517 another traveller, the cardinal of Aragon, was forced to side-step, en route from Rotterdam to Breda, an area being pillaged by the troops of the duke of

Guelders, and, later, to prolong his stay in Avignon rather than encounter Gascon soldiers returning home from their participation in Pope Leo X's campaign to install his nephew as duke of Urbino. Again, though officially Europe was at peace, the cardinal's chronicler took such interruptions in his stride. As in the interstices of domestic centralization, so in those between the radii of major wars, local antipathies and side-issues considerably broadened the scope of war or warlike violence. Interstitial wars, like that of Guelders, became less frequent; the last of note were the campaigns during which German princes like Albert Alcibiades of Brandenburg and Maurice of Saxony took advantage of Charles V's embroilment (while France armed behind his back) with the Lutheran factions in Germany to enlarge their own domains. Improved central administration reduced the number of Compostela incidents, though a whole infrastructure of local vengeances and private wars can be perceived in the guerrilla subplots of the main strategic story of the Netherlands wars and in the spaces between the 'official' civil wars of France, showing how fragile the state-building process still was, and how ready men were to resort to arms. 'And if it be well noted,' as Montaigne pointed out, 'it will be found, and experience doth teach it, that the least blazoned occasions are the most dangerous; and that in our late home-warres, more good men have perished in slight and little importing occasions, and in contention about a small cottage, than in worthy achievements and honourable places.' But that story could be told even more vividly in terms of those major revolts against economic or sectional injustice, as it was perceived, that involved mobilizations and casualties on a scale comparable to military expeditions or minor wars: the Spanish revolt of the Comuneros in 1520–1, the German 'Peasants' War' of 1524–5, the bitter, confused rising in the English south west in 1549 – and on through those revolts in the 1560s in Scotland, England, Corsica and southern Spain that can be seen as a premonition of the still more drastic grindings of the old domestic order against the new of the 1640s.

A distinction must be maintained between international and civil wars on the one hand, waged through formalized taxation and recruiting and accompanied by diplomatic activity representing a legally constituted or (in the case of civil wars) widely recognized political power, and, on the other, armed commotions varying in scale from major revolts to isolated riots over the exploitative price of bread or illegal land confiscations. However, as the size of armies and the number of ex-soldiers grew, and the peacetime practice of enrolling civilians in militias extended, from the point of view of weaponry and leadership even riots could look like the skirmishes that increasingly characterized wars of siege and stalemate. Not only war, then, but any form of violence organized to achieve a shared concern for rights can add a shading to 'war' as it concerned society. And each shading complicates the definition of 'peace'.

For statesmen whose imaginative grasp was extended by advances in cartography, by the need to imagine the extent of the Habsburgs' manifold inheritances and the Ottoman advance, and by the plugging in of a whole new religious circuit to the diplomatic wiring diagram of Europe, peace, overall peace, was a myth. A rare exception was the surprised comment made by Jean Barrillon, secretary to the French chancellor, Antoine Duprat, about the year 1517. 'There was . . . no noise or rumour of war, division or partisanship. Merchants plied their trade in perfect safety as well on land as on sea. Frenchmen, Englishmen, Spaniards, Germans and all other natives of Christendom traded peacefully together. This was a great favour bestowed by God.' Yet this was the year, as we have seen, of war in Guelders and in the duchy of Urbino. Wars, moreover, were seldom brought convincingly to a close. Summing up his experience of the last generation of the Hundred Years War, an English captain remarked, 'It is always necessary to double-bar the door in times of truce or peace treaty.' Neither oaths nor hostages prevented Francis I from renewing his campaigns against Charles V.

There was probably no single year throughout the period in which there was neither war nor occurrences that looked and felt remarkably like it. There were a number of unstable frontiers – Scotland/England, Spain/Portugal, France/Spain, French/Imperial Burgundy, Christian/Turkish Hungary – which were zones of constant raids and counter-raids, where no one worked unarmed and no garrison force could do what it liked best to do, namely, pawn its arms and make love to taverners' daughters. The practice of reprisal, whereby a shipowner was empowered by government to recover by violence the value of goods lost by piracy or unlawful sequestration in port, grew into the privateering, or piracy-by-licence that made marines, guns and convoys as necessary in peace as in open war. Moreover, as frontiers, after surveys by land commissioners and the construction of strong-points, did become more stable, especially in the later sixteenth century, their place as zones whence military escalation was always possible was taken by

piracy

political ganglia, inflamed trouble spots (of the sort to which we are all too accustomed today): Livonia, Piedmont, the duchy of Jülich (west of Cologne), Saluzzo (a marquisate on the French–Savoy frontier), the Valtelline (the valley linking Lombardy to the Tyrol). These were crossroads of strategic communications or of weak or disputed ownership which kept a sense of impending crisis a-boil. And warlike crisis, with its emergency taxation, partial mobilizations, recruiting drums, and fluctuations in normal food prices, is part of society's experience of a life conditioned by the existence of war. Of course the definition of 'war' must be kept in its place. But wars had preludes, aftermaths and simulacra, and for those far from the fronts of combat the effects could be much the same.

Why, then, were there so many wars? A library-ful of books answering this question in general, with shelves of debate about our animal inheritance and politicized psychosis, has not improved on the response formulated by Lorenzo Valla in 1440: wars are embarked on 'for desire of glory', 'for the hope of booty', 'for fear of incurring disaster later, if the strength of others is allowed to increase', and 'for avenging a wrong and defending friends'. Wars, that is, arise from the relationship, at any given moment and depending on the mood (and resources) of the decision-making authority, between greed, fear and altruism.

In our period greed can be defined very largely in terms of land. Status throughout the Middle Ages had been above all bound up with the ownership of land, the jurisdictional rights attached to it, the opportunities for patronage it offered and, a weaker motive almost always, to the profits obtainable from rents, fees and the acres farmed directly by the tenant-in-chief. The prestige attached to land lost none of its glamour; there was, indeed, a persistent increase of purchases by the urban patriciates of mercantile cities, London, Amsterdam, Lyons, Florence, Venice. With them the profit motive and the possession of an independent provision of foodstuffs ranked higher, but enhanced status was aimed at, too.

As the greatest landowners, monarchs acted as did lesser ones, and thus could usually be assured of the acceptance of their motives and methods: the revival of old family claims to estates lost in times of poverty, legal contest or violent occupation; the linking of properties through marriages; an indifference as to whether new acquisitions were contiguous to the old or contained populations different in speech or custom. Political Europe was like an estate map, and war was a socially acceptable form of property acquisition.

That it was not until 1802 that English kings ceased to claim on their coinage that they were also kings of France suggests something of the tenacity with which the monarch-tycoons of early modern Europe pursued their claims. For claims, based on rights, rather than illegitimized takeovers, they were. Henry VIII's repeated stabs of the carving knife into the northern flanks of France were but – in the values of the day – attempts to regain his, i.e. Edward III's, inheritance. It was in a rare extra-legal mood that he proposed to Charles V in 1525 that they should split the whole of France between them while Francis I languished in a Spanish prison, for Charles had no prior claim to French territory. Examples of 'pure' conquest are, in fact, few. Charles VIII embarked on his epoch-making invasion of Italy in 1494 after a careful checking of his claim (snaking back to the thirteenth century) to the throne of Naples. Louis XII conquered Milan by right of an ancestor's marriage to the daughter of a duke of Milan in 1389. Philip II's forcible annexation of Portugal to Spain in 1580 was similarly made with the excuse of a family claim to its throne which he (amongst others) had disinterred. Western Europe was, after all, too small a space for so many centuries of conquests, alliance trade-offs, and intermarriages, plus the vast claims of popes and emperors as feudal chieftains, not to have left a web of claims to be picked at by the lawyers of land-hungry rulers. Apart from the Swiss attempts to dominate Milan during the Wars of Italy and France's acquisition in 1552 of Metz, Toul and Verdun, only Turkish conquests in Europe and the Mediterranean and Spain's naval bases in north Africa lacked such precedents. But, as in the case of Spanish and Portuguese conquests in the New World and in the Far East, these were based on the still higher right of a true religion to occupy the domains of heretic or heathen.

Territory, then, was greed's object, and was expressed in the idiom of inheritance. Marriage, as a symptom of this dynasticizing view of the initiating and settlement of major property transfers by violence, extorted from a French professor of law who died in the year of the Peace of Cateau-Cambrésis (at which Charles V's son was contracted to Henry II's daughter), one of the age's few political jokes. 'We see very often', François Duaren wrote, 'that as of a comedy, so of a war, the final conclusion is a marriage.'

Land, and the 'glory' it brought with it, was a far more potent motive for war than any anticipated economic profit. Another Frenchman, Antoine de Montchretien, opened his pioneering work on 'l'oeconomie politique' in 1615 with the statement that 'those who are called to be the rulers of states should have glory, expansion and enrichment as their principal aims'. But he did not see expansion as leading to enrichment, though he hoped that wars of conquest might at least recover their costs. No government, no private theorist saw profit as a tenable aim of war; enrichment was to be achieved by a more methodical development of a country's own economic potential and the nurturing of a favourable balance of exports against imports. This process could be benefited by war, but only to the extent that a foreign war calmed, by diverting, civil passions and gave governments the excuse to pack off the unproductive elements in society – rogues, vagabonds and paupers – to be slaughtered.

These arguments had gained force after 1559. By then western Europe as a whole had come to resemble Italy between 1454 and 1494, with the chief power blocks so jammed together, and so in need of consolidation rather than accumulation, as to make voluntary expansion less a part of 'glory' than were internal stability and wealth and courtly splendour. And this mood was fostered by religious factionalism and the revolts and civil disturbances of the 1560s. But greed in the sense of monetary profits had always played a greater part in the calculations of those who joined or enjoined wars – soldiers and merchants – than of those who decided on them. Wars could be started, but could not have been carried on without the profit motive (and we shall see in later chapters how this operated); even those who fought for 'religion' expected to be paid. It is, however, only in this sense, and in a few specific instances – England's intervention in the Netherlands, and the Baltic campaigns among Muscovy, Poland, Denmark and Sweden, when trade was an important, though never single motive – that one can speak of 'economic warfare' in Europe. Ivan IV was not entirely disingenuous when he complained to Elizabeth, apropos the provocative incursion of the English Muscovy Company, that 'we had thought that you had been ruler over your land . . . but now we perceive that there be other men that do rule, and not men, but peasants and merchants'. When Henry IV settled his war with the duke of Savoy in 1600 by asking for fiscally profitable districts rather than the prestigious marquisate of Saluzzo, his own nobility, 'which more regard the honour of France than the profit of the King's purse, doe terme it a shamefull and dishonourable treaty', as Sir Ralph Winwood, Elizabeth's diplomatic agent, reported. Rulers were meant to have nobler motives than pecuniary profit. What conditioned warfare in the sixteenth century was not economic motives but economic resources. Larger armies and more extended campaigns were the result of an increase in taxable wealth caused by more effective centralized government, population growth, somewhat more cost-effective agriculture and the stimulus given to commerce and manufacture by the flow of gold and silver and the counterflow of manufactured goods across the Atlantic. The reach of war into European society would have been slighter had it not been for the American exploits of Columbus, Cortés and Pizarro.

'Fear' was the second of Valla's causes of war. Fear that the 'balance' between the Italian states was shifting against him caused Lodovico Sforza of Milan to egg Charles VIII on to the conquest of Naples. France feared the noose of Habsburg encirclement while Charles V feared the striking power of the better consolidated French monarchy. Henry VIII feared that a peace treaty between France and Spain in 1538 would lead to invasion from an unremittingly hostile coastline. Fear, feeding the desire to anticipate attack, was the most potent factor in fostering the development – a phenomenon of this period – of resident embassies at foreign courts, the employment of secret agents and the placing of local 'moles'. Diplomacy operated on the principle of mutual distrust. And fear operated ever more strongly as Counter-Reformation popes urged the Habsburg political power to become also a crusading one, and by excommunicating 'heretic' rulers (Elizabeth, Henry IV), encouraged their subjects to turn against them. On the whole, however, fear was more a part of the history of defence than of attack. Philip II decided on war in 1567 to suppress the revolt in the Netherlands out of fear lest it spread to other Habsburg territories, but pre-emptive strikes were few. All the same, defensive preparations involving fortifications, standing armies, trained militias, with costs passed on, as they were, to the populace at large, and with the dislocations of everyday life that they caused, were also part of war's impact on civilian society. These precautions did not in themselves make governments more prompt to go to war. Fortifications were expensive; new conquests would only mean new lines of them. A permanent military structure was never large enough to be more than the nucleus of a field army, and represented a standing charge on revenue which encouraged conservatism rather than recklessness. Centrally administered militias, as a charge on local authorities, were so far from representing a nation in arms as to encourage the appetite for peace.

There remains Valla's last cause: 'for avenging a wrong and defending friends'. The idea, as befits a humanist scholar, was the classical one that allies or buffer states must be assured of their major partner's support if they were attacked. It is difficult to think of an early modern example, though one or two might lurk in the small print of some regional interstitial conflict. The equivalent motive in this period is the supporting of foreign co-religionists, though because no impulse that involves spending large sums of money is simple, this was never an altruism unadulterated by other intentions.

The vivid and widespread response to Alternative Christianity, Protestantism in its various guises, chiefly Lutheran and Calvinist, owed something to better means of communication via the printing press than heresies had possessed in the past, and something to princes who, not necessarily sincere converts themselves, saw a fresh excuse to claim exemption from traditional overlordship. But its diffusion was based on a liberating response to a new and more congenial set of demands on individual conscience, challenges felt to be both more intense and more personal, and all the more committing because they came to be combated by a more stimulating form of the old faith, organizationally reformed and ethically tautened Catholicism.

The conflict led to no wars between a Protestant and a Catholic country waged solely on religious grounds. The faith-wars were internal, though there came to be an overall ideological conflict, powered from Calvin's Geneva and from Rome, that coarsened the mood of diplomacy everywhere and led to military intervention 'for defending friends'.

Lutheranism, working within the mosaic of Germany, forced Charles V to accept, as we have seen, the 'cuius regio eius religio' compromise of 1555. And this agreement to differ – which Charles was encouraged to accept because he needed uniform support against a third forceful militant faith, that of Islam (Russian Orthodoxy being non-expansive and Greek Orthodoxy practically obliterated by the Turks) – led to a reasonably unobstreperous co-habitation within the bounds of the German Empire.

Calvinism, the form of Protestantism that appealed more widely to individual need elsewhere, with its carefully monitored structure of local congregations and provincial synods, and its single doctrinal reference book, *The Institutes*, rather than the marvellous sprawl of Luther's religious journalism, was a more difficult spiritual neighbour to come to terms with. The weakness of the

French monarchy and the move in to control it by the most arrogantly Catholic grandees such as the Guises, coincided with the creep of Calvinism up the social scale from the townsmen and farmers who had been its initial converts to men of the territorial and clientage stature of Louis de Bourbon, prince of Condé, and Gaspard de Châtillon, count of Coligny. The resulting civil wars were fought for control of a crown which all accepted as the legitimate source of national administration, and whether fighting for toleration or suppression, the religious motive was probably dominant at first among those who summoned and paid and those who fought – apart from the foreign mercenaries employed by both sides.

From the Paris massacre of Huguenots on St Bartholomew's Day in 1572, and the wave of assassinations that spread outwards from it, the mood changed. It was as though the religious obsession, having discharged itself in an orgasm of terror, took on if not a disillusioned, a more calculating stance. Thereafter the spurts of war, and the local disturbances that thickeningly filled the spaces between them, became case-studies in the resentments – town v. country, rich v. poor, local magnate v. territorial chieftain – that could emerge when central government broke down and religious fervour faltered in its appeal to unity of purpose. It was different in the Netherlands. There the seven Calvinist provinces saw the repressive power as a remote and foreign one, and resistance, sustained by a flourishing overseas trade, was led by members of a family, the House of Nassau, under whom a sense of Dutch nationalism could develop a parallel momentum of defiance and a genuine sense of enduring political purpose.

The spores from these conflicts circled over the whole of the west. Catholicism was strengthened as a cause by its identity with crusade after the widely publicized Papal–Spanish–Venetian naval victory over the Turks off Lepanto in 1571, and with its deftest missionaries, the Jesuits, who scored a major victory in Poland, culminating in the reign from 1587 of Sigismund III, 'King of the Jesuits', and who covertly challenged consciences in whatever Protestant country they could gain access to. The image of Protestantism was somewhat weakened by the split between Calvinism and the more prosaic Lutheranism of Germany and Scandinavia and the middle-of-the-road church established in England. Nonetheless, its appeal was strengthened after the scandal of St Bartholomew and by its identification with opposition to the ever more terrifying apparition of Habsburg–Papal hegemony. Undoctrinaire dynastic hegemony had been alarming enough to those within its potential orbit, but the politico-religious version alerted a more complex panic.

Despite advocates on both sides, Europe did not split into two warring religious camps. The German cities and princes were happy to receive profit and lose sources of discontent by succeeding the Swiss as the prime exporters of mercenary companies and vagabonds-turned-soldiers. The Scandinavian–Baltic area was fully occupied with dynastic-economic broils of its own. The Italian states, though Catholic to a man, were quite without quixotry, and in any case were small and sufficiently diverted by Moslem pirate raids. Spain, in spite of freshets of spendable income from the New World, was aware that further takeovers and subsequent occupation were beyond its financial reach, in spite of the frail hope in 1588 that the Armada might bring back the days of English satellitism when Philip had been briefly married to Mary Tudor. France was incapable of corporate action. England was too poor, too preoccupied with a restless Scotland, an insurgent Ireland, and a Catholic Fifth Column of its own, as well as being all too aware of Henry VIII's failures to establish himself across the Channel, to adopt any leading role in forcing back the Whore of Babylon into the Roman stews with which polemicists identified her.

So instead of formal wars between creeds there were interventions and harassments. Thus in spite of Elizabeth's insistence in 1601 that she 'never gave just cause of war to any prince . . . nor had any greater ambition than to maintain my own State in security and peace', she had been maintaining an army in the Netherlands since 1585 to support the United Provinces (in exchange for control over the ports of Brill and Flushing); in 1589–90 she had not only sent an expedition under Sir Francis Drake to attack the survivors of the Armada and try to detach Portugal from its union with Spain, and fleets to trap Spanish silver convoys off the Azores, but had shipped 4000 troops to help Henry of Navarre's Huguenot forces in France; and in 1591 she had dispatched a further force under the earl of Leicester to assist Henry in the capture of Rouen, an attempt foiled by the appearance of a Spanish army led by Philip's commander-in-chief in the Netherlands, Alexander Farnese. Yet Elizabeth's statement was not disingenuous. It was not territory but security that she was after. If her words have an ironic ring it is because they coincided with the occupation by nearly 4000 Spanish troops of Kinsale, sent to hamper her general

Lord Mountjoy's attempts to tame the Catholic Irish.

Religion, then, poisoned – or exalted – domestic tensions, led to interventions 'for defending friends', and, if it did not constitute a cause of open war between nations, made the very name of war more alarming by broadening its associations from the territorial ambition of monarchs to threats to the personal convictions of individuals.

In whatever combinations greed, fear and the succour of friends led to military action, someone had to pull the trigger, and, outside the republic of Venice and the Swiss confederation, that person was the prince, whatever his title. It was Galileo, in 1610, who first referred to war as a 'royal sport'; but the inhabitants of More's *Utopia* (1516) 'know that the common folk do not go to war of their own accord but are driven to it by the madness of princes'. War – at least in its 'greed' aspect – was a continuation of litigation by other means, a way of settling claims to land, and these claims were those of princes. Your prime responsibility, wrote Machiavelli to a tyro diplomat en route for Spain in 1522, is to study the personality of Charles, to tell your government 'whether he loves war or peace, whether he is motivated by glory or some other passion'. The advice was sound, for however complex the bureaucracies, ministerial councils and consultative assemblies which grew up around rulers, their own prerogative to take decisions in foreign policy and war, while it may have been hemmed in by stonewalling and cautionary advice, was unchallenged. It was not merely a romantic-chivalrous gesture (though it was an unrealistic one) when on three occasions, in 1526, 1528 and 1536, Charles V sent heralds to challenge Francis I to settle their differences in a duel.

Francis declined, but his sense of personal responsibility for war is shown in a description of him written by the Venetian ambassador to France in 1546, one that holds good in this respect for his contemporary rulers as well. 'If the King endures bodily fatigues unflinchingly,' wrote Marino Cavalli, 'he finds mental preoccupations more difficult to bear and hands them over almost entirely to the cardinal of Tournon and the admiral [Claude d'Annebault; both were members of his council]. He takes no decision and gives no reply without first listening to their advice. . . . But in all the great matters of state, matters of peace and war, His Majesty, who is submissive in everything else, insists on his will being obeyed. In this event there is no one at court, however great his authority, who dares remonstrate with His Majesty.' It was in the same vein that in 1553 the duke of Alba, who had already established himself as an impressive – and was to become a notorious – military commander, wrote, not without some resentment, that 'Kings are born to do their will, and we, their vassals and servants, are born to do their will likewise.'

So it is not surprising that rulers found it advisable to wage 'their' wars in person. Only one pope did, an armoured Julius II in his anti-French campaign of 1511. But Dukes Philip and Charles of Burgundy commanded their armies (the former until he was in his late fifties). For Spain Ferdinand served as a young man. Charles V led his Tunis campaign, left sealed instructions to be opened only in case of his death or capture during his war in northern France, and Titian's Mühlberg portrait shows him in the armour he actually wore during the battle. His predecessor as emperor, Maximilian I, was nearly killed leading a cavalry charge in 1504 while trying to bring the expansionist Elector Palatine to heel, and went on to earn the soubriquet 'heart of steel'. Charles VIII and Louis XII personally led their invasions of Italy; Francis I owed his life at the battle of Marignano (1515) to the soundness of his protective carapace (no wonder rulers flattered one another with gifts of war chargers and suits of armour) before being taken captive ten years later while fighting at Pavia. Henry IV's expertise and bravery in battle mildly shocked another Venetian ambassador, Pietro Duodo. 'When it comes to making war,' he wrote in 1598, 'which is the real calling of a great captain and King, . . . he moves fearlessly under arquebus and cannon fire without giving it a thought and as gaily as if he were going to a wedding, and he often takes greater risks than he should.' And he goes on to comment: 'The fact that the King sets such an example is very important, but it is also true that it is something you look for and praise in a soldier or ordinary officer, but not in a great King like his Majesty. He knows this and apologizes for it. But as he said to me at Lyons, the only coin he can pay his soldiers in is the example he sets for them, and if he did not provide it, he would lose his troops and be unable to defend his country. Nor would any noble put on his breastplate if he did not see that the King had already armed.'

This suggestion that the warrior-monarch was by then something of an anachronism owes something to the Venetian ruling class's decision not to confuse political with military activity. But it reflects, too, the influence not only of Philip II, who directed the affairs of his great empire from his file-encumbered study, but of a curious concentration of women rulers around the mid-century: Mary Tudor and Elizabeth, Mary Queen of Scots, Catherine de

Medici, and – as Spanish deputies in the Netherlands – Mary of Hungary and Margaret of Parma. But these examples, and Duodo's reserve, did not check the assumption that wars were, ultimately, personal matters. It was demonstrated by the threats against Elizabeth's life, the successful assassinations of Henry III of France in 1589, of the incarnation of Netherlandish resistance to Spain, William of Orange, in 1584 and of Henry IV in 1610, and by the increase in princely guards and precautionary court etiquettes. By the time Christian IV of Denmark led his forces against Sweden in the 1611–12 War of Kalmar, personal service was coming to be considered something of an eccentricity. All the same, as rulers became lifted up higher than ever in public esteem by political theorists and by the appetite for a vision of personal leadership in times of increasing social, economic and religious complexity, there was no slackening in the belief that the decision, peace or war, lay properly in their hands.

Their attitudes to international affairs were affected by notions about leadership that looked outside the maintenance of domestic order. One was chivalry, the ethical etiquette of the international club of the well-born. Even though most of its code sagged into theoretical showmanship or the often criminous pursuit of personal honour (between 500 and 1000 French aristocrats died in duels in the years 1598–1610), it retained the core which equated glorious deeds with military ones from the campaigns of Charles the Bold at least until the mid-century. Wars were never undertaken simply in a spirit of derring-do. Charles VIII, though strongly influenced by the code, prepared his Italian expedition after elaborate diplomatic preparations to safeguard his flanks and careful strategic reconnoitrings of the terrain across which he proposed to march. All the same, chivalric values added their temptation to make warlike decisions. And they helped to prevent a resigned licking of wounds after a defeat. Claude de Seyssel wrote a hard-headed book of advice in 1515 for the new king of France, Francis I: *La monarchie de France*. But he remarked that 'it is never practical nor honourable, even for a great ruler, to accept humiliation at the hands of an enemy'. And an equally hard-headed Italian ex-diplomat, Francesco Vettori, wrote of Francis's decision to try again after his troops' expulsion from Milanese Lombardy, that 'with his indomitable nature, so unused to experiencing humiliation, he could not accept it'.

Princes between 1450 and 1550 had access to a particularly heady brew compounded of patriotic chronicles in which wars, on the principle that the devil has all the best tunes, bulked large, of chivalrous and crusading romances, and of humanistic potboilers which stressed the exploits of Alexander, Hannibal and Caesar. It is not altogether sensible to dismiss it as a mere stirrup-cup quaffed before riding off on campaign. The pro-peace movement, whose powerlessness we shall look at shortly, pointed to all these ingredients as inflaming the imagination of princes to seek war rather than peace.

With the shrinking of the acreage open to occupation in Europe from the mid-century, the chivalric-adventurous element in foreign policy became soberer; the temptation to acquire glory became transmuted into the determination to maintain reputation: through the retention of conquered or inherited lands ('honour and reputation are the things that most mark a man in the world', the embattled Ferdinand I of Austria told his sister in 1549), the impressing of neutrals, and through identification with a cause – Protestantism (somewhat reluctantly) in the case of Elizabeth, Catholicism in the case of Philip II, northern independence (against Muscovy) in that of successive kings of Sweden, guardian of the west (against the Turks) in that of Venice. Of two arguments by senior ministers urging Philip to press the war against the Dutch in 1577, one emphasized the importance of his 'honour and prestige', the other of his 'honour and reputation'. Wars came to be waged, or threatened, less to gain territory than to save face.

A problem of expansion had always been to combine conflicting demands on manpower: the need to increase the ruler's domestic control in the interest of security and the economy, versus the need to take over, or, at least, invigilate the administration of newly won territory. This conflict came to be rationalized by a grander version of the clientage systems managed by great regional families: the surrounding of the central power with satellites, 'friends', persuaded by marriages, subventions, fear and unremitting diplomatic pressure to be self-governing but dependent. 'For it is in this way', as another Spanish adviser put it to Philip in 1587 (advocating the subduing of England), 'that monarchs have increased their power and monarchies have grown – not by appropriating everything for themselves, but by distributing much of it among their creatures and dependants.' It is this move towards a Europe of ideologically defined power blocks, satellites and potential flash-points, that begins to give international relations a recognizably modern flavour. And the similarity was strengthened by the carrying of European rivalries overseas: English raids on the

Spanish Caribbean, the establishment of French bases in North America, Dutch competition in the East Indies with the Habsburg satellite Portugal.

Within this shift, the finger on the trigger of escalation or riposte remained that of the prince. It was seldom pressed as controversially as when Henry IV readied 55,000 troops in 1610 for a war on three fronts – the Spanish southern Netherlands, Navarre and Milan. Ostensibly this was to show that as a Catholic king he could still support a Protestant cause: a Lutheran successor to the vacant ducal throne of Jülich. But surprise at his choosing to put so much at stake in so crucial a moment of inter-block stability was lessened by suspicion that his covert motive was to punish the Habsburgs for giving shelter in Brussels to the latest object of his lust, the pretty young (she was fifteen) princess of Condé. The knife of his assassin, François Ravaillac, aborted the war. His true motives, therefore, remain obscure. But the Dutch ambassador's assumption that he was using his power, with the support of his ministers, to abduct 'the new Helen', at least suggests how far personal motives could be taken for granted.

By the early sixteenth century the relationship between rulers and their ministers had become the object of much concern. Machiavelli (in *The Prince*, 1513) and Seyssel took the line that foolish princes would not understand advice and that clever ones would not take it. In the 1520s Francesco Guicciardini, a senior minister in the service of two popes, Leo X and Clement VII, and a well-informed observer of the international scene, ruefully noted that 'in affairs of state, you should guide yourself not so much by what reason demonstrates a prince ought to do as by what he will most likely do according to his nature or habits'. In 1523 Thomas Cromwell, another great housekeeper who knew the glory-equals-conquest temperament of his monarch, Henry VIII, drafted a speech for parliament in which he warned against the cost of French adventures, the impossibility of small England ever occupying large France, the impracticability of assuming that the France of today was like the easily divided country of the days of Edward III or Henry V; now, 'there was never nation more marvellously linked together than they be amongst themselves'. This sort of commonsense did not prevent Henry from raising what was then the largest army in English history to invade France in 1544. Pained by the expense of the Armada scare preparations in 1588, Elizabeth's chief minister, Lord Burghley, jotted down one of his world-weary memoranda: 'To spend in time convenient is wisdom. To continue charges without needful cause bringeth repentance. To hold on to charges without the knowledge of the certainty whereof, and of means how to support them, is lack of wisdom.'

There were princely advisers who advocated risk in the cause of prestige and, more conjecturally, security. We have noted Juan de Idiáquez's suggestion that Philip should supplant Elizabeth by a Spanish placeman even if, as he granted, the cost of maintaining England as a friend would exceed that of the enterprise. But on the whole the two chief indicators of 'early modern' notions of the state, bureaucratic husbandry at home, and the maintenance of reputation and leadership abroad, developed in an irritable symbiosis all too recognizable in the later relationship between land agent and landowner (the cutting down of productive woodland to buy a yacht, the mortgaging of land to pursue an heiress) or between accountant and tycoon. The employer, of course, always wins; that is, his values do.

Ministerial caution seems amply justified if, for a moment, we indulge in a pointless, because anachronistic, review, territorial and fiscal, of profits and losses in war. On the political map, apart from the conquest of Granada, the passing of Milan and Naples–Sicily to Spain, of Siena to Tuscany, five more cantons to the Swiss confederation, a modest outwards creep of a few German principalities, the firming of Savoy–Piedmont into an independent duchy, and the slipping of the former 'middle kingdom' of Burgundy into French and (by inheritance) Spanish hands, the boundaries of western Europe remained remarkably stable between 1450 and 1618; startlingly so if we compare them with the massive stride of the Turks into the south-eastern land mass and the Mediterranean, or with the more fateful thrusts of fleet-borne European swords, guns and horses across the world's oceans. Fiscally, no campaign recouped its expenses, no occupation compensated for the cost of administering it. In these cool perspectives, war was not sensible. But as value-ridden imperatives, wars were embarked on in terms of whatever precipitated a sense of crisis at the time, and a prince's view of what was 'just and necessary' (a phrase commonly used to justify military action) could reckon on an adequate measure of support from ideas and emotions that had little to do with calculation or the long view, and were a necessary make-weight to his very restricted powers of compulsion.

Rulers needed the positive backing of the clergy. They needed the cooperation of the nobility, of the weighty landlord class as a whole: to serve as senior officers or field administrators, and to foster recruitment among their tenants; wars were seldom waged simply with permanent establishments and mercenaries. They also needed at least an acceptance of mobilization by the larger class of men of moderate status whose administrative and taxpaying support in towns and the countryside was essential in extending the recruitment network and raising money. In the third place, both recruiting and service morale benefited from some measure of patriotic motivation.

The clergy constituted not only one of Europe's most numerous non-agrarian occupation groups but its chief moulder of public opinion. On the whole, clerics favoured peace. The New Testament generally endorsed it. War and its soldiery led to the breach of the most socially interesting commandments. And it involved the taxation of clerical incomes. Yet everywhere, even in those Protestant countries whose faith was not established so closely under the wing of the state as was England's, the church lived in partnership with government. The sermons of John Colet, dean of St Paul's, against Henry VIII's invasion of France in 1512, were very rare examples of the chiding of princely militancy in sermons normally devoted to advocating joining up and paying up. It is revealing that, later, the one issue on which all Catholics and most Protestants were in accord was their denunciation of the Anabaptists' pacifist claim that Christ's 'Render therefore unto Caesar the things that are Caesar's' did not apply to military service or taxes. But it is not surprising. Popes raised armies and joined military alliances. German archbishops waged war to protect and extend their territories. Luther, needing political space cleared for his convictions, remarked that 'war is as necessary as eating, drinking or any other business'. Calvinist conviction that it was legitimate to fight to defend the faith extended in the 1560s to plead the right to wage war against a government that persecuted it. And in seeking to justify clerical belligerence, clerics of all persuasions could switch from the slightly tricky New to the reassuring Old Testament, that 'book of the battles of the Lord', as a devout author described it. And at a more popular level, an older tradition in which war was reluctantly accepted as God's plan for alternately chastising and rewarding his peccant creation, surfaced in sermons, diaries, correspondence and chronicles throughout the period.

Christianity, after all, had grown up with war, had needed it as much as it tried to check it, had become habituated to it. Conscious of its horrors, and the barriers it placed against man's spiritual development, theologians had developed a theory to limit its acceptability. Going back to the fifth-century St Augustine and refined by St Thomas Aquinas in the thirteenth, this was the doctrine of the Just War: wars were unsanctionable by the church unless they were waged on the authority of a legitimate ruler, for a just cause, and with righteous intent. Erasmus in 1510 put his finger on the theory's chief weakness: 'We will not attempt to discuss whether war is ever just; who does not think his own cause just? . . . Among so many treaties and agreements which are now entered into, now rescinded, who can lack a pretext of going to war?' The same point was acknowledged in 1593 by an English divine who was quite without Erasmus's loathing of war as such: 'Every man', he wrote, 'will seem to make his cause good, and to do nothing without good causes.' A fair example of such cause-glossing is the passage in Francis I's letter to his heir written during his captivity in Spain. He had been captured during an invasion which had for its sole intention 'to reconquer territory which belonged to us by right' – the 'right', as we have seen, of an ancestral claim by marriage. Where so much uncertainty existed as to the abstract justice of a ruler's cause, the clergy, in addressing their congregations, could at least fall back on the fail-safe principle that 'the duty of obedience doth make the soldier innocent', and thus could support opposing rulers within the same faith with no more than a warning to their flocks that as soldiers they should continue to behave as Christians.

This is not to say that individuals, clerics and laymen alike, did not suffer in conscience and intellect over the very idea of wars among Christians. But the case for inter-state conflict also gained some colour from the unarguable case for the justice of a general category of war, crusade. By the mid-fifteenth century the practicability of a pan-European crusade against the infidel occupiers of the Holy Land was, it is true, nil. A wave of crusading good intention had fluttered across Europe after the fall of Constantinople. Another followed the landing in 1480 of a Turkish army at Otranto, on the Italian Apulian coast. And successive popes tried to arouse crusading zeal, even those, like Alexander VI, Julius II and Leo X, who were also conducting wars of their own to reinforce political control within the Papal State. As late as 1578 King Sebastian of Portugal lost his life leading a crusade in Morocco – and thus enabled Spain to take over the throne he left to the short-lived Cardinal Henry. War against the Turks in

Hungary from 1593 was accompanied by a spirit of genuine crusading mission. It is true that the notion of crusade became diluted by the recognition that the Turks had come to form part of the geo-political European scene, to fight, trade and negotiate with; and it became diverted by the west's absorption in its own domestic problems. But the idea of crusade remained alive, and respected, and by inference it helped to validate other wars fought for causes pleasing in the eyes of God.

If the churches, with their immense opportunities for propaganda on the state's behalf, could be relied on to support wars (though on occasion protesting against additional taxation), the aristocracies of Europe were influenced in their favour by another ideology.

As with crusades, the hold of chivalry over the imagination long outlasted the withering away of the relevance of its international code of behaviour and training to the actual practice of war. The creation of new orders of knighthood by princes – 'national chivalries', as they have been called – enhanced this tendency by creating elite corps sworn to be loyal above all to the ruler. Chivalrous literature, which had never been so prolific, ceased – save in Tasso's Catholic-revivalist *Gerusalemme liberata* (1581) – to stress the spiritual goal of knightly quests. 'Chivalric' gestures remained: a challenge to single combat, the release without ransom of a particularly gallant foe, efforts to save civilians, especially women, from the horrors of sack. But most of these episodes are better seen within the context of the freemasonry of professional soldiers of fortune, or of the gentleman's code which was evolving through secularization of the chivalric one. Chivalry had seldom appeared in its most exemplary form on the battlefield, and as the role of infantry and firearms became predominant, the cult of the emblazoned individual heavy cavalryman in any case lost its focus. And in parallel with these changes in military practice, the characteristic recreations of the chivalric class – the joust, or single combat and the *mêlée*, or group engagement – became subject to rules (blunted lances and swords, the insulating barrier) which made them both safer for the combatants and more attractive as theatrical entertainments for the spectators. Danger remained. Skilled riding and hard hacking provided athletic training useful in war even if the techniques employed were not directly applicable. But the tournament, no matter how seductive the air of nostalgia that glamorized its choreography, could no longer be seen as an adequate training for war.

This shift from vocation to fashion, however, does not alter the part played by the chivalric tradition in getting support for a ruler's determination to go to war from the class whose cooperation he most relied on.

Chivalry had started as the coaxing by church and kings of violent instincts into ethically justifiable and politically useful courses. This institutionalization of recklessness had always produced strange bedfellows. By the late fifteenth century, for every *preux chevalier* there was a brigand, for a Bayard, 'chevalier sans peur et sans reproche', a Jean de Salazar, who named his children from the romances of chivalry, Tristan, Galeas, Hector and Lancelot, but robbed his way to supporting them. The idealization of violence, with hunt and tournament leading to battle, was still so pervasive in the lifetime of the pacific Sir Thomas More that one of the major themes in his *Utopia* is an attack on the whole range of chivalrous-aristocratic values and practices. As we shall see, personal military service came to appeal less and less to the aristocracy. But their values, as they modified into the gentleman's code, retained more than traces of chivalric ones: the right to hunt and to go armed, a class monopoly of the concept of honour, scorn of the timorous and unmartial qualities of bourgeois and peasant, belief that the battlefield, like the duelling ground, was the proper place to settle quarrels among equals. As a result, even though the number of the Second Estate willing to serve in person declined, rulers could broadly rely on this essential echelon in the mobilization process to support a call to war.

The larger echelon of men whose assent was necessary for running the war machine contained influential clerics, landowners and wealthy townsmen who either had, or had aspirations towards, aristocratic status, and a wide scattering of full- or part-time government officials. These groups could be expected to cooperate with a ruler's demands. But their local concerns were of livelier interest than decisions made in distant capitals, and they were reluctant to tip their private purses into the public one. It was a hesitation shared by other urban and rural members of this echelon who were concerned with tolls and taxes, and the cost of equipping local recruits and strengthening defence works.

This was, all the same, a literate sector. So it is at least interesting to glance at the reading matter of the period to catch the tone of what was written about war.

Its most notable feature is the growing treatment of war as a secular phenomenon, distinct from divine punishments like plague, murrain and successions of bad harvests. War may have been itself a plague, but it was a man-made one. That individual wars were the result of political decisions was, of course, clear enough from the preambles of alliances and in public proclamations explaining why a particular war was being embarked on. It was the linking of these instances into a concept of causation that was new. The popularization of interest in the wars of classical antiquity was influential here; for while ancient history as a whole may have been part of God's waiting game for the right moment to enter the world as Christ (as Dante had suggested), the actual campaigns were clearly motivated by fears and greeds readily compared by contemporaries to their own. By 1600 a novel, classically derived ethic of grin-and-bear-it positive pessimism was emerging, neo-Stoicism, which taught how men should adapt to the strains of a war-world of their own creation.

Humanism's main (and not unchallenged) contribution to much that was thought and written about war was, indeed, the enabling of the imagination to picture a world unpatrolled by the Christian God. It was this comparative vision that encouraged Renaissance writers to state clearly what had previously been known to men of affairs but not openly articulated. A conspiracy of silence about political self-determination, about the role of force in establishing states, extending and defending them, and maintaining law and order within them, was broken through by a wave of defiant pragmatism. Machiavelli's *The Prince* is only the best written of a whole wave of gloves-off works about the realities of political life. The disconnected wars of the medieval chronicle became, under the influence of classical historians (and, thanks similarly to the printing press, of a closer knowledge of contemporary nations, including the Turks), instances of an enduring human dilemma, 'war'; as Sir Walter Raleigh, early in the seventeenth century, put it as he summed up his favourite reading matter: 'The ordinary theme and argument of history is war.' We are not far, here, from Furió Ceriol's recommendation in 1559 that the Spanish Council of War should establish an archive of records relating to the conduct and results of ancient and contemporary wars.

Secularized interpretations of war's inevitability, given rulers' ambition and the nature of man as a political animal, led to cyclical theories on the lines of Luigi da Porto's 'peace brings riches, riches pride, pride wrath, wrath war, war poverty, poverty mildness, mildness peace, peace riches', and so on and on. It led to a steady emphasis on the need in peace to prepare for war. Shakespeare passed on a common assumption when in *Henry V* he made the heir to the French throne remind his father that

> It is most meet we arm us 'gainst the foe;
> For peace itself should not so dull a kingdom,
> Though war nor no known quarrel were in question,
> But that defences, musters, preparations,
> Should be maintain'd, assembled and collected,
> As were a war in expectation.

And it led, even more significantly, to the wide expression of reasons why war should actually be provoked, how it could be used to improve a national community: a foreign war diverted men from making trouble at home; it rid a country of social dross; it acted as a stimulating tonic to a lethargic body politic.

How far individuals within the sector we are considering came into contact with the ideas expressed in books is, naturally, impossible to say. The extent of interest in them is, however, suggested by a list of topics proposed for discussion in a mid-century (1551) Italian book about domestic pastimes: 'Why do all our lords and princes go to war?'; 'What is a legitimate war?'; 'May Christians wage war among one another?'; 'Whose victories are the greater, those of peace or war?'; 'Why do men set off in a spirit of glory to wars that are full of misfortunes?' That authors learned from other authors is, of course, clear enough. In 1606 Dudley Digges referred to the inevitability of being afflicted by war 'in this iron age' in the context of references to Aristotle, Xenophon and Quintilian and a quotation from a contemporary (and untranslated) French author. But books registered well beyond their readership. The remarkable range of Shakespeare's acquaintance with contemporary ideas about war and military theory and practice was not derived from active service or (as far as has been ascertained) paraphrased from specific books. His own ability to catch the drift from a wide miscellany of works dealing with war, and acquaintance with ex-soldiers, is no yardstick, but it does suggest how the transmission of ideas and information worked through browsing rather than reading, through conversation with those better informed, through listening to sermons or speeches in legal sessions or city councils.

What was passed down in these ways contained little denunciation of war as such. The international wave of quasi-pacifist feeling that for a generation stirred the writings of More in

England, Erasmus in Holland, Guillaume Budé in France, Juan Luis Vives in Spain, and, in a less systematic way, Baldassare Castiglione in Italy, soon died away. And even they had had to accept that in certain circumstances a ruler could be justified in using force, even though wars fought in a mood of aggression, out of a perverted sense of glory, could never be approved. Thereafter, though there were plenty of warnings against expecting campaigns to repay their costs, and against the evil consequences of awakening the licentiousness of the soldiery, authors (and not just because of a growing awareness of political censorship) accepted that wars would be called for and, if called for, would have to be fought. Influenced by the polarization of denominational and political enmities, the most concerned minds, instead of denouncing war, concentrated on ways of ameliorating it.

Accepting that, as in a court of law, opposing war leaders could both believe in the justice of their cause, and, perturbed in conscience by Spain's genocidal wars in the Americas, lawyers concentrated on working out principles that could encourage negotiation, limit the territorial scope of wars and mitigate their devastations and cruelties. Chivalrous notions of respect for the worthy adversary and gallantry towards the weak and helpless; humanistic emphasis on *concordia* and on magnanimity as the most praiseworthy quality in the ruler; Christian emphasis on mercy and the blessedness of peacemakers; political theorists' debates on the limits of sovereign authority; legal caution and tidy-mindedness: all these were components within a new approach to the international law of war which culminated in 1625 with Hugo Grotius's *De jure belli ac pacis*. This eclectic pragmatism is more impressive today, and was more appealing and influential then, than parallel suggestions as to how European warfare could be stopped altogether. In this latter vein Castiglione proposed that rulers should be content with making the best of what they had got, and direct warlike instincts into a shared crusade. Charles V's grand chancellor, Mercurino Gattinara, believed that peace could only come when every country accepted the overlordship and arbitration of the Holy Roman Emperor – an idea echoed by the Frenchman Guillaume Postel, but in terms of a revival of the idea of universal empire in Carolingian terms. Scarcely more likely to commend itself was the duke of Sully's proposal for a newly sliced-up Europe of fifteen equal powers, linked by freedom of trade, religious toleration and an agreed arbitration mechanism, or, in 1623, Emeric Crucé's more prophetic vision of a permanent organization in Venice comprising representatives from every important European court, which would settle international quarrels peacefully while the violence of individuals was channelled into sports, hunting and police work against pirates and brigands.

There was, then, a wide range of peace-seeking ideas which could filter down to the levels where support for war was considered. But no idea, of course, had greater influence than a calculation of gains and penalties in the immediate local context. Peace parties, whether in municipal or in princely or republican councils, were not formed from groups of idealists or philosophers but from practical men who drew different conclusions from the same set of facts and arguments that moved their more militant colleagues. The absorption of general ideas about war and peace was, in any case, pestered by proclamations, broadsheets, and pamphlets: the use of the press for propaganda purposes was becoming highly developed as early as the reigns of Charles VIII and Maximilian, as was the circulation of satirical political prints and woodcuts. And initial pressure to justify hostilities was sustained by a flow of slanted official bulletins and news-sheets reporting on the progress of campaigns.

Propaganda stressed the rightfulness and necessity of the national case and contempt for and hatred of the enemy. And certainly Europe could be represented as primed with national antipathies that could explode in war. Philippe de Commines, successively councillor of Duke Charles the Bold of Burgundy and Louis XI, and the trusted negotiator of Charles VIII, wrote that God had so planned history as to place a rival nation by each ruler's side: 'thus he has confronted the Kingdom of France with the English, the English with the Scots, the Kingdom of Spain with Portugal', and so forth. Erasmus wrote more bitterly: 'practically every Angle hates the Gaul, and every Gaul the Angle, for no other reason than that he is an Angle. The Irishman, just because he is an Irishman, hates the Briton; the Italian hates the German; the Swabian the Swiss; and so on throughout the list. District hates district and city hates city.' Both men exaggerated because they had axes to grind. Commines wished to indicate a providential plan which should, through the existence of checks and balances, lead to an orderly balance of powers. Erasmus wished to shame men for putting national and local rivalries before 'the common name of Christ'.

Antagonisms between nations there certainly were, but they

were neither so clearly defined nor so widely shared as to provide a cause of war or to guarantee automatic support for one, either among the sectors we have been looking at or the larger one into which governments delved for troops. Geo-political Europe had been shaped by centuries of wars, but they had never involved whole populations or broken down the enduring process whereby local resentments ('district hates district, and city hates city') fostered a satisfying sense of 'otherness'. Local patriotisms could merge into regional loyalties, and both at times could become aware of a larger shared identity: a history shaped by 'their' rulers; a common (or roughly common, for there was a dialectal mosaic within all frontiers) language; a shared space (most strongly felt in island England and peninsular Spain and Italy) which nature had appointed as a home; a sense that somehow 'they' had contributed something to the world that set them apart. It was this that, on occasion, led armies comprising mutually competitive peninsular units to battle against crude northerners with the cry of 'Italy!', and that prompted Budé to dedicate a treatise (on ancient Roman coinage) to 'The genius of France'.

Anti-foreigner feeling could break out violently when those at home thought that they were being excluded from privileges or positions that rightfully belonged to themselves. The importation by Charles V (himself a foreigner) of Burgundian administrators to Spain; the protection by Henry VIII of foreign merchants; the patronage extended by Catherine de Medici to her compatriots; these are all occasions that led to the expression of rampant national prejudice. The literary equivalent of this antipathy was the development of folk characterizations of foreigners (Germans sots, Florentines sodomites, the English with tails curled up inside their breeches, etc.) into a veritable *genre*, sometimes highly fantasticized, sometimes subtle. Neither instinctive resentment nor intellectual playfulness, however, suggests that countries went to war because they hated their stereotypes of one another.

But did wars, once started, acquire an impetus from nationalistic rancour?

In a country fought over by foreign armies there was a patternless series of relationships – fraternizations and business deals of mutual advantage, atrocities and deprivations, actions which now stimulated, now wounded local pride – which were further complicated, as we shall see, by the mongrel composition of armies and by the mutual respect that brought fighting men of both sides together in a shared contempt for civilians. These relationships, in spite of a flow of would-be unifying propaganda, expressed not just in government leaflets, but in commanders' pep-talks, never coalesced into a lastingly exacerbated nationalistic antagonism except in the Netherlands, where occupation and warfare lengthened over decades and where religious differences added a frantic ingredient to political-patriotic ones. Reformation religion, like the slow capillary growth of centralized administration, helped to pull towards a nationalistic mould a still very loose mixture of subjective patriotism and clearly realized regional self-identity. But it is very doubtful whether this process was encouraged on the spot by war.

It could, indeed, be argued that peace, fair administration, good policing, economic protectionism and restrictions on travel (all of which conditions obtained at intervals in most countries from the 1530s) did more to encourage a sense of nationhood than the jolting and cosmopolitan experience of men serving in armies abroad. Foreign wars were not waged by men whose patriotism – where it existed – was of a missionizing nature. Military service induced a restlessness and criminality that every country found it difficult to reabsorb. And war offered experiences and camaraderies that during its long inactions broke the spell of national identity. William Lambarde, a JP in Kent, the English county which saw the greatest outflow and return of soldiers serving on the continent, commented on this phenomenon in some despair in 1596. 'Since the time that our nation hath conversed with foreign people in the wars abroad, what Frenchman so garish and light in apparel, what Dutchman so daily drunken and given to the pot, what Irish more idle and thievishly disposed, what Scot more cowardly, sudden, and ready to stab, what Spaniard more insolent, fleshly, or blasphemous than be many of our own English, who have not only learned and transported hither all these vices of those other men, but are grown so perniciously cunning therein that they excel their teachers and teach it to others at home?'

Without the sort of nationalism that seeks and provides momentum for wars, and in the absence of an effective system of conscription, we cannot speak in this period of a militarized society, let alone of a militarized civilization. Thanks to the persistence of a sense of feudal loyalty and obligation, and to the firmer grip of central bureaucracies on regional administration, one can, nonetheless, speak of a society adequately organized to produce wars on demand, in spite, as we shall see, of a sluggish resistance to paying for or serving in them.

The rulers of early modern Europe had certain important advantages over their medieval predecessors when planning a campaign. Their sources of information were better, thanks largely to a greatly extended diplomatic service. They had – at least from the planning stage of Charles VIII's invasion of Italy – maps which enabled both major strategic moves and key tactical targets to be visualized more or less accurately. (The extent to which maps could whet appetite is suggested by Martin du Bellay's comment that when Charles V obtained a map of Provence in 1536 'he convinced himself that he already possessed the land in the same way that he owned the map'.) They had larger revenues and better facilities for obtaining credit – though the history of truces and peace treaties runs in tandem with that of periods of financial exhaustion. They had improved administrations and a new source of propaganda with which to bring pressure and cajolement to bear on larger enlistable populations – yet commanders were seldom content with the numbers, let alone the quality, of the troops they led.

For the central mystery of politicized conflict is not why wars took place but how enough men could be found to fight in them. That, and the repercussions of war through society as a whole, is the subject – after a look at the technical nature of combat – of the rest of this book.

2

The military reformation: techniques and organization

After a century-long apprenticeship (references to the use of guns in combat begin from the mid-fourteenth century) portable firearms and artillery came radically to affect the conduct and conditions of war. For the soldier they changed the equipment he wore and carried; the formations which affected his morale and practice in combat; the nature of his wounds, for they broke bones and led to the loss of limbs by gangrene; and, more conjecturally, his chances of being killed. Because the military engineers' response to artillery was to design stronger fortifications which could shelter forces an enemy would be unwise to leave intact behind him as he pressed forward, guns led to longer sieges, and these extended the campaigner's active year beyond the old rhythm of summer fighting followed by disbandment or winter-quarters ease. Men froze to death in the siege-lines outside Metz in 1552 and equipment ordered for Spanish armies in the Netherlands in the 1570s included skates.

For governments, firearms sharply increased the costs of war. As far as hand-held weapons were concerned, the soldier was supposed either to bring one with him or to repay its loan through a stoppage from his wages. But governments had to stockpile them and never recouped their investment. For artillery, they paid the full cost and it was high: as early as 1482 the artillery service of France accounted for 8 per cent of the military budget. Thereafter, for every government, the percentage, or at least the capital expenditure, increased. In peacetime there was the progressive accumulation of a 'park' of field and siege guns, and a growing establishment of men to serve, refashion and administer them; in wartime there were the formidable costs of ammunition. In 1589 a Venetian military adviser calculated that if Brescia were to be besieged, its 65 pieces of artillery should be able to fire 400 shots each; powder and ball for this would cost 43,000 ducats, more than half the entire annual wages of the 2347 infantry then in garrisons on the *terraferma*. From 1609 Venice earmarked 36,000 ducats a year for the purchase of saltpetre alone. War also brought the engagement of draught animals (some forty to each medium-calibre gun and its supplies), carts, drivers, pioneers, smiths, carpenters to repair gun-carriages, masons to make balls of stone if the supply of iron ones ran out; it also meant that members of the voluntary gunnery 'schools' now came on the pay-roll. Gunpowder weapons and their services may have added a third to the costs of a campaign. One estimate of *c.* 1600 put it as high as a half for an artillery train alone. It can be assumed that no battle and no siege, for this reason, ever fully demonstrated the power of the new weapons.

Finally, gunpowder was chiefly responsible for the most significant military development of all: the increased size of armies. Firearms became adopted as the standard missile weapon soon after the victories of the Swiss pike phalanxes over the Burgundian forces of Charles the Bold had led to a new respect for the infantry's power to resist cavalry charges. By the 1520s, when they came to be treated with a respect equal to that accorded to the pike (not only because of the hitting power of bullets but because guns could be poked through holes and rested on the parapets of field fortifications more conveniently than could cross- or longbows), this doubled proof of the foot soldier's effectiveness had led not only to the proportion of infantry to cavalry being steadily increased but to a demand for more and more of them. And this coincided with the realization that sieges were taking longer. The new bastioned fortifications were stronger in themselves, and both the artillery they mounted and the firearms used by their defenders tended to produce stalemates resolved more readily by starvation than by storming. To keep supplies from being forced into a besieged city and to counter sallies by the defenders against the siege-lines, while at the same time maintaining a field force, larger overall forces were required.

The increased costs of this growing reliance on gunpowder weapons were passed on to the population at large: they paid higher taxes, and, thanks to higher imposts on commodities, they paid more for what they wore, ate and drank. The increased size of armies was passed on still more personally through the voracious appetite of the recruiting process.

In 1521 the Venetian Council of Ten proclaimed that 'there can be no doubt whatsoever that one of the chief factors in the protection of lands and of armies is the artillery'. No one was going to shake his head over this weighty hindsight. Guns had contributed to the taking of English strongholds during the last stages of the Hundred Years War. The conquest of Granada was largely a process of reducing towns and castles. By 1500 every monarch had invested, and heavily. Wheeled, rather than sledded, carriages were introduced from the 1460s and made cannon easier to transport to siege or battlefield. One of the bulletins Charles VIII sent back to be printed and circulated in France by the regency during his triumphal campaign of 1494–5 showed with what nonchalance he was able to knock out one unmodified fortified place after another on his route to Naples:

> Today [4 February 1495] I besieged one of the strongest places in this whole region, both for its defences and its situation. It is called Monte San Giovanni. . . . My cousin Montpensier had arrived before me with my artillery . . . and after firing for four hours my said artillery had made a breach wide enough for an assault. I ordered it to be made by men-at-arms and others, and though the place was held by 5–600 good fighting men as well as its inhabitants, they went in in such a manner that, thanks to God, [the town] has been taken with little loss to me, and to the defenders great loss, punishment and great example to those others who might think of so obstructing me.

The first convincing demonstration that field artillery could determine the outcome of a battle also occurred in Italy: the forcing out near Ravenna in 1512 by Spanish gunfire of the securely entrenched French army of Louis XII. No campaigns had been recorded with such close contemporary attention as these earlier ones of the Thirty-six Years War, and their message seemed clear: artillery was transforming the conduct of war.

With our own hindsight, this opinion has to be nuanced. Guns were only one factor in the reduction of a city; the ability of Famagusta to hold out for months against a vastly superior and almost constantly cannonading Turkish army in 1571, or of Rouen to resist months of English bombardment in 1591–2 shows how crucial were other factors: morale, supply, defensive ingenuity, the skill with which the guns themselves were placed and handled. Similarly in battle: artillery could condition the timing of an action, to a lesser extent its tactics, but its outcome depended on numbers, experience, skill, command intelligence, and again, and above all, on morale. Charles the Bold had more cannon than any other power in Europe. They neither reduced the cities he besieged nor saved him from defeat in the field. It was the French who were the victors at Ravenna.

There was something not altogether rational about the way in which the alchemist's weapon came to win, as it were, its spurs. That Henry IV's grand master of the artillery should adopt around 1600 an eagle clutching the divine thunderbolts of Jove as his emblem is not surprising. It is more interesting that as early as 1465 the Burgundian grandee and jouster Louis de Bruges chose a bombard, and that around 1505 Duke Alfonso of Ferrara selected a bomb. In both cases the reference was to the power latent within the inert metal casing; rigid control, ignited by a spark of righteous passion, could lead to an explosion. The power of guns to release the imagination as well as projectiles is shown, too, in the names given them. Not just to types of artillery – basilisks, serpents, falcons, sparrow-hawks (*sacres* and sakers) – but to individual pieces: 'Mad Margaret', 'Lion', 'Monster', 'Messenger', 'No more words!' Many of these named guns of the fifteenth century were huge: 'Monster' – otherwise known as Mons Meg from its possible place of origin – weighed some five tons. It was hauled away from Edinburgh to the siege of Norham in 1479 to the accompaniment of the town band. These guns, which fired so slowly and inaccurately, were as much symbols as weapons. The great bombard commissioned by the city of Strasbourg was called 'The Ostrich' because it laid such tough and enormous eggs when its crop was full of powder. It was sent to the siege of Héricourt in 1474 less, surely, for the effectiveness of the fourteen shots it could belch forth in the course of a day, than for its reassuring potency as a mascot. The day of these impractical monsters was short. Mons Meg was laid up in 1501. But their fabrication, like the purchase and display to visitors of artillery parks containing more guns than were strictly justified by the current evidence of their usefulness, suggests an overreaction, at once awed and swaggering, that was an early means of emotionally coming to terms with the inevitability that gunpowder weapons as a whole had come to stay.

There followed a century of steady rationalization that was to leave little scope for further development until the introduction of the rifled barrel and the explosive shell in the nineteenth century. Rulers built up their own corps of gunfounders instead of relying on immigrant – chiefly Italian and German – specialists. They set up training 'schools' for gunners and formalized the financing and staffing of ordnance departments. By the mid-sixteenth century much had been done to reduce the number of types of gun and to standardize their calibres and ammunition. The 'proving' of guns became more methodical: charges were carefully weighed, ranges at different elevations measured. Books were published dealing with practical gunnery and the theory of ballistics. Inventors of new forms of propellant, or handier or more versatile types of gun, were given a hearing and sometimes financed to make prototypes for the proving ground. The relationship between a master gunner and his weapon remained a personal one, for no two guns performed identically and, thanks to the slew of the carriage on recoil, no shot could be fired without realignment. And the care lavished on the inscribing and embellishment of large bronze pieces still bore witness to the earlier instinct that guns did not only communicate prestige but could have a mysterious personality of their own. But the artillery, from its manufacture to its administration and – though less clearly – its employment, shows, as does the development of challenge-and-response military architecture, how 'scientific' the early modern treatment of war could be when it was dealing with materials rather than men.

While the most advanced and lovingly made cannon or culverin was intended to see service, only rich sportsmen and princely collectors got their hands on portable firearms of advanced and expensive design – rifled, multi-shot, with revolving barrels or chambers – and exquisite embellishment. Military firearms, though hand-made, were mass-produced, and this utilitarian characterlessness helped in the rapid growth of their use. When Louis XI, intent on employing pikes modelled on those which had given the Swiss their victories, rejected one batch after another of those submitted by French armourers as inadequate, an observer was moved to comment that the fuss would only be justified 'if he would also manufacture men capable of handling them'. The long-hafted Swiss pike was but the sharp end of high communal morale and much voluntary spare-time training; in a sense, the pike was a 'national' weapon. Other countries borrowed it. It became shortly after 1500 an essential supplement to shorter-hafted weapons like the halberd, and to the sword. But no other country used it with the confident ferocity of the Swiss. In the same way other regions, notably northern France and the Low Countries, had adopted the English longbow after its successes at Crécy and Agincourt, but, again, without the results due to English training and – on the battlefield, at least – patriotic identification with 'the weapon of English men'. But firearms could do appreciable damage with less training than was required for other arms and their spread had been so rapid and so universal that they had picked up no national overtones. It is true that behind the protection of their shores many of the English felt it safe to cling to their traditional weapon. It was only the need to cooperate with the Dutch from 1585 that led to definite orders to the trained bands – the pick of the militia reserve – to drop them. But in 1596 the Privy Council was still sending out orders to lords lieutenant urging them to proceed with 'changing your bowmen into muskets and your billmen into pikes'. Elsewhere, however, the progress of firearms was unchallenged. In 1543 Michel d'Amboise in his *Le guidon des gens de guerre* could think of little better advice to give a general who had fewer of them than his adversary than to try to force battle upon him on a rainy day.

From the last decades of the fifteenth century the triggerless handgun, held under the arm, was replaced by the arquebus and the slightly shorter caliver, both fired from the shoulder (though some had deep butts for steadying against the chest) through a trigger which lowered the end of a piece of slow-match into the priming pan. And from the 1540s the heavier musket, supported on a rest stuck into the ground, gained in acceptance because, in spite of its longer loading time, it could pierce all but specially reinforced siege armour at 200–240 paces.

An infantry of shot only would not have been able to protect themselves from cavalry who got through their fire, nor push home an attack or force a retreat into a rout, because they could not load or shoot when in movement and were too lightly protected to fight boldly hand to hand. To repel an attack, to attack in turn, pikemen were essential, as were halberdiers who, with their heavier breastplates and handier weapons, could deal with troops, horse or foot, who got in among the unwieldy pikes and could not be reached by the shot. The real casualty among practitioners of the *arme blanche* were swordsmen. The first to go were those two-handers whose strength in the swinging of their huge weapons made them, especially in Germany, the most respected of footmen. Vulnerable to fire while a-whirling, they are difficult to trace after 1515, though artists continued to associate them, along with pike and halberd, with the burly image of the *Landsknecht*. Then followed the sword-and-buckler men, though Machiavelli's belief that, sent against pike, they could knock the point aside with their shield and then strike home with the sword, was revived experimentally by Prince Maurice of Nassau late in the sixteenth century. Swords were demoted to weapons of self-defence or finishing off:

another victory over the Middle Ages, like that over the slow battle-charger, that was hastened by the freer use of gunpowder.

The proportion of arms within the infantry – halberdiers, pikemen, arquebusiers (from the mid-sixteenth century used mainly as skirmishers) and musketeers – is difficult to establish with any degree of certainty. Governmental decisions, like Louis XI's orders for the fabrication of pikes and the Venetian decision to issue practically the whole of its newly formed militia in 1508 with firearms, could slowly influence the traditional pattern, and the fact that so many recruits turned up weaponless helped foster this redistribution. But the majority came with the arms their ancestors or their region had been used to. And it was long before there was any agreement about what the ideal combination was.

In Venice the proportion was first fixed in 1548, at 10 per cent halberds, 30 per cent arquebuses, 60 per cent pikes. French contracts of 1562 simply specified 33 per cent of arquebusiers. For the English 1571–2 campaign in France the recommended balance in newly formed companies was 6 per cent halberds, 20 per cent muskets, 34 per cent calivers and 40 per cent pikes; this was adjusted in 1589 to 10 per cent halberds, 30 per cent pikes and 60 per cent unspecified shot. By 1600 France was aiming for equal proportions of pike and shot, and Spain for 10 per cent halberds, 30 per cent pikes, 25 per cent muskets and 35 per cent arquebuses. Overall, the century was marked not only by a notable increase in the proportion of shot but an equally strongly confirmed preference for the pike over other forms of hafted weapons. The chief discrepancies between numbers called for and the arms that actually appeared concern muskets; communities responsible for equipping contingents tried to stick to the cheaper caliver or arquebus, and governments jibbed at the higher wage due to musketeers.

That this concern for exact proportions should emerge only from the mid-century is not surprising. Getting small (100–150 men was the norm) companies of mixed arms into battle position was a highly complex task for the campmaster or sergeant-major. But it was becoming apparent that while large-scale engagements were always a possibility and sometimes a need, most service time was spent in raids, skirmishes, counterattacks against attempts to break siege-lines, or small-front operations against breaches. And here the self-sufficiency of companies operating on their own or in small groups was all important. All the same, save in the long-service Spanish army in the Netherlands, where deaths and desertions and the steady arrival of recruits dependent on government issue helped the actual distribution of arms to resemble what theory called for, none of these proportions was achieved in practice; they represent tendencies but do not freeze the real state of affairs at any given time.

The proportion of cavalry (of all sorts) to infantry was even more dependent on the availability of horsemen and the ability to pay their higher wages; even ideal proportions were not laid down. What happened in practice can be seen from some figures, given in rounded thousands.

Year		Cavalry	Infantry
1475	Castile–Aragon v. Portugal	12	30
1485	Castile v. Granada	11	25
1489	Castile v. Granada	13	40
1494	France, invasion of Italy	13	15
1509	France, battle of Agnadello	14	16
1509	Venice, battle of Agnadello	9	20
1515	France, battle of Pavia	5	24
1552	France, Metz campaign	6	32
c. 1555	Venice, standing army	1.5	5
1562	Battle of Dreux. Protestants	4.5	7
	Catholics	2	15
1590	Battle of Ivry. Protestants	3	8
	Catholics	4	12
1610	French effectives	6.5	62

Perhaps the best comparison among these confusing figures is that between the French armies of 1494 and 1552, the composition of both of which was carefully negotiated. The others reflect a variety of factors that make comparison hazardous: declining 'feudal' participation (1475 and 1489); length of service, cavalry being more difficult to replace than infantry (1515); the nature of the terrain to be patrolled and policed by peacetime forces (1555: most were deployed overseas in Dalmatia, Crete and Cyprus); fluctuations in local resources (1562 and 1590); specific conditions: the proportion of horse in Spain's forces in the Netherlands was abnormally low because of the canal-ridden nature of the countryside and the concentration on sieges. While overall the proportion of horse in armies undoubtedly declined during the period, there is no other aspect of the game of military statistics that has to be played with such caution; and not only with respect to numbers, but to the military value represented by them.

The heavy cavalryman, or man-at-arms, was at peak efficiency in 1450. No longer cramped by a heavy mail undergarment, he was more at ease within a self-sufficient plate armour which, although heavier, was suspended, as it were, from the shoulders, and allowed the body's musculature to work fairly freely. The *arrêt*, the projecting hook riveted to the right side of his breastplate, assisted him to cradle the lance for support and balance and, therefore, aim. With lance shattered, he could fall back on his sword or, against a disarmed but still armoured foe, his lobster-cracking tool, the mace.

It was a highly specialized branch of the service. The man-at-arms had to be one of a class that could choose to buy either a new suit of armour or a small farm at an equivalent price. To protect his throat from missiles he wore a collar fixed to the breastplate which made it almost impossible to move his head from side to side. To protect his eyes his helm provided mere slits or a honeycomb of holes to peer through. He needed, then, the leisure and training of the tournament to accustom himself to turning his torso rather than his head and to navigating through the equivalent of a starred windscreen. Thus accoutred, and riding a charger 'barded' with plate or leather (as much against the sword thrusts of footmen as against missiles), the man-at-arms himself was a slow, weighty missile, very difficult to resist and as near invulnerable as any soldier could be amidst the chances of the battlefield.

This picture had many variants. Not all men-at-arms could afford full plate, let alone replace a suit with the newly fashionable Italianate or south German armours. Not all could bear its constriction: some were killed by missiles because they had removed gorget or bevor. The supply of war-chargers varied from country to country. Only France, Burgundy and Italy had as many as were needed. Worst off was Spain where the shortage had led the aristocracy to take unashamedly to the mule as their usual mode of transport. Isabella tried by legislation to enforce the adoption of the war-horse of at least fifteen hands in the north, where her armies could expect to encounter the heavy cavalry of France, and in the south the fleeter steeds employed by Castile's other adversary, the Moors of Granada. But legislation could not produce horses and as a result Spanish armies contained a higher proportion of infantry than others of the late fifteenth century.

The man-at-arms had always needed to be accompanied by a squire or page to help him dress and undress and a servant-groom to supervise his baggage, pitch his tent or prepare his quarters and, at need, help the squire to protect him, sword in hand. He was the head of a small family unit, the 'lance', and as the numbers and hazard of infantry increased he acknowledged the changing conditions of battle by adding to it. From the mid-fifteenth century the French 'lance' comprised man-at-arms, squire, page (increasingly useful to keep him in touch with messages from the higher command as tactics became rather more flexible), servant and two archers or crossbowmen who dismounted to fight. In still more 'chivalrous' Burgundy, the 'lance' contained up to six potential infantrymen: three or four archers, a handgunman and a halberdier. How far these extended 'families' kept together to support their chief if he were hard-pressed or isolated, or were diverted into separate detachments of horse and foot, is unclear. The Burgundian 'lance' was exceptionally large, but in general the most tradition-conscious type of medieval warrior showed a capacity to adapt. He was prepared to dismount and rally shaken infantry. He was quick to draft the new firepower into his own entourage – while, by so doing, putting an additional pressure on a never adequate supply of horses that helped to limit the number of cavalrymen of his own stamp that could be put into the field.

As pike and shot became more numerous and influential, the all-purpose 'lance' became decreasingly relevant. Bands of mounted crossbowmen and handgunmen were raised on their own account, capable of firing from the saddle but, except in the case of highly trained units like Charles VIII's 'poudriers' (so named in exaggeration of their gunpowder-grained faces), usually employing the horse merely as a means of quick deployment. By the 1520s the 'lance' had been drained of its horse-propelled infantrymen and the 'heavies' were progressively challenged by the introduction of medium cavalry, lancers and pistoleers (from the 1540s, though preceded by a few experimental companies), and by growing numbers of light cavalry, miscellaneous in equipment and armament but progressively valued as raiders, scouts, supply interceptors and dispatch riders. The role of cavalry remained essential even while numbers dropped proportionately to the infantry, but it became a more flexible one, based on harassment, the quick relief of pressure-points, effective pursuit. Permanent heavy cavalry units survived in a few countries – France, Venice, Milan – as prestige guards or to satisfy noble pretensions and as a sop to men who, like Scipio Costanzo, claimed (in a memorandum of 1577 to the doge of Venice arguing against their disbandment) that while governments seemed to think that the future lay with infantry and defence works they still needed 'this mass of steel, this fortress of armour'. Besides, he argued, 'innovations have always been pernicious, or at least hazardous'. Venice kept them in being, and in 1616, after less than a year of the War of Gradisca, the doge received their casualty figures: out of some 750 men 190 were dead, 48 ill or wounded, 82 absent without leave. This is due, the report said, to their continually being engaged in standing guard, clearing roads, patrolling, turning out with the other cavalry for night alarms and being ready to fight by day; this sort of cavalry, 'whose role in an army is to take part in battles and stiffen the light cavalry', is unsuited to a campaign of skirmish and siege and vulnerable to sickness in bad weather.

This was not quite an epitaph on the Venetian men-at-arms, who only disappeared in the 1620s, but it helps to explain why they were retained only as a tolerated anachronism among a more up-to-date cavalry with pistol-proof helmet, a cuirass arquebus-proof on the front and pistol-proof in the back, but otherwise lightly equipped, and flexibly armed with pistols plus sword or lance or carbine.

The steady increase in the numbers and use of the artillery (though it remained more effective in sieges than in the field), changes in the roles and weaponry of foot and horse; these developments caused war to be treated as a self-sufficient subject. From a manuscript dribble, treatises on war became a printed flood. From the 1550s, books covered every aspect of warfare (except strategy): weapons, tactics, company drill, battle formations, siegecraft and defence, the ideal characteristics of officers and men. Word by word, woodblock by woodblock, diagram by diagram, from tourneying dolls to full formations of lead soldiers, 'war' was studied and discussed throughout the west. And not only among professional soldiers; the prevalent humanistic strain in learning emphasized how much modern soldiering had to learn from ancient example, Roman, Greek, Byzantine. The armchair soldier, the scholarly or merely enthusiastic military buff, emerged as a type, seeking out the company of captains and badgering governments with advice. Increasingly war was referred to as an 'art' in the modern sense, and not simply in that of its original meaning of 'craft' or 'trade'; the first published large-scale and systematic treatment of warfare, complete with tactical diagrams, was Machiavelli's *Art of War* of 1522. Young men of birth, applying for leave to travel abroad, said they were going to learn from campaigns – those of Henry II in France, Maximilian II and Rudolf II against the Turk, as well as those of Philip II in the

Netherlands – referred to as 'schools' of warfare. 'The art of war is now such that men be fain to learn it anew at every two years' end,' as Charles V's minister Antoine de Granvelle pointed out in 1559, and the pace of change quickened; there are 'evrie day newe inventions, strategems of warres, change of weapons, munition, and all sorts of engins newlie invented and corrected dailie', noted Captain Sir Roger Williams in 1590.

From the 1449 *Ten Books on Machines* by Mariano di Jacopo, Il Taccola, the 'inventions' had come thick, fast and often fantastic. The Sienese sculptor and architect Francesco di Giorgio designed new forms of cannon in the 1460s. Leonardo da Vinci, seeking employment with the duke of Milan, Lodovico Sforza, represented himself first and foremost as a designer of new instruments of war, and among his notebooks are drawings of explosive projectiles, multiple-fire artillery and a steam cannon as well as an accurate anticipation of the wheel-lock. And from 1500 the pace quickened: handguns with protective shields, crossbows and swords incorporating tiny gun-barrels, repeating-shot arquebuses, a combination bow and pike. There are probably more of these inventions than of weapons actually used in war to be seen in museums today. The latter were used, re-used and then discarded; the inventions, complex, expensive and difficult to mass-produce, were retained as ingenious and often beautiful curiosities. The same ingenuity expressed itself in a search for stupefying or poisonous gases, and in the sphere of siegecraft: inflatable boats, prefabricated pontoons, elevatable fire platforms, earth-shifting machinery. Ben Jonson knew that a smile of recognition would greet Fitton's anxious question in *A Staple of News* about the Spanish general in the Netherlands:

> But what if Spinola have a new project:
> To bring an army over in cork-shoes,
> And land them here, at Harwich? All his horse
> Are shod with cork, and fourscore pieces of ordnance
> Mounted upon cork carriages, with bladders
> Instead of wheels, to run the passage over
> At a spring tide.

But the inventions, if only rarely affecting the conduct of war (as did the wheel-lock, and trunnions plus the gun-carriage), did help to establish 'war' as a branch of knowledge.

And, like other branches, it had its pedagogues, the military reformers. Some, like Machiavelli, had witnessed war but not handled a weapon. Others were professional senior officers: the reformers of Spanish military methods in the late fifteenth and early sixteenth centuries, Gonzalo de Cordoba and Gonzalo de Ayora, Lazarus von Schwendi, tirelessly working for rationalization in mid-sixteenth-century Germany, François de la Noue, sharpening his memoirs as a spur to reform in the France of the 1580s. Yet others were princes who, from Charles the Bold of Burgundy at the beginning of the period to Maurice of Nassau and Gustavus Adolphus of Sweden towards its end, were in the best position of all to meet the challenge of changing methods and expanding numbers that so persistently called for further military reformation.

All were sensitive to the need for the most necessary reform of all, that of formations and tactics. The balance between horse and foot, the emergence within both of men performing increasingly specialized functions, the predominance of firearms among the weaponry of both which led an English writer to comment in 1598 that 'it is rarely seen in our days that men come often to hand blows as in old times they did': all called for a rethinking of how armies were brigaded for administrative purposes, formed up in battle array, and divided into tactical units upon whose interdependence and flexibility an army's capacity to adjust to the circumstances of combat depended.

We shall see, shortly, how armies were composed. The combination of long-service troops gathered from scattered garrison towns with mercenary bands and flocks of native recruits made for a mixture impossible to slice into equal portions for the convenience of paymasters, commissariat officials and campmasters. Though the terms 'colonelcy', 'battalion' and 'regiment' were bandied about, they had little numerical consistency. Muster lists rarely mentioned them, referring simply to the number of men under each captain of a company; even senior officers, from colonel to sergeant-major or captain-general, were listed as captains of their own companies within their wider command. Government cash flowed not through colonels but through captains. Battle plans were discussed not by the heads of 'regiments' but by commanding officers and political agents who convened captains selected for their birth or experience on an ad hoc basis. War, though constituting the most serious business conducted by the state, remained a strongly personalized one. Only in Spain's armies in the Netherlands was there an organization regularly based on self-contained units of 'regimental' size: the *tercio*, comprising 1200 to

1600 men, and this was the result of campaigns renewed over decades and the periodical drafting of large bodies of men from such similarly organized permanent garrisons as those of Lombardy, Naples and Sicily.

The process whereby an army was lined out into battle array is difficult to seize. It is concerning that tensest moment, the dusk or dawn deployment before the adrenalin-assisted hour of battle itself, that the sources are most silent. Something can be caught of tented conferences receiving the reports of scouts, spies and prisoners taken from the enemy's advance parties, of the consultation of sketch-maps of the terrain, of the opinions of veterans on the preparedness or morale of individual units on either side, of the advice of the political commissioners – wait for reinforcements from an ally, don't risk an engagement while we can afford to stay in the field and wear them down, seize this moment because beyond it we have no means of paying the troops – but of the waking-up, briefing and herding of tens of thousands of footmen and horsemen bearing a wide variety of arms into their battle positions we know almost nothing. Military memoir-writers took it as a matter of course and did not anticipate our ignorance.

One principle does, however, emerge as a consistent guideline throughout the period: the preference for linear deployment over that of large blocks. With many exceptions due to terrain, numbers or confidence (that of the English in their archers at Agincourt, for instance), the medieval preference was for an order of march and subsequent deployment of three massive, homogeneous units, or 'battles': main body, vanguard, rearguard, usually so manoeuvred as to serve as shock-absorber, flanking diversion and support. As early as 1476, however, Charles the Bold suggested four successive lines (each three ranks deep, infantry in the centre, with archers on either side flanked by cavalry) which, according to the fortune of the day, could either implode inwards to envelop successive breakthroughs, or press forward, the footmen seconded by missile troops and horses positioned to make flanking attacks. This experiment in linearity was not followed up, first because of the difficulty of stopping the Swiss pike phalanx from steamrollering its way right through, then because of the preference for defensive and, if possible, fortified positions that increased as firearms became more and more effective during the Italian Wars.

From Machiavelli onwards, however, every theorist of the open battle stressed the advantages of linear formations. They had brought success to the legions of Rome; and as heavy cavalry declined and missiles became more dominating, warfare was coming to resemble more that of the ancient than the medieval world. Longer, thinner lines made it easier for troops of different types to cooperate, reduced the density of targets for cannon or musket ball, and, above all, cut out the multitude of passengers: rear-rank pikemen who never reached the enemy, rear-rank arquebusiers who never got a clear view for a shot.

Linearity involved one major difficulty. If a square or deep rectangle of men were challenged in flank, each man had but to turn left or right in his own ground to preserve the fighting front. Long lines had to pivot, a laborious and time-consuming manoeuvre. It could be done, but only if the line comprised numerous small, well-drilled units, each controlled by a non-commissioned officer. And this is the point at which theory failed to touch hands with practice.

Machiavelli, again, had anticipated the need for many well-led units if the linear formations he recommended were to succeed: 'For a wall that is weak and tottering in every part, may be better supported by many props and buttresses, though they are but feeble ones, than by a few, be they ever so substantial; because their strength cannot be of much service at any considerable distance.' That is: use many NCOs (heads of 100, of 50 and of 10) instead of a few captains. But no army achieved a full complement of NCOs – the Elizabethan ideal was a lieutenant assisted by two sergeants and six corporals for every company of 150 men – because of captains' reluctance to pass on the bonuses that would have made their extra duties worthwhile. Even in the Dutch forces raised by William Lodovick and Maurice of Nassau, princes thoroughly convinced by Machiavelli's ideas (as re-emphasized by their own classically influenced military theorist, Justus Lipsius), full complements of NCOs and ideally linear formations were probably only achieved on the parade ground. It is significant that the Spanish tercios, though they included more veterans than did other armies, retained a fairly deep, square formation.

Thus although by the early seventeenth century there was a formidable equipment of drill books, formation diagrams and military texts which took flexible, linear, well-disciplined small units for granted, the doctrine of tactical reformation was, as we shall see, preached rather than practised; its success lay in the near future, however, with the armies of Gustavus Adolphus, Louis XIII and Cromwell. The age may have had an itch for orderliness – Machiavelli was one of those who advocated marching in step – but there was too much financial corruption, too little training and thus too much fearfulness for the deep, companionable, passenger-accommodating, comparatively easily led deep formations to be given up. Just as no army was composed by the book, no battle was fought by it. There were, of course, old soldiers who resented the application of bookish theories to the traditional approach to war; of Guise's meticulous (and successful) plans for the capture of Calais in 1558, the anti-bookish captain Blaise de Monluc remarked scornfully that the duke would have made a good 'clerk of the Parlement of Paris'. And coinciding with the reformist movement was the realistic assessment of success in war as resulting from a strategy of envelopment, attrition and siege rather than from a seeking of pitched battle; governments' attitude to calculation reduced that of the reformers to the status of gambling. Even Maurice saw mass engagement as a last, chancy resource.

It can also be said that an incipiently 'scientific' approach to the handling of men foundered in the rising sea of numbers. As the old warrior Jean de Bueil said to Louis XI in 1471, 'War has become very different. In those days [of the late campaigns of the Hundred Years War], when you had eight or ten thousand men, you considered that a very large number; today it is quite another matter. . . . I am not accustomed to see so many troops together. How do you prevent confusion in such a mass?'

The miscellaneous figures on pages 62–3, which include both cavalry and infantry, have varying credentials. Some are based on a cautious use of contemporary chroniclers and military memoir-writers, others on government calculations, a few on muster lists. No source is trustworthy. Chroniclers and participants guessed abnormally high or low for dramatic effect. No government knew more than roughly how many men estimated for were actually on active service; to give but two instances, in 1592 the paper strength of the duke of Parma's army sent to relieve Rouen from the English siege was 17,500 while its effective strength was about 10,000; in 1616 out of 7737 infantry estimated to be in camp at Mariano, during Venice's War of Gradisca, only 2700 could be traced. Muster lists were full of connivances and concealments. Some of the high early figures (1475, 1491) include feudal levies which were only in the field for a few weeks. For defensive or border campaigns it was easier to raise native troops than for foreign expeditions: 50,000 of the Imperial troops mustered in 1532 were Germans who, when the Turks began to withdraw, went home, claiming that they had been engaged only to fight in a defensive war. So many of the others, from Bohemia, Silesia, Moravia and Austria, then deserted that the campaign had to be called off. Campaigns in occupied territories needed troops in garrison to pin down local populations as well as forces available for combat (1574, 1590s). 'Little war' forces are omitted: the 8000 troops employed by Duke Cosimo I of Florence against Siena in 1554, the 7400 sent by Elizabeth to succour the Dutch in 1585 (when there were already 8000 serving unofficially), for instance. So are other instances when paper strengths (no fewer than 50,000 contracted for the Florence–Milan–Naples alliance against Venice–the Papacy in 1482) cannot, to any satisfactory extent, be followed into action.

Men estimated to be on active service

Year	Country	Nature of force	Total numbers (approx.)
1450	Venice	Troops in being	21,000
1451	France	Troops in being	20,000
1475	Castile/Aragon	Against Portuguese	42,000
1476	Swiss (and allies)	Battle of Murten	25,000
1480	France	Campaign against Maximilian I	25,000
1491	France	Brittany expedition	20,000
1491	Castile/Aragon	War of Granada	60,000
1494	France	Invasion of Italy	28,000
1499	France	Invasion of Italy	27,000
1509	France	Battle of Agnadello	30,000
1509	Venice	Battle of Agnadello	29,500
1510	Castile/Aragon	Expedition to Tripoli	34,500
1512	France (and allies)	Effectives in Italy	29,000
1512	Swiss cantons	Expedition to Italy	24,000
1525	France	Battle of Pavia	28,000
1528	Empire (Charles V)	Battle of Pavia	28,000
1532	Empire	Mustered against Turks	100,000
1536	France	Defence of Provence	45,000
1536–7	France (Charles V)	Effectives, Lombardy and expedition to Provence	60,000
1544	France (Charles V)	French campaign	35,000
1544	England (and allies)	French campaign	48,000
1552	Empire (Charles V)	Effectives throughout Empire	150,000
1552	Empire (Charles V)	Metz campaign	50,000
1552	France	Metz campaign	38,000
1557	Spain	S. Quentin campaign	45,000

Year	Country	Nature of force	Total numbers (approx.)
1558	France	Troops in being	50,000
1574	Spain	Army in Netherlands	86,000
1580	Spain	Conquest of Portugal	35,000
1590s	Spain	Army in Netherlands	85,000
1591	England	Brittany campaigns	20,000
1595	England	Troops in Ireland	17,000
1607	United Provinces	Troops in being	51,000
1610	France	Troops in being	68,500
1617	Venice	War of Gradisca	26,000

All the same, discounting the fifteenth-century Iberian figures as relating to bodies resembling the medieval temporary 'host', it can be said that the size of major field armies remained fairly steady at 25,000 to 30,000 between 1476 and 1528 (Spain, again, providing the exception with the Tripoli expedition), sharply increased from 1536 to 1558, and increased again with Spain's deepening commitment in the Netherlands from the 1570s (average size 65,000) and with France's recovery from civil wars in the early seventeenth century. And these two periods of expanding numbers looked towards further growth. At Henry IV's death in 1610 the duke of Sully was planning an army which, with contingents from allies, would comprise 190,000 men; in 1625 Philip IV's minister, the count-duke of Olivares, was planning to *supplement* Spain's armies by enrolling 140,000 men in a new militia. These were paper plans, but they anticipated the armies of over 100,000 men led by Gustavus Adolphus and Wallenstein in 1631–2. In contrast, the largest force led to France from England in the Hundred Years War was (in 1346) 32,000 and its major battles were fought with armies of 7000 to 15,000 men.

The growth in the size of armies towards the middle of the sixteenth century reflects the appetite for more and more infantry, especially arquebusiers, and the need for numbers rather than concentrated weight that followed from the virtual disuse of heavy cavalry and the proven vulnerability of the pike phalanx. And while the battle tactic of wearing down rather than driving in wedges required more men, so did the similar bias in siegecraft towards blockade rather than assault. But numbers were also determined by governments' ability to pay, and this capacity to raise money by taxation, and on credit from financiers, depended on the wealth judged to be available in the country at large. Army numbers grew along with increases in population and in prosperity and with the development of administrative machines better able to tap it. There was no uniform correlation between numbers, population, wealth and bureaucracy; a prosperous and comparatively elaborately governed country like Elizabethan and Jacobean England was averse to war and, being an island, could afford to be. The Spanish sense of imperial religious and political mission led to large armies and repeated state bankruptcies.

And the upwards surges in numbers, which bore into combat so many men who were unsuited to it, did not go uncriticized. Typical of such criticism was the opinion of the earl of Essex while planning Elizabeth's expedition: 'An army well chosen of 3000 is able for numbers to undertake any action or to fight with any army in the world . . . and wheresoever such an army consisting most of disciplined men shall invade, the defendant's state is desperate if he only trust to numbers.' The contested zone between Habsburg and Turkish control in the south east was not only defined by the effective limits of Ottoman supply routes but by the inability of successive emperors to pay large armies for long enough to push them back towards Constantinople and hold the territory gained. More generally, when the strategic pace of war slowed, as it did in the Netherlands, this was not just because of improved fortifications and longer sieges. Battles came to be avoided because larger armies contained so many unsuitable, untrained and untrustworthy men. And larger armies cost so much that war could become – though never as a matter of initial decision – a Fabian game to see whose forces broke up first from lack of pay.

The changes in methods of fighting that led to increased numbers also brought into sharper focus another controversial element within the military reformation, the composition of armies in terms of their conditions of service.

Leaving aside the borrowing (and paying) of auxiliary troops from allies, armies were composed of natives, largely inexperienced and raised for a single campaign and turned off at the end of it, stiffened by a small permanent establishment, supplemented by hired professional mercenaries, and backed up in a real emergency by drafts from part-time militias.

The most original element in the organizational aspect of reformation was the emergence, from its start, of the realization of a need for permanent military establishments more formal than a cluster of princely guards and reliable tenants-in-chief. By the mid-fifteenth century the lesson had at last been learned that whether a ruler was striving to keep the advantage in recurrences of civil war, as in England and Spain, or regarding warily the uncertain outcome of an inter-state peace treaty, as after the Peace of Lodi of 1454 in Italy, or planning the forcible consolidation or protection of his lands, as in the case of the kings of France and the dukes of Burgundy, a quick take-off based on a permanent force was more advantageous than the old practice of raising a whole army from scratch and dismissing it at a fighting season's end. There were other considerations. Rulers' attacks by force or legislation against dangerously militant subjects cut into the most readily mobilizable sector of the population. Changes in weaponry and tactics called at least for a core of trained men who could help recruits to adapt to methods no longer part of quasi-folklore behaviour (mercenaries kept to their own units and could not perform this function). The eager adoption by rulers of artillery, and the need to have a permanent corps of officials and craftsmen to administer and service it – some 4000 men were in Charles VII's employ at his death in 1461 – helped establish the notion of earmarked funds for consistent annual military expenditure.

During the second half of the fifteenth century only three governments, however, had permanent establishments on a significant scale. Thanks to the setting up of the companies of the *ordonnance* in 1445, the kings of France had a force of some 9000 men, a third of them heavy cavalry, the others mounted archers. From 1471 Charles the Bold followed suit with an ordinance calling for the establishment of a body of 8400 men, 1200 heavy cavalry, 3600 mounted archers and 3600 infantry. After the Peace of Lodi Venice retained the service of some 8000 men, mostly heavy cavalry and infantry provided with horses; this followed a deliberate policy of giving fiefs on the mainland while it was conquered earlier in the century, in return for a guarantee of military service with a set number of men. Milan had a similar, though smaller body of fiefholders and troops on half-pay. Progress towards a standing force was slower in Spain; though certain captains and a few of their men were retained during lulls in the war against Granada, and captains were drafted from the permanent law and order organization, the Santa Hermandad, it was not until 1493 that Ferdinand and Isabella faced the financial drain of a permanently ready establishment, the 2500 cavalry 'lances' of the *guardas viejas*; in the case of long-service infantry garrisons in key frontier cities, they tried to compel local grandees to foot the bill.

Every country, of course, had small numbers of troops in

garrison to supplement citizen local defence forces, but they were engaged by the month and their wages came from ad hoc central financing or charges on the cities themselves. The permanent establishments that emerged from the mid-fifteenth century represented a change in attitude both to military preparedness and government finance. All these establishments differed in their composition, and some governments – Florence (until the 1530s), Sweden (in spite of a brief experiment in the 1540s), England, the German Empire – could not, or did not see the point of meeting their cost.

Tedious though the term 'permanent establishments' may be, it is preferable to 'standing armies' with its associations of barracks, training programmes, career structure, regularly topped-up quotas and regimental uniforms and traditions; only prophetic flickers of these features yet existed.

There were signs, too, that their development was premature. Princely guards were increased in size at the very time when they might have been thought less necessary. In pioneering France, experiments were made with putting a cadre of officers from the feudal cavalry militia, the *ban* and *arrière ban*, and the archery militia, the *francs-archers*, under permanent contracts to buttress the never very steady fabric of the *compagnies d'ordonnance*. Louis XI, in the teeth of advisers aghast at the expense, even undertook to raise and keep in being a force of 14,000 infantry. From 1481 until his death two years later, when they were disbanded, the royal revenues were supporting, on paper at least, 23,600 men (including the 9000 troops of the *ordonnance* and a guard of 600), a force almost as large as the average combat army was to be for the next fifty years. As in the case of early artillery, a form of gigantism accompanied the introduction of a new military concept, in this case especially inappropriate because men were not yet adjusted to the idea of remaining 'soldiers' in peacetime. And just as the Mons Megs were slimmed down to more practical and transportable dimensions, so in the sixteenth century permanent establishments came to move towards the standing armies of the seventeenth century and today in pace with the realities of finance and politico-military circumstance.

Spain's conquest and enduring occupation of Naples from 1504 and Milan from 1535 called for large permanent garrisons; in addition, mounting tension between its Mediterranean coast and the Moslem corsair ports of north Africa, and its Pyrenean frontier and successive French monarchs, led to the engagement on a permanent basis of nearly 17,500 troops (mostly infantry) by the 1590s. The persisting wars in the Netherlands came to be seen as necessitating a permanent nucleus of 13,000 to 15,000 men topped up annually by far larger numbers for combat in the field, many of whom, by staying on year after year, did much to create the true atmosphere, if not the institutionalized actuality, of a modern standing army.

Spain's financial resources, thanks first to the gold and then, far more impressively, the silver of the New World, were totally exceptional; even successive state bankruptcies did not erode faith in the silver income measured against the underrealized real wealth of the peninsula itself. France, on the eve of its civil wars, was supporting perhaps 10,000 men in 1562 between the *ordonnance* companies (shrunken by the declining value of heavy cavalry), long-term garrison troops – concentrated in recaptured Calais – the royal guard, and the officer cadre of the *légions*, the revamped (in 1534) version of the withered-away *francs-archers*. Battered thereafter by civil war, the permanent establishment practically disappeared. Twenty-five years later François de la Noue pleaded for the revival of a modest nucleus of 6500 troops: 'Many think the French nation to be so well enured to wars that they need but stamp on the ground (as Pompey said) to bring forth whole legions armed, howbeit they are deceived.' In the euphoria that attended the reunification of the nation under Henry IV, Sully proposed paying 56,000 troops (6000 of them cavalry) on a permanent basis.

By then Venice was maintaining 9300 in garrisons scattered from Bergamo to Crete. In the German Empire successive Reichstags legislated to bring the mercenary bands of *Landsknechts* under closer Imperial control but stopped short at voting the taxation necessary to keep them at home and in pay. On the other hand, continual campaigning on the Croatian and Hungarian frontiers was leading, as with Spain's commitment in the Netherlands, to the creation of a permanent army which, though unintentional, conditioned future German thinking about the desirability of maintaining a standing force.

Two additional factors had come to strengthen the arguments which led to the creation of such forces in the fifteenth century. One was the increasing difficulty of raising short-service troops of adequate quality, the other was a growing awareness that the new tactics required an investment in training that could only be justified if men were not turned off at the very moment they had learned to use their experience with confidence. Even in England, where the permanent force had been kept to a few slender garrisons and a small body of yeomen, there were proposals to extend it radically. Sir Roger Williams suggested in 1590 a permanent establishment of 10,000 men; this would enable England to keep abreast of tactical developments, stiffen the ranks of new, part-time recruits in case of war, and lessen the country's dependence on costly and, worse, unreliable mercenaries. Above all, 'It is an error to think that experimented soldiers are suddenly made like glasses, in blowing them out of an iron instrument.' Similar considerations had led, and were to lead, to other proposals: 24,000 for Imperial Germany in 1521, and, by a process that would doubtless be less uncannily similar were it methodically traced, 24,000 for Savoy in 1560, 24,000 for France in 1576, and for Venice 28,000 in 1606 and 27,500 in 1621.

This continental infection, caught by Englishmen who, like Williams, served in the Netherlands, contradicted a deep insular prejudice. In *A Discourse of the Commonweal*, written in *c.* 1549, the characters of the dialogue discuss the *ordonnance* cavalry of France. 'God forbid', said the Husbandman, 'that we have any such tyrants come among us, for, as they say, such will in the country of France take poor men's hens, chickens, pigs and other provision and pay nothing for it, except it were an evil turn, as to ravish his wife or daughter for it.' The French put up with it, added the Merchant, but they are a cowed and abject lot, 'in reproach of whom we call them peasants'. In vain the Doctor pointed out that 'It is not for commotions of subjects that France keepeth such, but the estate and necessity of the country, which is environed about with enemies, and [has] neither sea nor wall between.' Here is the self-image of the freeborn Englishman who saw a permanent army as a source of pillage, which it was, and of tyranny, which it was not. Even in France voices had been raised against the 'tyrannous' *ordonnance*, but in its context the word referred to a tax burden imposed by the monarch, not to the added power of political control the force could give him. The only outright identification of standing forces with tyranny was made when the States General of the Netherlands refused in 1534 Charles V's request that they should contribute to one: 'If we accept the project we shall undoubtedly be more united, but we shall be dealt with in the manner of France.' Both in parliamentary England and the conciliar Netherlands the *ordonnance* bogey reflected its association more with a monarchy that taxed without consent than with one that had used it to overcome the particularism of, especially, Guyenne and Brittany. In any case, its role was not essential to the reunification of France after the Hundred Years War. This could have been carried through without armies containing a permanent core. And looked at closely, the standing establishments simply could not, in the period as a whole, have been instruments of absolutism. In peace they were scattered, inefficient; already small, they were never up to strength. Living on peacetime pay which forced many of them to take on part-time civilian work, their discipline, never adequate to the stiffening of combat armies, also made it impossible for them to become the blind instruments of their paymasters, who anyway used them rather as instruments of patronage than of oppression. In war they were locked up within the larger military organization of combat armies. They did have a local police function, though it would seem – the subject is unexplored – a feeble one. But as yet the significance of the 'no standing armies!' slogan had only been adumbrated and no constitutional changes were forced through by them.

In any case, controversy over this issue was minuscule in comparison to the unceasing arguments over the employment of mercenaries.

All countries used them throughout the period. Without effective conscription, and with but scant anticipations of the jingoism that was eventually to be the chief assistant of the recruiter of volunteers, there were seldom enough men effectively to bridge the gap between permanent nuclei, where they existed, and the required combat strength: in the case of large-scale campaigns, never.

It was natural for cities striving to assert their independence from local seigneurial or ecclesiastical control to eke out their own forces with hired help. Thus Liège employed German, Swiss and French mercenaries in the 1480s and 1490s; Metz, in its struggle against Duke René of Lorraine in 1490, cast its net wider among the military job-hunters whose ears were attuned to the hint of profitable trouble: French, Burgundians, Spaniards, Germans, Italians, even the swarthier migrants known collectively as Slavs or Albanians. The proud *ordonnance* companies of France and Burgundy themselves had to accept foreigners, perhaps 15 per cent, to keep their numbers reasonably full. In time of war some 30 per cent of Burgundian troops were foreigners: French, English and Flemish for the most part. From 1474 France negotiated a long-term stand-by contract for 6000 Swiss. During the War of Granada Ferdinand and Isabella snapped up the contingents and individuals attracted to the war theatre from England, France, Germany and Flanders.

The sixteenth century saw no halt in the process whereby 'national' wars were fought by international, mongrel armies – 'Noah's ark' armies, as the Venetian diarist Marin Sanuto called them. Henry VIII's French invasion army of 1544–5 contained, according to a sour Welsh professional, 'depraved brutish foreign soldiers from all nations under the sun . . . Scots, Spaniards, Gascons, Portingals, Italians, Albanians, Greeks, Turks, Tartars, Germans, Burgundians, Flemings'. In this list 'Tartars' were probably Balkan migrants, but otherwise it does fair justice to the assiduity and, at times, desperation of Henry's recruiting agents on the continent. During the domestic troubles that followed Henry's death, Protector Somerset brought in some 7500 mercenaries to patrol the interests of the young Edward VI: chiefly Germans, Italians, Burgundians and Albanians – the last universally sought after as the liveliest light cavalry outside southern Spain. Later in the century King Sebastian of Portugal's expedition against the Moorish Moroccan base of Alcazarquivir in 1578, because of the reluctance of his own subjects to serve, was heavily padded with German, Flemish, Italian and Spanish contingents. Spain's own forces in the Netherlands contained but a small minority of Spaniards; even though the larger number of Italians, Germans, Burgundians and Catholic Netherlanders fought as Habsburg subjects and, indeed, were conscious of some political unity, they formed a motley, if not mongrel combination. And they were opposed by 'Dutch' armies that were predominantly English, French and German, plus some Danes. Swedish dependence on Germans from the 1520s had changed by Gustavus Adolphus's reign to a reliance on Scottish captains that amounted to a 'special relationship' with that country.

The Noah's ark nature of large armies was so consistent that it needs no further emphasis. It meant that men of the same nation were brought into confrontation in other than civil wars. Englishmen fought on both sides in the Netherlands. The chronicler of the Venetian–Austrian War of Gradisca in 1615–17 noted that each side employed Germans, French, Croats and Dalmatians and that only Austria's Spaniards and Venice's Greeks (he might have added the republic's English and Dutch troops) did not face one another as antagonistic co-nationals. The duke of Sully's *Memoirs* pointed to one of the disadvantages that followed. At the battle of Dreux in 1562, for instance, 'the Swiss soldiers of the two armies meeting, bullied each other with their pikes lowered without striking a blow', and 'the Germans, who professed the same religion as our soldiers, fired, as it were, in the air'.

That was only one of the snags involved in the use of mercenaries. The most constant accusation was financial fraud. Early in the sixteenth century the Florentine army commissioner Antonio Giacomini advised his government how to check this. As many 'constables' (leaders of mercenary infantry) were pure entrepreneurs, with little or no military experience, they should be submitted to a viva voce test of their competence before engagement. A physical description of their men should be made to prevent the paying of substitutes or non-combatants. No excuses for men being on leave or sick should be accepted. Money should not be handed to the constable to pay his men with, but given directly by a Florentine paymaster. Well aware that these abuses had become so ingrained as to have become traditional perquisites, the government did not dare to implement his proposals.

It is true that these abuses were practised everywhere by native captains as well; in all military operations there was more graft than gore. But mercenary bands were more resistant to bureaucratic invigilation, and as they were frequently paid at a somewhat higher rate than native troops (if not through the base rate, to avoid jealousy, then through the officers' salaries and the bonus fund) their employers faced a greater loss. And whereas native troops could usually be persuaded to continue to campaign when their wages were in arrears, mercenaries were liable to demand an immediate action with the prospect of spoils (as the Swiss, it was widely believed, forced their French employers into the defeat at Bicocca), to mutiny and to hold commissioners, commanding officers or local dignitaries as hostages for payment, or simply to desert en masse. Voltaire's 'point d'argent, point de Suisses' was anticipated by La Noue's 'tant qu'argent dure, on ne manque point d'en avoir'. Mercenaries could drive hard bargains in other ways. In order to contract with Melchior Lusi, entrepreneur colonel of 6500 Grisons infantry in 1571, Venice was forced to agree that an extra pay would be given after every successful engagement, that if they had to entrench themselves they would receive additional money after two days' digging, that while they could be transported to an overseas theatre they would not fight while at sea, and that they would not be expected to take part in siege operations. The loss, and subsequent dreadful sack of Famagusta by the Turks later that year, was at least in part due to other mercenary captains in Crete who, when asked to go to its relief, replied that 'they had been engaged to serve in the fleet and not in Cyprus'.

There were less rational complaints that mercenaries acted as spies or spread heresy, or that they damaged an economy by milking specie from it to be spent elsewhere. Loudest and commonest were accusations of lawlessness and cruelty. In his description of the sack of Rome in 1527 (brought about by Charles V's inability to pay his German mercenaries), Thomas More reached out to an audience which would be horrified but unsurprised. 'And old ancient honourable men, those fierce heretics letted not to hang up by the privy members, and from many they pulled them off and cast them in the streets. And some brought out naked with his hands bound behind him, and a cord tied fast unto his privy members. Then would they set before him in his way other of those tyrants with their moorish pikes . . . and draw the poor souls by the members towards them. Now was all their cruel sport and laughter, either to see the silly [simple] naked men in shrinking from the pikes to tear off their members, or for pain of that pulling, to run their naked bodies in deep upon the pikes.' In a book entitled *A Dialogue concerning Heresies* we are not to expect a lack of prejudice against Lutherans, but it was the fact that they were mercenaries as well that lent verisimilitude to the atrocity.

Yet for all these complaints, such was the need for mercenaries that the chief grievance was that there were never enough of them. Since the single, and entirely *sui generis* instance of Francesco Sforza, using the troops he had been hired to command to supplant his employer, the tottering republican government of Milan, in 1450, there had been no suspicion of mercenaries on political grounds. Indeed, paid from central treasuries, their use aroused less widespread resentment than did national recruiting, which burdened local ones. The difficulty of obtaining them started to become acute when an entrenched Habsburg–Valois rivalry led to the sealing of mother-countries and their satellites to recruiters and to bans on natives leaving to serve the rival power. Such precautions were as ineffective as were all frontier controls. But they could pinch. To look again at Venice. For the War of Gradisca the republic's recruiting agents signed contracts, and made the down-payments, for 17,000 non-Italian mercenaries (the Italian states were either Habsburg governed or fearful of incurring Spanish displeasure). These included men from Savoy, Corsica, Graubünden, the Swiss cantons, France and Saxony. Only some 3000 got through frontiers 'sealed' by pro-Habsburg policies. Venice had to turn to Dutch troops (with their high transport costs) and, on an unprecedented scale, to its own subjects in Italy and overseas.

Almost every criticism of mercenaries was accompanied by arguments in favour of using native troops instead. Although less abreast of changes in methods of fighting than mercenary bands, and bringing home the wounds and the violent manners learned in camp instead of bearing them elsewhere at a campaign's end, native troops, it was argued, would be more faithful, more conscious that they were fighting for fatherland, family and possessions; less – in a word – mercenary. Machiavelli's eloquence in pleading the cause of a native soldiery as against cynical and treacherous mercenaries passed into international currency with the translations not only of *The Art of War* but of his *Prince*, *Discourses on Livy* and *Florentine History*. His arguments had been anticipated in Italy, and also in France, England and Burgundy among those intelligent soldier-aristocrats who, though otherwise hardly touched by humanism, knew enough of Roman history and the treatise of Vegetius on Roman armies to believe that Rome's victories had been won largely by its own citizens. And his views were sustained and further developed by authors – such as Lipsius in the Netherlands – who otherwise flinched from them and cited his military opinions with a fastidious lack of acknowledgement. Francis Bacon was led into a rare error of judgement when he pronounced of mercenaries that 'all examples show that whatsoever estate or prince doth rest upon them, he may spread his feathers for a time, but he will mew them soon after'.

At the same time, however, there was a consciousness that to arm subjects more methodically than they already were could be dangerous; it might imperil local law and order, rebellion could be more readily mobilized and more difficult to suppress. Machiavelli himself was ambivalent on this point. In the 1470s Sir John Fortescue, in his *The Governance of England*, had reasoned that the threat of rebellion was nothing to the importance of having a population armed to defend itself from foreigners. But Bishop Seyssel, always alert to the political consequences of types of army organization, insisted that some mercenaries were necessary so that a native, and potentially revolutionary infantry, would not be too numerous. And Lipsius was forced to claim that as only bad government led men to rebel, wise rulers had nothing to fear from subjects prepared for military service.

Though theoretical, discussion of this topic was shaped by men in a position to make their views known in council or court, and by actual institutions and events: it was not just an intellectual issue but a running comment on facts. This is not the place to review them, for they form part of a wider prospect: the soldier as policeman as well as warrior, a government's relationship to its subjects in peace as well as through war. As far as the composition of armies was concerned it is enough to note that from the setting up of the *francs-archers* in France in 1448 every country came to establish national militias. It was a rough world. Practically all non-clerical males had some sort of weapon to defend themselves on the road, when working in the fields or to bring to the self-defence posses of rural communities and the citizen guards of towns. Central governments encouraged such resourcefulness; a Spanish decree of 1495 ordered all, except the clergy, suspected malefactors and Moors, to have 'in their houses or available, defensive arms according to their station, aptitude and substance'. They also intervened to enrol a select number whose equipment and spare-time training was intended to form them into a national military reserve. They had privileges – exemption from certain labour and tax burdens, a licence rather than a self-appointed 'right' to carry arms – that symbolized the priority of their relationship to the state over that to local magnate or community. The lessons of actual warfare, weaponry and tactics, were filtered down to them slowly and with the patchily effective nature of every initiative that involved spending money. In any case, militiamen were conceived of primarily as a home guard to defend coasts, patrol communications and replace troops drafted from garrisons; their dispatch to reinforce field armies pending the arrival of more mercenaries or native volunteers was ordered only in moments of extremity.

When reviewing the composition of a combat army we are left, then, with the missing link between permanent core and mercenary supplement on the one hand and the latent usefulness of militias on the other. The link, the utterly necessary component, was the body of native troops. This most natural, obvious, component was also the most complex in its motivation and performance; its recruitment, without which most wars could not have taken place, calls therefore for a somewhat extended review of the relationship between wars and the men who accepted and fought in them.

3

Recruitment: personal and organized violence; the Second Estate

If armies became larger, in the eyes of those who conjured them up they were usually still too small. Perhaps with the exception of Charles VIII's 1494 invasion of Italy, no campaign was fought with men in the numbers, let alone of the quality, its planners had hoped for. And this was in spite of the low ratio of the demand for combatants to the population as a whole: it is doubtful whether this amounted to more than 0.5 to 0.75 per cent in general, or more than 2 per cent in regions where either civil war, or the neighbourhood of threatened frontiers, had a particular stimulus on recruitment. Field armies probably never drew on more than 5 per cent of the recruitable sector of a population.

With permanent forces restricted, and the availability of mercenaries uncertain, governments naturally looked to their own citizens. The tradition that members of the Second Estate were 'those who fight' continued to bring, if with decreasing alacrity, members of the landed classes into the field. Legally, most able-bodied males of all classes between the ages of fifteen or sixteen and sixty were liable to serve (with regional exceptions made for certain occupations or civil states: clergy, magistrates, heads of households, gentlemen's domestic servants, for instance). There might be objections to service 'out of the realm' but in most parts of Europe the lawyers – almost everywhere exempt themselves – could quote precedents in rebuttal. So it was into the populous gap between the permanent garrisons and the part-time, mainly home-defence militia that the recruiters rode, armed with their licences to raise men, pay them and in many cases personally to command them.

Whoever the recruiting agent was – the agent of a regional magnate or of a supplier with a stand-by contract to raise men on demand, a local authority or a roving captain who had petitioned for a recruiting licence – the approach, save to the few who positively welcomed the chance to enlist, was an identical mixture of cajolement and pressure. Magnates called on their clientage groups of tenants and retainers to honour obligations, sometimes written, sometimes simply assumed, to serve them in arms along with their own tenants or servants; kinsmen were urged to support them in the same fashion, for the honour of the family and the favour of the king. Local authorities, in rural parish or urban ward, consulted registers of adult males, selected the number they had been charged to send, and sent the constable to summon them in the name of the monarch's wage, the justice of his cause and the reputation of a community only too well aware of its vulnerability to punitive taxation. The captain submitted his patent, had his mission proclaimed by the cryer at church, market and through the streets, set up his standard, had his drummer beat, and waited for custom in an inn or the more supportive house of a justice or alderman; serve the king was his message, too: let him pay you, enter that alternative society of warfarers which promises freedom from the humdrum, penurious, hen- and priest-pecked life of everyday.

To all these approaches the majority response, unless the war was one for which the locality had an emotional or economic sympathy, was reluctant. Spring mobilizations for summer campaigns were hardly convenient for magnates whose incomes depended on the following by their tenants and labourers of the routines of the agricultural year. In towns and cities the promises of support expressed by civic councils were not subscribed to by the community at large or necessarily by the civic fathers themselves. The men they were required to select had to be equipped and given an initial wage and conduct money to get them to embarkation port or theatre of war. Not all communities were bound to provide these advances, but in practice they had to. Recruiters avoided the risk of travelling with cash; recompense from a government whose own resources dipped as a campaign went on, might be anticipated but could not be relied on. Moreover, governments wanted the very men – especially carpenters, masons, blacksmiths, leatherworkers and bakers – whose labour provided a prime base for urban comfort and profit. The capitalistic measurement of productive time which had led medieval mercantile societies to pay others to fight their wars was more nagging than ever in an age when there was a wider urban prosperity and fewer mercenaries to go round.

The result, in countryside and town, was a response of buck-passing, blackmail and litigation.

The great magnate would normally serve in person with his closest associates; he would not have been chosen as a noble recruiter if the government had not been sure of this. But as his own summonses radiated out they encountered prevarications and excuses as well as downright refusals side-stepped by the cowing of others to serve as substitutes. Local authorities encountered a flurry of protests: men could not forsake a sick wife or a foundering business; the lists of able-bodied men were out of date; men were summoned who were too old, frail or responsible for households of minors to serve. Besides, was there not the case in which some long-dead monarch had granted absolution from future service because of one conspicuously useful contribution of men? Had not relief from foreign service been granted to a community because of its abidingly crucial role in the local defence of a river-crossing, or harbour or frontier? Back along the roads recently traversed by the recruiters hurried petitioners for redress.

Meanwhile, amidst the reasoned protests, the consciousness of magnate displeasure, or the power of central government to label recalcitrance treason, led to the production of troops. But not, as far as the majority was concerned, of potentially the best soldiers.

Save in personal indentures, individuals were not named in call-ups but only quotas (in Spain and Sweden, 10 per cent of those registered as fit to serve) so the pressure exerted by government could easily be taken over and pushed downwards through the layers of society in town and country: past those who could afford to pay for substitutes, or bully or litigate their way out of the draft, to those who were too poor, too stupid or too universally disliked to put up a fight against having to fight. Men did come forward out of a sense of duty, for adventure or because joining up suited their convenience at the moment, but the turning screw also drove through a society that relished the picking of scapegoats for the majority's unreadiness to accept risk. The process of recruitment shows as clearly as does the persecution of witches and the harassment of Jews and Gipsies, the callousness whereby a changing, but still tradition-conscious society protected its increasingly cherished self-interests.

Both the buck-passing and its consequences, the transference into armies of men who had no business to be there, was the result of an abstinence on the part of the governments from what we would properly understand as conscription.

Conscription in wartime has come to mean the compulsory call-up, on an age basis, of named men of all stations. There will be exempt occupations, a machinery for dealing with challenges on moral grounds. But conscription garners a cross-section of society and relies on a military establishment large enough, and training programmes organized by it sufficiently defined, to ensure that a high proportion of recruits will be turned into effective and perhaps promotable, even if temporary, soldiers.

Then, however, no government knew enough about its subjects to send them call-up papers addressed to the right name at the right abode, or had enough clerks to check that the men addressed were the ones who answered the call, let alone enough career officers and NCOs to arrange a training-conditioning programme for them after recruitment. The legal power to conscript was there. It was on occasion used: by magistrates pinpointing undesirables, by landlords wanting to eject men whose tenancies, if they failed to return, could be renewed on better terms. Henry VIII revenged himself on a merchant who refused to offer an unconstitutional forced loan by 'sentencing' him to military service in Scotland. The aldermen of London posted guards on church doors during the Easter communion of 1596 until they had persuaded enough men in the congregation to make up a force of 1000 they had been ordered to produce for service in France. 'Prest' men, 'forçats': there were men all over Europe who were left no choice but to enlist. But given the hit-or-miss methods employed, it is misleading to describe them as conscripts. No government had such power or persuasiveness as to compel any large number of non-helpless men to do what they did not want to do; the pained response to demands to pay for wars through taxes showed how unwise it would have been to compel payment in terms of named lives as well. So reliance was put on pressure. And because it was only pressure, it could be transferred downwards, squeezing out the making-up-numbers dross whom literature's most memorable recruiter, Sir John Falstaff, not unreasonably described as 'food for powder, food for worms'.

It is true that at times of domestic strife or civil war the language of conscription could be used in writs to regional and civic administrators ordering them to produce 'all and every' subject capable of bearing arms. On occasion, the penalties of death and the forfeiture of property were invoked. But the response still depended on the degree of pressure judged practicable by local authorities. Understandably, the summonses most widely obeyed by a cross-section of the community were those calling on them to man walls and beacon stations, and patrol coasts and valleys in their own defence. Though even here, as in Elizabeth's call-up to counter the threat of Spanish invasion in 1588, there were many who dodged the draft or snatched up a first month's pay and at once absconded with it. Ten years previously Geoffrey Gates had referred despairingly to 'the rurall man [who] by bribes, by a livery coat, by frank laboured friendship, by counterfeit sickness, or by starting from his house under colour of far business doth shift himself from the ordinances of the prince'. Witness such as this is abundant, and it is hardly worth adducing from muster after muster the complaints of local authorities that men turned out without the basic arms they were by law required to possess in the event of mobilization.

Recruiting policy was thus uneasily poised between implying compulsion and accepting voluntarism. It was a voluntarism that became even more fictitious as pressure was applied lower and lower on the social scale, but even there we are rarely dealing with armies stuffed with the gleanings of the press-gang. Of the resentful groups forced out by their neighbours and herded at the start of the long march towards what they dreaded, only a proportion arrived anywhere near an army. Many of those that did soon poured themselves into the staunchless flux of deserters who weakened the physique of every fighting force. Those who had crept away en route, and were too scared to return home, contributed to the social cost of criminous vagrancy. With such limits on the effectiveness of compulsion we cannot speak of conscription. As late as 1626 we find the count-duke of Olivares, arguably the toughest-minded administrator in Europe, accepting that 'it is no use having men extracted by force'.

Indeed, the inflated numbers of men a government commissioned its recruiters to raise tacitly allowed for its own weakness. Thanks to evasion, bribery and colourable legal challenge, the number actually enrolled represented a shortfall of perhaps one-fifth. Desertion en route accounted for the loss of between a seventh and a third, depending on the length of the journey, the desperation of the men and the corrupt connivance of their escorts. And by mid-campaign an army could expect to have lost a further quarter of its new recruits from desertion alone. If we add losses from disease, and from fatal or debilitating wounds (the smallest of these categories), the shrinking in effectives is so dramatic as to call for a cluster of specific instances: 50 per cent in the case of the force that Parma led into France in 1592, 75 per cent in the short (three months) expedition of Lord Willoughby into Brittany in 1589; the reduction of the force Essex led against Rouen in 1591 from 4000 to 380.

Of course there were enough recruits who enlisted willingly or were at least determined to make the best of it (plus a number of the unwilling who became infected by the positive aspects of military service) so to supplement ex-garrison and mercenary troops as to get wars started, and, with greater difficulty, to keep them going. But the process of recruitment revealed a society which was, as we shall see, insufficiently militant to allow them to be waged on the scale envisaged by rulers or according to the methods advocated by military reformers.

Yet that society was, even by modern standards, a violent one; why did not the summons to be licitly violent find a sufficient response to solve the problem of recruitment? Certainly it did not. There was, in any case, little likelihood that men showing violent behaviour in one context would carry it intact to another, and no evidence that authority believed that criminousness could be channelled productively into armies, though we shall see that the emptying of gaols was occasionally resorted to in order to make up numbers. Yet the question is worth putting because there were some centres of violence that did attract 'recruits'.

At sea, where undeclared rivalries were pursued by privateering under letters of marque on an almost perennial basis, the period saw a gradual, and from the later sixteenth century, really notable, increase in this activity. The categories were blurred. Privateers interrupted a rival's trade, raided his shores, sank his naval shipping in a form of pre-bout sparring permitted by the rules of war, and borne with because of the horrendous costs of ending it with war itself.

By the 1580s, however, when the vessels calling themselves privateers were at sea in hundreds – chiefly English, French and Dutch – many were unlicensed, not following government objectives and not declaring cargoes and prizes. They became, save in name, pirates, as likely to attack the shipping of a neutral power, like Portugal (before its conquest by Philip II in 1580), Denmark or Venice, as that of the common enemy, Spain.

At least the corsairs, the Moslem raiders operating from fortified ports – in north Africa, with Algiers the wealthiest and the most frightening symbol of them – preserved a steadily ideological policy. They preyed neither on one another nor on vessels belonging to their nominal overlord and occasional employer, the sultan. But their attacks on Christian coasts and shipping were checked neither by truces nor peace treaties between the two faiths. And the success of their unremitting pursuit of loot and slaves infected the motives of galley captains operating out of such 'crusading' ports as the Knights of St John's Valetta in Malta and the Tuscan Knights of Santo Stefano's headquarters, Pisa; in spite of the crosses on their backs and banners, they came to make little distinction between Christian and Moslem. When sea banditry lost its original privateering-crusading image, maritime insurance rates soared in recognition of the fact that the Mediterranean had become a den of thieves. Were the lean and overarmed vessels berthed in Valencia, Palma, Palermo, Naples and Cosimo I of Tuscany's only too well designated 'free port' of Livorno privateers, corsairs, anti-corsairs or mere priates? Their owners themselves would have given different answers in different circumstances. The population of Senj, the little port protected by the islands in the crook of the Istrian peninsula, knew, from parish priest to old-clothes vendor, that their entire economy was dependent on sea robbery. They were believed to drink their victims' blood as a solemn acknowledgement that theirs was a creed of one against all. Yet they captured Turks in the guise of Christians, and Venetians in that of zealous servants of the Austrian Habsburgs.

Outside the Mediterranean the same phenomenon occurred and at about the same time. Sea ports which originally concentrated – together with their normal fishing and trading activity – on licensed raiding, like Bayonne (anti-Spain), La Rochelle (anti-French Catholic vessels) and Dunkirk (anti-English), became the Livornos of the north, attracting immigrants drawn by the lure of the profit to be derived from an undiscriminating life of violence at sea.

Piracy was, of course, as endemic as smuggling. But normally it had been – as it remained in little ports all the way from the islands of the Aegean to the harbours of Devon – an activity of secluded communities living on the marine margins of policed life. With the sixteenth century it became a trade. Always the gallows shadowed it. But at least in the Mafia-like confusion of roles and protections offered in the 'corsair' ports it offered a new chance to hounded or restless men: not just overambitious shipmasters and naval captains reluctant to be turned off at the end of a campaign, but bankrupt gentry, broken merchants, shoemakers and men whose nicknames commemorate not their previous occupations but the braggartry of rejection: the Penniless, Big-thirst, Gambled-it-away, Unwashed.

For these men, homing in on centres of violence, the recruiter's drum had little music. We know about them chiefly from inquests on their washed-up bodies, complaints from merchantmen who had fought them off, judicial records of their trial and execution. Life in the pirates' nests was probably more hazardous than it was in any army. But they were real communities. Seamen, fences, ransom-brokers, bent law-officers, chandlers, these interdependencies on land, and the close-quarters sharing of dangers and loot on board, provided a heightened substitute for a community life that had proved too dull or ostracizing. Probably very few men in 'the age of individualism' were temperamentally loners. To some, as we shall see, the army did offer the lure of an alternative society, but with its pittance-pay and alternating recruitments and disbandments, it could not rival the appeal of the pirates' nests, as long as these remained capable of absorbing newcomers.

If piracy is one example of capacities for violence not diverted towards war, another is brigandage. This was also an activity that increased in step with the growth of armies without contributing to them. It is true that some bandit chiefs, in Catalonia and the Romagna, for instance, were forced to seek pardons in return for military service, but brigandage, whether open road highway-manry or a defiant harassment from frontier forests or mountain hide-outs of an authority that taxed too hard and judged too harshly, was essentially a local, community-linked phenomenon. The brigands needed contact with the lands they had chosen to leave; and the cowed and the law-abiding stay-at-homes there, whom they alternately pillaged and protected, glamorized their leaders and very seldom betrayed them.

Similarly inward-turning were the brigandlike practices of those French *gentilshommes* who turned – as the contemporary pun had it – into *gens-pille-hommes* during lulls in the Wars of Religion. These outbursts of neo-feudal robber-baronry (revealing a strong nostalgia for the outlawed private armies of the Middle Ages) drew on purely local and personal loyalties as an excuse to release behaviour often as deliberately cruel as it was violent. But this is not to suggest that this behaviour, or that of the *bravi*-surrounded lordlings who swaggered it over the priests and peasants of isolated villages in Piedmont and Lombardy, could be diverted away from local ties into distant armies. *Bravi*, as the Venetians found, might enrol as cavalrymen of the republic, but only in order to gain permits to carry guns and pistols at home.

Similarly a third, and more widely distributed type of violence displayed by groups – rioting – cannot be represented as a strain within society which would relish the more formalized riot of the battlefield. Sparked off by new taxes, fear of grain-hoarding or a rise in the price of bread, enforced changes in religious practice, new regulations favouring masters against men in a high-employment trade, riot was a form of battle waged against authority with stones and swords, clubs and pitchforks. But it was a fight to preserve ancient, 'honest', traditionally protective ways of life; it expressed the panic of men who wanted life to go on, not necessarily very comfortably, but stably, fairly, and, above all, at home.

In all these forms of group violence there were acts of outrageous, supererogatory cruelty. Not only there. The age in general had a twist of sadism. Victory in a family feud could be celebrated by rape, castration, ritual gnawings on dead bodies, the macabre humiliation of using heads as footballs. In 1500 the Florentine pharmacist Luca Landucci described what happened when the cart bearing two murderers towards the place where they were to be hanged stopped outside his shop; the brazier to heat the pincers with which they were being tortured on the way had gone out. 'The beadle shouted at the executioner who went for charcoal to the charcoal-burner, and for fire to Malcinto the baker, making a great fire. The beadle kept shouting "make it red hot!" and all the people wanted them to be tortured without pity. The very boys were ready to kill the executioner if he did not do his work well, so they shrieked in a most terrible way.' Leonardo da Vinci recommended to the ruler of Milan that one good way to deal with a hungry enemy was to poison the fruit trees on his line of march. Later in the century the jurist and classical scholar Girolamo Maggi proposed first to Duke Cosimo and then to the government of Venice the manufacture of a novel weapon. It comprised a lance-point which, on being stuck into an adversary, would activate two spring-mechanisms; one would grip him close with two toothed arms, the other would discharge against him a foam of liquid fire.

These random examples from Italy could be readily paralleled elsewhere. They serve only to raise a question. Savagery and the swift violence of emotional response to an insult or threat or fear were constants. Judicial cruelty, at least that of secular justice, did increase: breaking on the wheel, and leaving the victim to a lingering death there, was, for instance, introduced early in the sixteenth century. Perhaps in this period there was a new cynicism, in addition to an increase in an old relish, brought to the idea of the suffering and death of others. Charles the Bold laughed off the slaughter of a third of his men when after the debacle at Murten (1476) they were shot in the trees where they had taken refuge, and as they waded clumsily into the lake. According to the army surgeon Ambroise Paré, Charles V's reaction to the loss of men through disease at the siege of Metz in 1552 was to enquire whether the casualties included men of birth. When assured that they were all 'poor soldiers', 'said he it makes no matter if they die, comparing them to caterpillars and grasshoppers which eat the buds of the earth.' 'Food for worms', as Falstaff might blithely add. Was life now held cheaper?

During the disequilibrium between earlier armies that contained large contingents of neighbours-in-arms and later ones – after this period – comprising long-service regiments that constituted affective groupings, the answer is probably yes. We are not to expect village war memorials, let alone tombs for the 'unknown soldier' until the maturing of nationalism. All the same, an unnatural anonymity marks late Renaissance battlefields and siege trenches. Scarcely regretted when they left home, treated as pickings rather than persons by unprecedentedly rapacious generations of entrepreneur captains, unbemedalled after a victory, shovelled into mass graves; it is difficult not to compensate with indignation for careers so brushed aside. Of course, though rulers might hold humble lives cheap no individual did. Yet this was a world which took cruelty and early deaths from natural causes (at a median age in the mid-twenties) for granted, and offered the possibility of escape into an occupation that measured the chances of death not from the regular observation of neighbours' funerals but from the average-free trajectory of bullets and, moreover, offered a moral void (as long as the eyes of the provost and his informer-hangmen did not penetrate it). Were there not, then, conditions to attract the freelance, as opposed to the group-seeking or group-generated, criminal into army service?

The number of crimes committed relative to the size of the population before and during the early modern period is impossible to establish: statistics concerning both are frailly trustworthy. It is still more difficult to compare the number of individuals who, when convicted of crimes, can usefully be called criminals. But this was a constant from medieval to early modern times. Changes have been noted in the incidence and nature of crimes: in rural areas a shift from intra-class 'borrowing' to stealing from those better-off, peasant-proprietor or landlord; in towns an increase not only in theft but in crimes like swindling, forging and gang muggings that seem to reflect the increasing cash-mindedness and the stretch in fortunes between poor and medium-rich that accompanied the continuing economic development of urban communities. The popularization of 'short' firearms (dags), and the even shorter pistols of the mid-sixteenth century, led to assaults being possibly more lethal. All governments from the 1530s forbade their subjects to carry such readily concealable weapons. Even nobles and professional soldiers not on duty were forbidden to take guns less than three-quarters of a yard with them. In an English proclamation of 1559, which repeated earlier legislation, it was pointed out that such weapons were used 'in time of peace to execute great and notable robberies and horrible murders'. And the spread – among the few who could afford or steal them – of wheel-lock weapons, which could be fired instantly without lighting a fuse, led to such legislation being repeated with all the more fervour.

More was written about crime in the sixteenth than in the fifteenth century. But then more came to be written about everything, and more of what was written survives. Changes in criminal procedure – in England, France and Germany at least – made it more difficult for plaintiffs, whether in person or, in the case of murder, through representatives, to settle out of court or simply cancel an action: a less personalized justice may have caused the intending criminal to think of himself as such, rather than as a man with a wrong to right by illegal means within a society which, if he were caught, might settle the matter with a bargain rather than a brand, or worse.

We may give weight to the coming into existence of a literature about the underworld – the English rogue, the Spanish picaro – and see harsher punishments as a lightly policed world's answer to a rising wave of crime, and conjecture that the scanty evidence for recidivism simply means that released criminals thereafter kept on the move. But in seeking a connection between private and publicly organized violence, we must recognize that probably less than a third of all crimes involved violence to persons: rape, murder, assault and robbery with violence. And we would have to assume that of those who were not executed or disabled by maiming or by long pre-trial imprisonment, the undetected or lightly sentenced would break the multitude of congenial ties to the scene of their crime and, rejecting the subworld of the picaro, go off to the distant and less calculable violence of war.

We have seen that foreign war as a means of getting rid of the danger of rebellion at home became a truism. From the 1470s, however, there was a novel emphasis on the use of war as purgative or laxative to evacuate criminals from the body politic. A spokesman in 1474 for Edward IV's attempt to get an anti-French war subsidy out of the Commons pointed out that this would draw away those who were every day committing 'extortions, oppressions, robberies and other great mischiefs'. In 1607, when England was at peace with Spain, a poetaster drew attention to domestic riots and mourned:

O had we never ended Spanish jars,
Then these had never been our English wars.

Governments did not invent wars to rid the body politic of riff-raff, but there is no doubt that convicted criminals did enlist. Pierre de Bourdeille, seigneur de Brantôme remarked jeeringly that one of the reasons why so many soldiers wore their hair long was to conceal the fact that their ears had been cropped by the hangman. The medieval precedent for granting a pardon for men banished for crimes in return for military service was continued, though if the example of Venice is anything to generalize from, a high proportion of men who had committed crimes of violence treated their safe-conduct simply as a means of slipping safely home and did not go near the army.

To reinforce the troops besieged in Le Havre, Elizabeth I licensed the export of men from Newgate; in 1596 criminals were released from the royal prison in Seville on condition that they helped beat back the English raid on Cadiz. Justice Lambarde glumly contrasted the days of yore when armies composed of great landlords and their dependants blended easily back into civilian life with the present, 'when not only our gaols are scoured and our highways swept but also the cannels of our streets be raked for soldiers', and asked, 'What marvel is it if after their return from the wars they do either lead their lives in beggery or end them by hanging?' The appointment of civilian provost-marshals to herd ex-soldiers back to their places of origin defends Lambarde from the charge of exaggeration.

No military man believed – or, at least, said that he did – that criminals made good soldiers. The earl of Leicester, who had been sent some of the wide boys of London to join his expeditionary force in the Netherlands in 1585, indignantly pointed out that however good they might be with a bludgeon in London they were useless with a pike in the field. The man who was prone to cocky, personal, flare-up violence was unsuited to violence-to-order. Commanders knew well enough that they lacked the disciplinary resources to turn scum into cream.

Scum they certainly got. The duke of Alba's letters from the Netherlands were as bitter on this topic as were Leicester's. Claude Haton noted in his memoirs that all too many of the soldiers in the Catholic armies of the French civil wars were 'outlaws, vagabonds, thieves, murderers, deniers of God, renouncers of debts'. But – on, it is true, insufficient evidence – it seems likely that the scum that drifted, or was blown by authority towards armies, contained few criminals who were violent by nature. These men could do better elsewhere. Through the recruiting procedure, armies got vagrants; men forced on to the roads by enclosures, population increase, rising prices – factors they could not adapt to. And because jobless men on the move were popularly thought of as potential criminals, crime became associated with the army service they were too weak to avoid. For many, begging was far preferable to military service; that is how they caught the eye of local authority and were rounded off to war. Among the criminous who actually sought out armies, the likelihood – again, it can be no more than that – is that they moved not to the army itself but to its service fringes. Here, around a mass of men usually ignobly poor but sometimes fortuitously wealthy, short of women, for much of the time underworked and bored, was an environment on which bogus money-lenders, unlicensed pawnbrokers, pimps, card-sharps, rogues of all sorts could batten.

However, if it is uncertain how far armies attracted criminals or had them forced into them, it is clear that they sent back more than they received. On this score the evidence comes helter-skelter. In 1535 Robert Copland wrote of those

That have served the King beyond the sea,
And now that they out of wages be
They must beg, or else go bribe and steal.

This but anticipates the explanation given by a London merchant in December 1543 for his not having gone abroad. Troops were returning discharged from France: 'There is robbing on the ways now at the coming home of the soldiers, and therefore I stayed.'

Worse was to come. On 25 September 1550 the Common Council of the City of London received the following letter, probably from the mayor and aldermen. It related to the troops discharged from France under the Treaty of Boulogne and from the precautionary garrisons in the east and north of England.

'There be such a number of soldiers at this present within this city that unless speedy order be taken to rid and bestow them into the country, great danger will thereby ensue, for we are perfectly informed by such as heard some of them speak that their report is this: that they cannot work, nor will not work, and if they cannot obtain living [a livelihood] at the King's hands in consideration that they have long served the King's Highness and the King his father, that they will appoint themselves in several companies in London and come out of several lanes and streets in London and meet all together in some one place in the said city and thereupon set upon the citizens and their houses and take there such booties and spoil . . . they can lay hand upon and . . . that if it shall fortune them not to be ordered somewhat after their expectation, that then they will turn all England upside down at their pleasures.' And when in 1589 troops were returning from the expedition to Portugal, a mob of 500 of them were only prevented from looting Bartholomew Fair by the call-up of 2000 of the London militia. Given scares of this sort it is not surprising that the assassins of *Arden of Faversham* (1592), Black Will and Shakebag, were discharged soldiers.

In France the problem of military vagrancy in the wake of campaigns was grave enough by 1537 for Francis I to impose the death penalty for any ex-soldier who was not heading directly for home. François de la Noue urged the soldier readers he wrote for not to think it degrading to take up civilian occupations again at a war's end. Cervantes's story 'The dog's colloquy', with its account of men from the civilian underworld joining the gangs of vagrant ex-soldiers, could be readily supported from Spanish judicial records of ex-soldiers hung for theft, rape and murder.

This picture is confused by the overlap between vagrancy as an endemic problem and specifically ex-military vagrancy. Civilian vagabonds posed as ex-soldiers (Thomas Dekker gave the formulas of the toxic dressings they used in order to simulate unhealed wounds) in the hope of being more feared or of calling up some spark of charity. But even allowing for this in those who wrote about or legislated for vagabondage, there remains good reason to accept that armies functioned as crime machines. As the Venetian Senate recorded in 1599, it was better to use foreigners as garrison troops than natives of the *terraferma*: on discharge they took their criminous habits back to their countries of origin. Erasmus had not been writing just as a pacifistic dreamer when he made one of the objections to war that 'out of this fountain springs so great a company of thieves, robbers, sacrilegious men and murderers'.

As the same complaints were made when soldiers were turned off from abortive, bloodless campaigns as from ones that had seen battles or sieges, it is clear that what confirmed or awakened criminal tendencies was not the experience of butchery. A whiff of excitement, caused by the possibility of action and death, pervaded all armies, but from the tone of disciplinary ordinances and the very fragmentary records of military punishments, it seems likely that the gains of orderly civilian socialization, fragilely renewed generation by settled generation, were more easily negated by the dice, drink, scrounging, 'laundresses' and civilian-bashing of military leisure than by the sobering, if for some exalting, experience of combat. For those uneasy amidst the constraints of civilian life, an army provided, however shoddily, a Land of Cockayne. And even though it was as heartless in throwing out as it had been in wooing while enticing in, for some its glamour remained. So the military vagrants padded on from tavern to tavern, brawl to brawl, in danger of arrest but at least still on holiday from the routine of families, porters' baskets, mattocks and ploughs.

In all those countries which relied heavily on native subjects to make up armies, rulers used the social system itself as a recruiting device.

In the mid-fifteenth century, when princes were the residual landlords of vast tracts of essentially rural national economies, they could invoke written agreements with tenants-in-chief – and the holders of royal offices and the recipients of grants or annuities – whereby military service in person or by substitute was agreed, plus the obligation to pass the duty down the line of subtenancies and thus into the population at large. Primary recruitment, its incidence based on revenue, was routed through land grants and leaseholds. And except in times of incipient or actual civil war, it also tapped those informal and often illegal contracts whereby magnates protected their investments and standing with promises of protection or subsidy in return for local armed support. Royal rewards, in the shape of yet more land, an enhanced title or an office of dignity like the grand constableship, were most likely to be given in return for service in war. So contracts with 'retainers' or with equal-status brothers-in-arms were not only a local safeguard; they were the means of achieving the swift mobilization that could catch a prince's eye and was difficult to achieve through subtenancies which produced as many excuses as men.

For sovereignty, or the right and ability to demand, was at all levels a concept fighting for definition within a matrix of contingent self-interest and legal bluster. No wonder that Machiavelli identified law with the power to enforce it. And in no area of secular life was the issue of sovereignty more sharply challenged than in the raising of armies: a forcing of men to take pills some of which would contain poison. Significantly large standing armies; centrally paid police forces; an acceptance that 'the state' has a reasoned life of its own: all these were lacking. In an age of acutely personalized social relationships, monarchs and tenants-in-chief could issue orders based on promises made in writing. Tradition and a not-quite-institutionalized impulse to obey went some way to providing the quota. But the personal 'right' to avoid a response remained as valid – almost – as the institutionalized right to require it. As it happened, as far as leasehold military service was concerned, any crucial test of society's response to orders from above was diverted by changes in the composition of armies. The growing need for infantry, hauliers of artillery and diggers of field- and siegeworks led rulers to turn increasingly to mercenaries and to urban and rural communities as well as to the heavy cavalry 'lances' and the mounted bow- and crossbowmen called for by landholding contracts.

It may be true that in moving from the mid-fifteenth century to the eve of the Thirty Years War we cross a tract of time so lacking in major and enduring changes in the way life was organized and lived as to justify the term 'transition'. All the same, because a crucial element in recruiting remained identified with social structure, changes within that structure over five or six generations, changes that had subchronologies for each country and within them for regions nearer or farther from the punitive reach of central government, were marked; so marked as to make it a matter for some wonder that recruiting retained so strong a land-mediated element. Royal lands were sold, and a multitude of subsidiary property transfers and purchases were made which ignored military service as part of title. Yet the unwritten lines had been filled by a less tangible but to some extent compensatory sense of honour. Property still carried the connotation of service. Monarchs, of course, judged its nuances, increasingly summoning only those most likely to respond and not always permitting a grandee to appoint his own nominees to subordinate commands. They could expect most in countries – France, Spain, Naples and Sicily, parts of Germany – where men of noble lineage were exempt from ordinary taxation because of the still-living convention that their purses were spared because they were prepared to contribute their lives. Time apparently stood still in the declaration of the French States General of 1614 that 'the nobility [*noblesse*] is the one among the orders [of society] to which has been committed the possession and handling of arms for the defence and protection of the kingdom'.

Apart from dealing with epidemics, raising armies was the most onerous duty undertaken by governments. So it was only natural that the greater landowners should still be called on to help bureaucracies too small to do the job by themselves. But among the changes during these generations were shifts in the education, habits and aims of the aristocracy. By the early sixteenth century the practice whereby aristocratic youths were packed off to a noble household to learn the crafts of combat while serving as page-servants was dwindling. Fewer nobles maintained both a scholarly and an arms-and-athletics tutor to prepare their sons for war. It was unusual that the future duke of Alba's uncle took him on the Navarre campaign to harden him to scenes of war at the age of six, and that, in his turn, Alba sent his son García on the Tunis expedition when he was only five. How far did the Second Estate still lead as well as raise men? Speaking of the 1491 campaign against the Moors of Granada, the chronicler Bernáldez complained that 'many of *los grandes de Castilla*, tired of coming so far to this and other wars, would not serve in person but simply sent captains and men'. In 1509 the Venetian Girolamo Priuli, aghast at the defeat of the republic's army at Agnadello, groused in his diary at the patriciate's reliance on mercenaries and peasants while their ancestors' armour rusted in their lavish palaces. Later in the century Michel de l'Hôpital noted with alarm that so many of the French *noblesse* were abandoning arms and turning 'to the various branches of knowledge [*sciences*], to the arts and to agriculture' that it was necessary to look for leaders 'beyond the Rhine and Elbe to save our country from becoming the prey of the Spaniards'. And in 1600 Thomas Wilson, in his *The State of England*, noted that 'gentlemen who were wont to addict themselves to wars are now grown good husbands, and well know how to improve their lands'.

Evidence of the 'civilianization' of the armoured castes of western Europe is widespread. The retreat from militant values was vainly muffled by the camouflage of ever more elaborate heraldry, genealogical apologetics and the spurious, 'romantic' imagery of upper-class street theatre: tilts, progresses, the ceremonial 'entries' of rulers, escorted by their local nobility, into provincial capitals. The process was encouraged by external factors: the more effective protests of governments against local bellicosity, the shrinking acreage of lands held by aristocrats of the old martial stamp; the shortage of royal estates available as gifts in return for military service; but it also reflected redefinitions of its members' roles that emerged within the Second Estate itself.

Quantitative tests can be applied in the case of France to test the response of an aristocracy to the military functions which were the pledges for its privileges. The fifteenth-century *compagnies d'ordonnance* were designed with a dual purpose: to divert local aristocratic buccaneering into royal service, and to provide a permanent cavalry corps to speed the process of mobilization for war. The monarch's personal interest ensured that the *ordonnance* companies constituted a crack corps. It was a route to high office at court. Membership was held to confirm titles to nobility upon which lawyers and heralds had cast some doubt. It could be costly. Men-at-arms were paid; but their stipend did not stretch to the required expenditure on lavish armours, tentage and entertainment: Jean de Chabannes, grumbled his secretary, held open house in his billet to every military stray who wanted food, drink and good company: 'French, Gascon, Piedmontese, Swiss, Spaniard, anyone who came along'. But this was the 'crack' norm, from the *ordonnance* to those aristocratic companies of men-at-arms maintained anachronistically into the 1620s by the Venetians and on to the smarter regiments of regular armies up to the close of the Second World War. Expenditure (which possibly could, after all, be compensated for by a plum ransom or a sinecure like the mastership of the stables) was then a test of castehood. Nevertheless, the *ordonnance* companies had had by the 1490s to accept between 30 and 40 per cent of non-aristocrats.

A more instinctive test of a military caste's willingness to spend money and risk life is provided by the French response to call-ups of military-service tenants as a whole to musters of the *ban* and *arrière ban* (chief and 'rear' tenants of fiefs).

These human harvests were not, of course, complete. Swathes had to be exempted lest to reap an army would be to crop many of the fiefholders through whom the country was judged, taxed and defended from counterattack. And excuses to avoid the summons were also to be expected: illness (forms of dropsy were so prevalent that kings of France drew some of their sacral specialness from their claims to be able to cure them), uxoriousness or other sexual preoccupations, inability to redeem pawned armour, straight cowardice: allowance was made for these afflictions as long as their victims sent effective substitutes. No one believed that an entire section of society, albeit a professedly militant one, could be swept out of its private concerns into public service at the blast of a trumpet. A king had the right to claim that he would call spirits from the vasty deep, but so did a Hotspur to put the mocking question: 'But will they come when you do call for them?'

Even in genetic terms we are not to suppose that the militant impulse within a military caste would be uniformly self-perpetuating over many generations. For the *noblesse de l'épée*, arrears of pay which had seemed tolerable when due to the financial embarrassment of the king himself, were less supportable when it could be attributed to the defalcations of a swarming and contemned *noblesse de la robe*; financially and numerically they were losing ground to the sons of grocers and pen-pushers. Enough of them remained faithful to the hereditary code to man the military offices at court and in the provinces and to fill higher commands in the field, but the *noblesse* by the mid-sixteenth century felt itself to be mongrelized. It was happening everywhere: in England knights who could not ride, in Spain *hidalgos* who could not shoot, in Milan and Naples *conti* whose sword-hands stank of trade. Only on the eastern German marches were *Gräfen* and *Ritter* men any of whom one would willingly challenge to a duel as an equal. The fine old-fashioned definition of the 1614 States General was an attempt to put the clock back. Its declaration went on to call for a purge of foreigners from commands and an ousting from the Estate of those who had bought their titles of nobility. Even so, it was as much an argument to preserve the tax-exempt status of an allegedly militant class as to restore its status as the armed guardian of those who prayed and worked. The Second Estate had never, quite, been that. It certainly could not now be made over in the image of its own nostalgia.

For whether we look to the closing stages of the Hundred Years War or to the Wars of the Roses, or to the 1482–3 War of Ferrara (that horse-mad principality), or to the Genoa of the Italian Wars – the republic which, uniquely, was dominated by a militant nobility – or to Sweden or western and central Germany where the service of nobles smothered with armorial bearings had to be commuted for cash, or to the Spain of summonses to serve in Italy or in the early amphibious campaigns in north Africa, we find an opting-out.

Substitutes were often of high calibre, younger sons, whose numbers grew ahead of the base rate of population growth, or valorous non-aristocratic neighbours, but the Second Estate, from the early stages of our period, did not see itself as automatically bound to fight. And as it became progressively diluted by titles of nobility given for financial and administrative services, the proportion of those 'of the sword' dwindled, and the relish for behaviour based on that earlier exclusiveness declined still further. The profit motive, too, was less attractive. The possible recouping, and more, of the capital expenditure on equipment and entourage involved in competing on the international jousting circuit – with the rewards in gifts, trophies and offers of employment – had faded. Government intervention cut the proceeds of ransom and booty. The epitaph of Sir Thomas Cokayne, who served in Henry VIII's French campaign of 1513, on his tomb in Ashbourne church in Derbyshire reads:

Here lieth Sir Thomas Cokayne,
Made knight at Turney [Tournai] and Turwyne [Thérouanne]
Who builded here fayre houses twayne
With many profettes that remayne;
And three fayre parkes impaled he
For his successors here to be,
And did his house and name restore
Which others had decayed before.

It is also an epitaph on the general grave of aristocratic hopes of restorative profit to be derived from fighting. His successors preferred the prestige and favour that accrued from helping to administer the recruitment of others.

It has been suggested that the adoption of 'unchivalrous' gunpowder weapons and the declining importance of cavalry led to a decreasing appetite for military service among the aristocracies of Europe. Neither assumption can be taken seriously.

By the mid-century the finest and largest store of artillery belonged to the dukes of 'chivalrous' Burgundy. Descriptions of Edward IV's expedition to France in 1475 concentrate on the size and variety of his artillery train: would he have had two of his cannon named 'Edward' if they were thought to be unchivalrous? The Italians, from 1494, were astounded by the superiority of the field artillery and handguns of their 'chivalrous' French invaders. In Spain handguns had been used from the late fourteenth century and figured largely in the forces provided for the 'crusading' War of

Granada by the military orders. At the war's end Ferdinand ennobled his chief artillerist, Francisco Ramírez, and praised him for having 'rendered memorable service to God and to me'. Great nobles did not consider it dishonourable to be appointed master of a ruler's artillery service. Galiot de Genouillac, Francis I's master and captain-general of artillery, was further honoured by being appointed *grand écuyer de France*. But it was as an artillerist, standing beside a cannon, that he had himself portrayed in the bas-relief on his tomb. Nobles eagerly bought guns to strengthen their own castles. In 1470 Viscount Lisle challenged his rival in the Wars of the Roses, Lord Berkely: 'I marvel you come not forth with all your carts of guns, bows and other ordnance . . . to my manor of Wotton to beat it down upon my head.' And, later, it was the aristocratic sportsman and weapons connoisseur who challenged gunsmiths to refine the techniques and beauty of barrel, lock and stock.

But if there was an acceptance of firearms as such, was there a reluctance to run the risk of being killed by one? It is true that guns, because the force of their bullets owed nothing to the muscle power that tensed a bow-stave or wound the string of a crossbow into its notch, were looked on by some as unnatural. And on a few occasions this led to captured handgunners being treated with especial cruelty. And there were times when a selective hindsight that imagined wars of the past to have been all handstrokes caused writers to revile the 'coward's weapon'. But the man-at-arms and his horse had been vulnerable to missiles for centuries; his armour had become heavier up to the very verge of practicality long before there were more bullets than steel crossbow bolts in the air. Until well into the sixteenth century armours were regularly 'proofed' by firing crossbows, not guns, at them before they were stamped and passed for sale. Men of birth did not refuse to lead infantry companies, all of which came to include arquebusiers, against other companies similarly equipped. It was the duke of Guise who (according to Brantôme) through his own example helped to popularize the musket. It was as the baron of Rosny that the future duke of Sully caught Henry IV's eye while serving as a gunner.

It is similarly hard to believe that the changing role of cavalry kept aristocrats from accepting or seeking military service.

Certainly men of breeding associated fighting with their chosen vehicle and recreation, the horse, though nowhere exclusively and least of all in Spain, where gentlefolk normally rode mules. And thanks to changes in armament which enabled the lance to be held steady, the physical and psychological weight of a cavalry 'charge' (a formidable trot) had never been so effective as when opportunities to use it became rarer in the face of the pike phalanx and an increasing use of shot protected by field fortifications. The spectacle of armoured man on armoured horse was the most riveting personalized image of conflict before the masked riot-police of today. An image as potent as its opposite, the nude (with which, thanks to Venus's affair with Mars, it was often linked), it was kept alive in memory and mores by art, by the elaborately splendid accoutrements of the tournament and through the prestige establishments of heavy cavalry, long after it had ceased to be relevant to the actuality of war.

The evidence of a reluctance to serve as a man-at-arms had emerged, however, before the lessons of pike and gun had been absorbed. If the heavy cavalry was the most honourable arm, it was also the most expensive; professional men-at-arms could expect compensation for a slain horse but this was rarely true for the reservists of the *ban* and *arrière ban* or for the one-campaign volunteer. On the other hand, it did not prove difficult to find aristocratic officers for the companies of horsed crossbowmen and arquebusiers, and then the cuirassiers and pistoleers who transformed the place of horses in combat by the 1540s. Indeed, Louis Gonzaga, duke of Nevers, recalled young men of quality 'dipping into their pockets, as well as their pay, in order to have their companies [of light horse] fine, and to cover themselves in glory'.

If there was any element of aristocratic prejudice against changed modes of fighting, for a while it concerned the infantry. It can be traced, I think, only in Germany and France where men-at-arms were reluctant (as was not the case in England, Burgundy, Spain or Italy) to dismount in order to stiffen foot soldiery, and in France alone where royal pressure had to be applied to get gentlemen to command bands of foot. Even here, however, when the infantry had proved its worth time after time (and become more native in make-up) the prejudice yielded to Brantôme's glorious celebration, *The Lives of the Colonels of Infantry*.

Deaths in wars and the succession of minors; the shrinkage of land-based fortunes as the real value of money declined; the gaining of titles of honour by men without a militant heredity; the virtual absence – given the smallness of permanent military establishments and the way they were run – of a military career structure that could allow an aristocrat to be 'in the army' while still agreeably responding to changes in the peacetime manners of his class: all played some part in the process of civilianization. None has yet been given sufficient quantification (save the war experience of the English peerage) to be trusted. Perhaps the most important factor of all – after state moderation of persistent unruliness – was the notion of peace itself, peace which, in spite of the distrust we have noticed, was now more generally seen as a positive, attainable, prolongable, above all profitable and interesting phase of national life. For the appeal of 'peace', to a traditionally martial class, depends on what it has to offer. There had, clearly, been periods of non-war before. But swords had not rusted during them. Paradoxically, the period of what has been called (though not in these pages) 'the military revolution' was one that saw a true revolution in the connotations of peace, not just as a pause between wars or a phrase in the mouths of a higher clergy, all too prone to militant apoplexy, but as a positively attractive alternative to the perpetual preparation for recurrences of violence. The very monotony of the sixteenth-century advice given to rulers – 'in peace prepare for war' – suggests that the former was becoming perilously seductive. When Francis of Alençon was invested in Antwerp in 1582 with the propaganda titles of duke of Brabant and count of Burgundy as part of William of Orange's efforts to strengthen the Netherlands' opposition to Spain, the new duke was warned by the clerics of the reformed churches that 'we have seen many commonwealths flourish so long as they professed chivalry and learning together, and yet have fallen into the hands of their enemies . . . by reason of their discontinuing of their former trade of arms'.

The essential material base for a shift in the significance of 'peace' was a greater variety of occupations and honours: estate management, regional administration, court service and diplomacy. Connected to these, though less tangible, was a desire to live more comfortably, with larger windows, wider stairs, less of the perpetually on-guard associations of keep, barbican and manned gatehouse; and an appetite to vary the reading of family records, genealogies and chivalric chronicles and romances (though this taste died lingeringly) with translations and popularizations that represented the new humanist outpouring of books.

The world of upper-class culture is too well charted to be due more than a glance here. It is also too complex. Of all 'lifestyle' books aimed at an aristocratic audience, the most widely read – in the Italian, in translations and a host of plagiaries – was Castiglione's *The Courtier* of 1528. It expressed his opinion that society by now ought to have grown out of warfare, except against the infidel, and it describes the social and learned graces whereby time could be passed fruitfully and delightfully in peace while not neglecting training the body against the eventuality of war. Yet for Montaigne, the most bookish and intellectually sophisticated of country squires, the spectacle of the great nobles around him reverting to the crude posture of warlords made him wryly conclude that, after all, 'the only suitable and essential role for the *noblesse* of France is the profession of arms'.

From the 1560s, the proliferation of plans for military schools and academies for well-born youths (that led a few to be actually founded) were not based on the fear that aristocracies were going morally soft or turning into bookish recluses. They had in mind that 'a great sort of our gentlemen', as Sir William Segar wrote in 1590, 'do take more comfort to be called good falconers or expert woodmen than either skilful soldiers or learned scholars', and that both the increasing complexity of large-scale military operations, and continuing changes in armament and formations, suggested the usefulness of a more formal training than had been available hitherto. And the ever-increasing volume of aristocratic duelling does not suggest a failure of hardihood.

The problem was that when periods of peace were more orderly and, for England, Germany, Italy and mainland Spain, more prolonged, there was a greater temptation to use them more wholeheartedly, whether through a devotion to sport, lands and family, through studying at the English Inns of Court or by imitating those German landowners who studiously exploited their mineral rights. Thus in proportion to the size of the Second Estate as a whole, fewer sought military careers. Alba in the Netherlands could never obtain enough gentlemen volunteers from Spain although, as he wrote home, it is 'soldiers of this calibre [who] are the men who win victory in the actions and with whom the general establishes the requisite discipline among the troops. In our nation nothing is more important than to introduce gentlemen and men of substance into the infantry so that all is not left in the hands of labourers and lackeys.' Blaise de Monluc made the same point for France: nobles can be found to command whole armies and regiments of cavalry and infantry because they will be directly appointed to charges they know it is their duty to accept, but not enough members of the lesser *noblesse* come forward to accept minor commands. There is no gleam from the Age of Chivalry in Lord Burghley's advice to his son Robert on his children's education: 'Neither, by my consent, shalt thou train them up in wars. For he that sets up his rest to live by that profession can hardly be an honest man or a good Christian. Besides, it is a science no longer in request than [during its] use. For soldiers in peace are like chimneys in summer.'

Faith in the great nobles' sense of duty, natural authority and ability to learn as he went along, kept the highest commands in their hands throughout the period. Some saw royal favours as the best way to finance the clientage systems on which their regional repute depended. Some served with gritted teeth, aware that their armies would be underfinanced and inadequately manned. A few, like Elizabeth's earls of Essex and Leicester, pushed for the honour in a spirit of ambition and daring. In all armies there were gentlemen veterans who had seen war from the start as a profession suited to their temperament and prospects. And as for volunteers, Essex's expedition to Rouen had both a cause and a leader of exceptional glamour; he was able to pick twenty captains from nearly seventy applications for commands. Normally, however, in England as elsewhere, civilianization meant that the motives which led an aristocrat to fight had become declassed, that is, had become much like anyone else's.

4

Recruitment:
the reaction of the
Third Estate

The higher reaches of the Third Estate, which provided the mass of the armies which the Second led into wars, was already complex in composition at the start of the period and became more so, as well as more numerous, by its end.

The associations of the word 'bourgeoisie' are too restricted to describe the leading spirits who by the mid-fifteenth century had made Florence, Venice and Siena the tamers of the aristocracies whose broad lands they brought under civic control, or who, from Nuremberg and Augsburg to Ghent and Lübeck, had established economies and communal governments that had to be treated if not as separate powers, at least with caution and respect by central governments which needed to tap their wealth.

Certainly the standing of these elites, in their own eyes and those of others, was based on wealth, primarily accumulated through regional and international commerce and banking, and their control of industrial operations like clothmaking, shipbuilding and mining. But contemporaries did not only call them 'the rich' or 'the plump ones' (*grassi*) but fumbled for broader labels: 'the great ones', 'the weightier' or 'the better ones'. For wealth was not the only criterion. There was 'new' money and 'old' money, 'good' money (owning a row of goldsmith's shops) and 'bad' (an abattoir or a string of brothels); marriage connections; a family's tradition of public service; the image projected by an individual's personality, influence outside the city, style of life. And there was little in common between members of the dominant trading class in Venice, who belonged to a legally defined and closed caste and referred to themselves as nobles, and the men of highest standing in a port like Bristol.

What all these urban social elites had in common, however, was an in-built pacificity. The independent cities of Italy and the semi-independent ones of Germany and the Netherlands had won their territories or shown their determination to conduct their own affairs mainly by hiring others, mercenaries, to do the actual fighting. By 1450 such elites had almost defined themselves within society as the sector that did *not* fight. Part of that self-definition involved a deliberate rejection of the values of the traditionally dominant class; part arose from the time-consuming fascination of the money-earning process itself; part, again, perhaps the major part, was due to the necessity of a wholehearted immersion in the developing communal life of cities and large towns in order to grasp the opportunities they offered and dominate the rivalries which arose within them.

This preoccupation, and the accompanying absorption into so crowded and various a mode of life, which informs the gossip of urban diarists and chroniclers, could but grow during the next hundred years. It grew as city populations expanded. This was not a uniform process, but out of a generally burgeoning population a relatively high proportion survived after birth or were attracted to the job opportunities in towns. Naples, Venice, Antwerp, Seville, Augsburg, London: these are only a few of the great cities that had expanded notably by 1550; the population of Lyon increased by a third between 1530 and 1555. And a larger population brought new opportunities, more competition, the greater likelihood of threatening social disturbance from the deprived.

It grew as the elites absorbed an increasing number of fee-rich lawyers employed either by merchants themselves or by local corporations or central government. And the elites absorbed, too, into their houses if not quite into their ranks, along with a few well-mannered artists, some of those men of letters and scholars on whom they relied to provide themselves and their sons with the classical culture that provided yet another sense of proud self-distancing from the Second Estate, which could still command so much respect – and royal favour and employment – by right and not through work.

As the elite groups expanded, the pecking orders within them became more diversified. Those with leisure derived from the unassailable magnitude of their wealth, the trustworthiness of their associates or simply an adequately financed weariness with the routines and decisions of constant business preoccupations, moved into the enemy's orbit, as it were, by miming some of the distinguishing habits of the aristocracy. They built extravagant town houses designed to signal their separateness from 'bourgeois' canniness. They bought land and built villas in the countryside not as an investment, or not only as an investment, but as a way of showing that they too could be at home far from counting house and council chamber, in the world of cows and vineyards, bailiffs and tenantry. They bought fiefs that carried with them titles to aristocratic status, or, with the same intent, placed the cards of their credit on the princely gambling tables whence honours were distributed. These last were tendencies which became more marked in the second half of the sixteenth century, as the elites continued to expand.

But in seeking prestige of a sort that neither the profits nor cultural tone of cities could offer, they stopped short, at least in the first generation, of accepting the militant overtones of aristocratic life. They did not hunt. When they bought land owing military service they had it performed by substitutes.

This is not to suggest any personal timidity. In his account of Florentine resistance to the Imperial siege of 1529–30, Jacopo Nardi remarks on the previous pacific nature of his fellow citizens: 'As an adolescent I saw fathers and mothers confiscating anything like a weapon from their sons' rooms in the interest of good discipline and of checking their wildness.' Now these youths were following the example of Francesco Ferrucci who, without previous military experience, became a bold and admired captain. When Francesco was captured by professional troops, Nardi recorded that he was not only stripped of his equipment but jeered at and insulted 'for being a merchant turned soldier, almost as if he had committed some hitherto unheard-of crime'. Members of the urban elites elsewhere played their part in those civic guards and watch and ward companies later so wonderfully commemorated in Rembrandt's 'The Night Watch'. In time of siege they led the non-professional defenders. In the French Wars of Religion they could put cause above cash, and enough gained military commands under the crown to cause a rash of outraged aristocratic petitions to have them cashiered. But as a series of groups linked by business contacts and a common conditioning, they represented an important element in society that was not prepared to wage aggressive war in person. There was little pacifism in this pacificity. The elites paid, through taxes and hazardously secured loans, a stiff proportion of the money needed to launch armies. Some of them, as we shall see, increased their fortunes by supplying armies with weapons, clothing and provisions. Others, by bridging with their capital the gap between the passing and raising of a war-tax, actually made mobilizations possible. From top to bottom, great noble to earth-shifter, war was a paid occupation. The noble may have spent more than he received, the pioneer would have been lucky if he got more than a meagre daily ration of food. But all constituted a cost to government, and to meet it recourse was had to the least pugnacious strain in society. And that strain, the urban elite, reflected, as it on the whole confirmed, the stay-at-your-desk mentality of the true bourgeoisie, the much larger class of middle merchants and guildsmen, who, together with their clerks, accountants, notaries and trusted journeymen, ensured that the most prosperous cities were the most reluctant producers of sound battle material.

There was some irony here. The money-greed of the bourgeois reflected, after all, the land-greed of the aristocrat. Among the military entrepreneurs who made fortunes by raising and delivering mercenaries to manpower-starved rulers, the majority were members of the lesser nobilities of Germany, non-confederate Switzerland and central Italy. The itch for profit, financial acumen: these were not the prerogative of townsmen; they can also be seen at work in the careers of those profiteering abbots, bishops, archbishops and cardinals which gave the Catholic First Estate so scandalously money-contaminated an image in the eyes of the urban Reformers. But only in towns were these instincts institutionalized and, even if they were much reviled by satirists of all persuasions, perceived as a fact of life that grew more necessary as wars grew more hideously expensive.

There remains a question. If the upper slice of the Third Estate contributed, financially in person and through the influence it exerted on the bourgeoisie, to making wars possible, did it incite governments to wage them?

Surely, no. Since the pre-1450 Venetian conquests (those of a mercantile oligarchy) of Dalmatian coastal regions and Mediterranean islands that offered ports of call en route to trade with the Levant and of mainland areas that gave unchallenged access to northern passes over the Alps, the capitalistic strategy of governments had steadied. Charles VIII's invasion plans could awaken financial support throughout the Midi from Lyons to Marseilles among those who resented Genoa's hampering of Provençal trade with western Italy. The Spanish mercantile elite could see some point in wars with an England and a France whose privateers were chopping at vessels bringing back those cargoes (often undeclared) from the New World that were not earmarked for the crown. Elizabeth gained support from London merchants for her Netherlands campaigns; it was not in their interest that

Spain should control the outlets for North Sea trade.

Yet, as we have seen, the rulers who could alone decide whether to wage war did not have economic advantage primarily in mind in Europe (imperial conquests overseas were another matter). And when an economic benefit did flow, as when Spain's victory over Portugal assured Philip of an enhanced grain supply, this was not necessarily an advantage to merchants. Government conquest meant government control. Though hampered here by an embargo on the export of a raw material, there by a monopoly or by excessive customs dues, the techniques of international trade were flexible and cunning enough for the elite to make their fortunes without clamouring for war. War, indeed, spelled loss more clearly than gain: loss through the interruption of commerce, the impoverishing of markets, the uncertain returns on the loans that would have to be provided to promote the wars. Insofar as the mentality and influence of its chief representatives were concerned, increased prosperity meant decreased militancy.

It was from the remainder of the Third Estate, chiefly rural peasants, small proprietors and craftsmen, then urban journeymen, labourers, porters, drifters, that the bulk of armies was made up. How large was this pool of potential recruits? Patchy as the evidence is, it is clear that it became broader. In England, Castile and Naples the population may even have doubled during the sixteenth century; in the territory around Zürich it grew by some 45 per cent between 1529 and 1585. Conflating the most optimistic of such figures, it is not unlikely that the population of western Europe overall grew by some 45 to 50 per cent between 1450 and 1600; more cautiously it can be said that at least it kept up with the growth in size of armies.

Of course this growth was not uniform either between or within countries. In 1558 English county authorities explained their inability to fill their military quotas as due to the famine of the previous year, and to outbreaks of epidemic disease. And, indeed, between 1556 and 1560, from both these causes, the population fell by some 20 per cent. The French Wars of Religion were accompanied, especially in the south, by a fall in population due not only to battles and the blood-lust killings of civilians but to devastated fields, slain or stolen draught animals, ransacked seed: side-products of war at home that caused early deaths through malnutrition and disease and checked the impulse to bring more children into so bleak a world. Spain's, or at least Castile's, population growth was sent into reverse by fierce epidemics in the

1590s at the very time when Philip II needed more soldiers than ever.

To connect army targets with the size of the available pool of recruits for any particular campaign or reinforcement is difficult now because of the incompleteness of demographic records. It was as difficult then because of the incalculable appearance of those epidemics – plague and influenzas – and barren harvests that killed so many more than did the age's wars.

Even so, and allowing for the probability, given the high incidence of adult mortality, of the proportion of the population under the age of fifteen as being as high as one-third, the pool should have been large enough. In 1491 the population of France was at least 10 million, and rising. Preparing for his campaign against Brittany, Charles VIII's preparations envisaged a fighting force of 20,000 together with around 28,000 supporting non-combatants – draymen, sutlers, smiths, saddlers, armourers, farriers and the like: the *équipe* necessary to service an army which had a heavy armoured component was only less complex than that escorting a modern racing car to Le Mans. His plans thus envisaged provisioning at least 48,000 men. The current rule-of-thumb was that able-bodied non-clerical males who were not in exempt occupations made up 10 per cent of the population: in this case, a round million. There was plenty of manpower on hand. If men had wanted to fight, statistically there should have been no problem in getting them to, famines and plagues notwithstanding. Yet contemporaries registered alarm not only on the score of overpopulation but on that of the difficulty of obtaining enough men for armies and navies.

The problem of recruitment seems to shrink to zero when we look at some of the consequences of the growth in population. In the countryside it led to a new attack on marginal lands left untilled in the wake of that real demographic catastrophe: the Black Death of 1348 and its repercussions, striking, again and again, at a workforce initially reduced by two-fifths. But that land could not support enough of the refugees forced out from the 'easy' lands of pasture and tillage. The towns absorbed – alarmedly – some of the spillage from rural desperation. But urban service needs were soon swamped, and their productive sector was inadequately stimulated by a population surge which threw up so many who were too poor to purchase and sought only work and a wage. By the late sixteenth century certain cities were frantically inventing public works, like fortifications, as a way of absorbing the energies of an otherwise dangerous percentage of the populace: 20 per cent in 1586 in Rouen. Certainly the situation worsened generally in the last decades of the sixteenth century, but comparable figures for Louvain (18 per cent) and Hamburg (20 per cent) for the late fifteenth suggest that the number of jobless and propertyless in towns moved up to peaks of this sort from a base of 8 to 10 per cent, throughout the early modern period. And though information about rural population is scanty, there are indications that similar figures apply there too. In August 1586 – after sunless months – a Parisian recorded that 'the poor people of the countryside, dying of hunger, went about in gangs and cut the half-ripe grain in the fields, then ate it on the spot . . . in spite of the measures taken by those who owned the fields. Sometimes they threatened to eat [the owners] too, if they would not allow them to eat the grain.'

The hold on the means of keeping alive in country or town for the feeblest wrack within the tide of new births was shaken further by inflation. Halting, difficult to follow as its progress is, inflation – reflected in the difference between a wage and what it could buy – took serious hold from the 1490s. It was exacerbated by the cheapening of the precious metal content of high-value coins that followed the import of gold and silver from the New World, but did not begin with it. By 1568 Jean Bodin was writing, impressionistically, it is true, that 'the price of things fifty or sixty years ago was ten times less than at present'. Everywhere – except in areas where it was customary to pay labour in kind (foodstuffs) rather than cash – it pushed wage-earners into pauperism. In France as a whole the purchasing power of wages fell during the sixteenth century by 40 per cent, in Normandy by about 70 per cent, in the English midlands by 50 per cent. The conjunction of inflation with the un- or underemployment caused by the population surge created an unprecedented proportion of the Third Estate who were not only available for but who, it might be thought, actually needed military service.

A connection between the economy and recruitment had become clear by 1500. It was the labour-unintensive pastoral agriculture of the confederation that had encouraged the Swiss to serve abroad. The same was true in the large tracts of Castile given over to sheepfarming. The slowing of industrial activity in the German towns and the early signs of inflation in the countryside were important factors in the formation of the *Landsknecht* companies. Kings of France had long relied on the service of men from the less productive agricultural parts of Gascony, Italian rulers on men from the harsh lands of the Marche, Romagna and Abruzzi. And to look forward: in Spain it was the fall in population from the 1590s and the consequent rise in wages that made the recruiters' task sharply more difficult than it had been before.

Yet on the whole, while distress increased all over western Europe during the century, it was only in those regions which had already acquired a tradition of exporting soldiers that the connection between economic conditions at home and military service abroad emerges at all directly. Elsewhere the chief reactions were to stay put and suffer or to take to the roads – but not those that led to armies.

One of the chief reasons for staying put was the family. The evidence which shows a deepening sense of the satisfactions of family relationships, between husbands and wives, parents and children, the absorption of the majority of bastards, relates to the more prosperous, and chiefly urban, sectors of society. But to judge from applications from common soldiers for leave or discharge, the desire to rejoin their families was probably not only the chief motive behind these 'legal' applications but affected the desertion rate as well. The Utopian troops fought well because 'the absence of worry about livelihood at home, as well as the removal of that worry which troubles men about the future of their families (for such solicitude everywhere breaks the highest courage), makes their spirit so exalted and disdainful of defeat'. Send me no more married men, Leicester begged Walsingham from the un-Utopian Netherlands in 1586.

This homesickness emerges as a much stronger element than the rough popular humour bewailing the nagging, the sexual voraciousness of wives and their insistence on wearing the trousers, would suggest. Partly uxoriousness, it must have been heightened by concern for the vulnerability of spouses left with small children: the average age in armies, from very fragmentary evidence, was twenty to thirty-five (higher in garrisons, but there men could be joined by their families); so given an average age on marriage for males of twenty-five to twenty-eight, there was a strong chance that many men volunteering for service would leave very young children behind them. And this was at a time when a low life-expectation meant that support for wives from grandparents and other older relatives could not be relied on. All these remarks of a demographic nature are flimsily supported by the available figures. However, the picture they suggest does square with at least one aspect of the reluctance to continue in service long after enlistment – and, presumably, to join up in the first place. Soldiers themselves were best placed to know how vulnerable wives (five years younger than husbands, to cite another average) were to the streams of disorderly men pushed towards war or blustering home from it. We have seen that community ties – even criminous ones – were among the recruiter's enemies. We must add the most poignantly affective of them all, the family.

Of course no individual family situation at any particular moment is 'average'. Men did leave their wives, and thoughtfully, making their wills before they left. But at the moment we are not considering those who enabled armies to be assembled, but the far greater number who preferred to stay at home in spite of poverty, or to seek other ways of coping with hard times.

Some chose total emigration, but not many; a few hundreds a year to Spanish America, an unascertainable but certainly lower figure to Portuguese India, a mere trickle to France's possessions in Canada and England's first footholds across the Atlantic. The far greater tides of religious refugees and the forced-out poor crossed less dramatic frontiers. The way in which the prosperous (merchants and bankers) or those representing rare skills (scholars, silk-weavers, printers, glassworkers, gun-casters) found niches in countries other than their own is well-documented and familiar. The resettlement patterns of men and their families self-exiled for religious reasons is similarly fairly well traced because the sense of conviction that led them to break home ties also caused them to show up as property-owners or agitators in their place of adoption. Only recently have historians recognized the extent to which the new poor burrowed under frontiers, regularly migrating between south-western France and Catalonia, for instance, or finding relief amidst the less buoyant populations of central Europe. The tracing of these émigré routes has only begun.

More readily traceable, in masses if not by name, are the hordes who, often after travelling long distances, presented themselves at the gates of towns or within the streets of large villages within their own countries. These were the vagrants of contemporary panic and of vain legislation concerned with prisons, poor-houses and subsidized repatriation. Some could be absorbed. Some forced their way in and sank like stones to the very dungeons of the social fabric, outnumbered or outsmarted by their fellow beggars. Others were employed for a pittance on some public work (drain-cleaning or earth-shifting) and then, when it was done, ejected with a coin in one hand and a loaf in the other to try again elsewhere.

So much misery! And if the vagrant's country were not at any given moment looking for soldiers it was the common knowledge of taverns and street corners that somewhere – and these were travelling men – armies were fighting or needing replacements for their dwindling human assets. Why did not the sinking stay-at-home, the rejected vagrant, join up?

In 1572 the veteran Venetian commander Giulio Savorgnan explained why the doge could not expect too much of the troops he had engaged to serve in Dalmatia during the renewed Turkish threat that followed the battle of Lepanto. Why had they enlisted in the first place? 'To escape from being craftsmen, working in a shop; to avoid a criminal sentence; to see new things; to pursue honour – but these are very few. The rest join in the hope of having enough to live on and a bit over for shoes or some other trifle that will make life supportable.' We can expect the anti-militaristic intellectual Erasmus to take a sardonic view: men become soldiers to obtain booty and to be licensed to live in defiance of the laws of church and state. But Savorgnan's opinion was backed by other professional soldiers. For La Noue the incentives were cash and 'la licence soldatesque'; these were the chief reasons, 'though almost all say that it is to pursue honour'. Honour, duty: Sir Roger Williams recognized that these motivated some, but he put them (even for gentlemen) below gain.

What, then, was the cash incentive to serve?

Methods and standards of pay were roughly equal throughout the west. Venetian practice, for which the evidence is fullest, may be taken as the norm. Though pay in England was expressed in terms of a daily rate, most countries, like Venice, calculated pay by the month or, rather, 'month': for it suited the convenience of governments to spread the 'month' and thus hand out pay less frequently. Angelo Beolco's peasant soldier, Ruzante, when asked if he would serve again, replied, 'How do I know? If they paid up, and didn't stretch a month to 100 days, I might think of going back.' Though exaggerated for comic effect, this merely distorts common knowledge.

In peacetime, Venice gave out monthly pay every forty-five days, or eight times a year, up to 1589, when ten pays became the norm on the *terraferma*. Overseas, where the cost of living was higher, ten pays were occasionally given as a temporary measure to attract new drafts; it became the norm only from 1573. By 1601 it had been found impossible to attract men to serve unless pay was given by the calendar month both overseas and on the *terraferma*.

In wartime, or during precautionary mobilizations, the Venetian rate was ten pays a year until 1570, when the calendar month was adopted. Venice was at peace between 1540 and 1570; in other countries peacetime 'months' continued to vary, but by the mid-sixteenth century nearly all war-service pay was based on the 'real' month of thirty to thirty-one days.

In Venice the basic infantryman's monthly pay remained unchanged from 1509 to 1599 at 3 ducats. Its equivalent, 3 escudos, remained unchanged for Spanish troops from 1534 until after 1620. The Englishman's 6d. (old pence) a day of 1450 was retained in Thomas Cromwell's unrealized project for a small standing army of 1536–7, became 8d. in the 1550s and stayed there for the rest of the period. This is what seven-year-old children earned in Norwich by knitting stockings. The French infantryman's 4 livres tournois per 'month' increased to 6 or 7 in the 1530s and appears to have stuck there. By 1521 the German *Landsknecht* was receiving 4 gulden, and there is no evidence that this increased save through bonuses when mercenaries were in particularly acute demand.

There is no doubt that this inflexibility did, during an inflationary period, mean a progressive fall in the purchasing power of the military wage. All the same, wages were expressed not in terms of actual coins, but in moneys of account, moneys, that is, whose value in terms of actual cash reflected the monetary policies of the employing government. Thus the apparently unyielding Spanish 3 escudos were revalued upwards by 28 per cent between the 1560s and 1590s while still falling behind in purchasing power, and the Venetian ducat (under other names: scudo, zecchino) similarly rose in face value. Translating the vagaries of the Venetian monetary system into the smallest money of account, the soldo, and accepting changes in the length of the 'month', we get figures showing at least an increase in the cash value of the infantryman's basic wage.

Peacetime rate (soli per day)

1509–1588	8.15
1589–1598	10.19
1599–1605	13.8
1606–1615	15.78

Wartime or mobilization (new troops) rate (soldi per day)

1509–1569	10.19
1570–1598	12.23
1599–1605	13.8
1606–1615	15.78
1616–1617	18.41

On pay days, the men were issued with small change (piccoli, quatrini, bagatini, sesini and the like) which could be used in market and inn and which the pay clerks represented as equivalent to the number of soldi of account due.

Comparative figures are scarce, but nonetheless suggestive. In the mid-century, unskilled workers in the state dockyard, the Arsenal, received 8–10 soldi a day. Between 1545 and 1615 the average daily wage of building labourers rose from 18 soldi to 41.63. In terms of wages, then, Venice's soldiers came well towards the bottom of the social ladder.

And not only in Venice. In Florence the building labourer's wage rose from 20.5 soldi in 1543 to 51 in 1599. By the 1540s the English soldier's wage also was dropping behind that of unskilled craftsmen, and the pay rise of the 1550s did not bring him level for long. In France in 1500 the building worker's daily wage of 4 sous and 6 derniers tournois was already ahead of the infantryman's 3 sous and 4 derniers, and the discrepancy widened during the rest of the century. Even when allowance has been made for the numerous feast days on which in Catholic countries workers (in theory, at least) could not earn a wage, the soldier's trade, especially from the 1540s, steadily worsened in comparison with those in other low-paid occupations.

Like theirs, the military wage was not 'all in'. The builder's labourer had to house, clothe and feed himself and supply his tools. So did the soldier, apart from his lodging, which was free. But the equipment he had to bring to the job was more expensive than that of his best-paid civilian opposite number. By 1560 a characteristic form of military service was as an arquebusier. Leaving aside hose, shirt, tunic and shoes (commonly worn out during the joining-up march), he needed his weapon, a helmet, a sword and a breastplate or cuirass. If he already possessed them, well and good. If not, and few did, their issue would involve a deduction from his wage. And so would their replacement if lost, stolen or damaged: nearly a month's wage for an arquebus, three months' for a cuirass. Because governments seldom knew how long a mobilization or campaign would last, they sought to get back from captains the sums they advanced for equipping troops as quickly as possible – and captains were anxious to recoup their loans before men fell sick or deserted. So the stoppage on pay could be imposed at as high a rate as 25 per cent in each pay.

Giulio Savorgnan described the result in another letter to the doge from Dalmatia. We have seen that the pay due was 12.23 soldi. Stoppages of other sorts reduced this to 11: a service charge to the pay clerk, contributions to surgeon and priest, even the purchase of gunpowder (in England it was only in 1601 that arquebusiers were released from – in effect – fining themselves every time they fired). Savorgnan describes how he had gone round the market in Zara (Zadar) with a pair of scales pricing the bread, cheese, sardines and wine that the soldier's basic diet was based on: meat he ignored as too expensive, as was the wood required to cook it. He found that the minimum price of such a regime was 12½ soldi a day. 'So what soldier', he asked, 'would leave Italy for Dalmatia knowing that he would not be able to feed himself?' What is more, he added, the captains, 'aware that the infantry cannot hang on like this', stop so much of their pay for the arms they have issued that the men have no recourse but to desert.

It is true that supplements were paid to pikemen wearing the heavier body armour necessary for men in the front or wing of a formation and, from the 1540s, to musketeers, partly as a compensation for carrying heavier equipment, partly to help them pay for it. All the same, in Venetian service the maximum daily wage an infantryman so armed could earn was 23 soldi before stoppages at a time (1616) when a building labourer could expect 41.63. And because Venice drew recruits from many different nations – in that year France, Holland, England, Switzerland, Savoy, Germany and Corsica – its rates perforce reflected the European norm.

The pay of NCOs was better. Notionally each company of 100–150 men had, in addition to the captain who had raised or was appointed to command it, an ensign, a sergeant, at least one corporal, and a drummer. The guidelines were, in terms of base pay: ensign ×4, sergeant ×3, corporal ×2, drummer ×1½. These rates do not quite define a pay-in-pocket hierarchy. Ensigns and sergeants were expected to support batmen to look after them, cook and run errands (mystery enshrouds the corporal). The base-pay principle ran throughout the service, including the cavalry. The man-at-arms in French *ordonnance* companies, for instance, received 15 livres tournois a month: three times the pay of an infantryman. But out of it he was expected to maintain a swordsman and a page. Army pay, in fact, appears to have been calculated as a subsistence wage only; it has been estimated that at mid-sixteenth-century prices a balanced diet would have mopped up a *Landsknecht*'s whole pay and left nothing over for beer. Perhaps this was a belated, curiously long-enduring homage to the notion that military service was not an opportunity for profit but a labour service owed to the sovereign. That the pay of mercenaries, though often contracted at a slightly higher rate than that of native troops, did not soar above the subsistence rates, indicates the breadline base from which they, too, had been recruited. And the difference appears to have been treated as a recruiter's perquisite.

The peacetime captain, who was generally paid at base rate ×8, was moderately well-off, though he was expected to maintain a small personal staff. It was only senior officers, the colonels and captains responsible for enrolling new companies and, usually, commanding them, who were able to go to war with any anticipation of profiting from it. They were paid well, about twice as much as permanent captains, but this was because by raising, paying, equipping and disciplining their men they were crucial to the administration of an army. They, too, needed personal staffs to enable them to perform these functions. Their real profits were made illegally. Two chief devices were employed: falsifying numbers in order to receive money for non-existent men, and manipulating the company bonus fund.

The first abuse is graphically elaborated in a 1549 proclamation of Edward VI. It was aimed at 'captains [who], having not so much before their eyes their duty towards their sovereign lord and country . . . as a vile mind and filthy respect to their own gain . . . do not only diminish their numbers appointed to serve under them (saving that for a colour at the muster day they have some others to supply the void places) but also, by patisement [illicit connivance] with unmeet and unserviceable men for a less wage than his highness alloweth, do in such sort disguise their numbers . . . as, in a manner, the third part of the number which his majesty appointeth and payeth for is not ready, able, or sufficiently furnished to do that service which is looked for.'

This abuse – punishable with death in France from 1527 but which remained rife throughout Europe – contributed to the shortfall in numbers and quality that habitually characterized armies. Another version of it is illustrated by a report of 1596. 'Of all the captains in Ireland, Sir Thomas North hath from the beginning kept a most miserable, unfurnished, naked and hunger-starven band. Many of his soldiers died woefully at Dublin, some whose feet and legs rotted off for want of shoes; and albeit these poor souls were left thus at random, uncared for and unrelieved, yet were their names retained in the muster-roll.' The second abuse maimed the troops' fighting efficiency. The extra wages due to NCOs, pikemen and musketeers were given to captains either in the form of a block bonus fund, or of 'dead pays', that is, wages for men who did not exist: normally 10 per cent of company strength. It was clearly in the captain's interest to pocket this instead of passing it on. The resultant shortage of NCOs led to disorder on the march, confusion in camp and the near-impossibility of introducing tactical changes dependent on NCO-led small units.

These major abuses were at the expense of an impersonal fisc. But they contaminated captains' attitudes to their men, who could, moreover, be exploited in pettier but still damaging ways: excessive stoppages, falsified exchange rates, arbitrary fines. Perhaps in no other occupation were men so unsupportedly at the mercy of an employer, for though wages flowed from above, they were distributed at the captain's pay table.

Governments did what they could. To prevent falsifications at musters their paymasters, who were supposed to sit beside the captain at his table, were instructed to check men not only by name but by warts, wounds, squints and complexion. Bonus or dead-pay funds were cut from the 1570s so that real NCOs, rather than men bribed to masquerade as them, could be identified and paid directly. But shoestring military budgeting meant that no government employed enough men to administer its army in a way that would protect its own interests and ensure those of its soldiers.

Indeed, governments were so ill equipped even to raise money for the wars they decided on that those 'months' sometimes stretched into years. An extreme case was a German corps dismissed with the promise of their back-pay by Parma from the Netherlands in 1579; they did not receive it in full until 1591. But the problem of arrears goes back at least to Charles the Bold's campaigns in the 1470s and those of Spain in north Africa from the 1490s and in Italy from 1502; it probably dogged every campaign after its first months. Arrears might be partially bridged by intermediate 'lendings'. Living on hand-to-mouth transactions – food for work performed, petty credit tidings-over: this was familiar enough perhaps from troops' civilian backgrounds. But when governments could dole out nothing to captains, men sickened, deserted, or turned on their officers or, as we shall see, on non-combatants. Troops in garrison could to some extent compensate for arrears by taking a second job – that blending into the civilian population that so distressed local authorities from Berwick to Bergamo; frontier garrisons were, after all, also policemen: how could they control a population they had married or mistressed into, and whose bread they helped to bake? Not all could blend; from Spain there were reports from the 1550s not only of desertion but of starvation, even what was then a rare last resort, suicide. Troops on long-term service away from home, in addition to pillage could mutiny; not just packing up and going home but, as in the case, time after time, of the Spanish in the Netherlands, staying put, and, with an organization and ideological determination that anticipated trades union strikes of the nineteenth century, extorting at least a tithe of what they were owed.

Subsistence pay, worsened by captains' peculations and governments' defalcations: these were matters of common gossip. Whether in quarters or in the field, armies were not insulated from the eyes of the civilians who were necessary to feed them, billet them, wash their clothes and bury their dead. There can have been few hamlets so remote that the deserter had not touched them for a crust of bread or the disconsolate ex-volunteer regaled them with stories of the occasional splendours but more frequent miseries of war. Short-term service was the norm, the traffic to and from campaigns was constant. In an age when printed books had not yet diverted the habit of absorbing information chiefly from gossip or spectacle, the dark image of war was hardly lightened by the efforts of official published propaganda or the instinct of high art and prestige literature to present it, by and large, as predominantly glorious. Ruzante's hundred-day month was designed to evoke a chuckle of recognition. So was, in Shakespeare's *Pericles*, the response of the brothel-keeper's tout to Marina's challenge to find a better occupation:

> What would you have me do? Go to the wars, would you? Where a man may serve seven years for the loss of a leg, and have not money enough in the end to buy him a wooden one?

Or, to take again the correspondence of the earl of Leicester who, as an unhardened commander, was alert to the connection between the summons to service and the anticipation of its conditions: 'Very hard it will be, certainly,' he wrote in 1586, 'to levy many voluntaries; the journey [campaign] standeth so slandered here and men stand in doubt of good usage, and especially of pay.' And two years later, haunted by Elizabeth's reluctance or inability to disgorge pay: 'It is no marvel that our men run fast away. I am ashamed to write it, there were 500 ran away in two days, and a great many to the enemy. . . . Divers I hanged before the rest, and I assure you they would have been content all to have been hanged rather than tarry.'

We can be fairly sure that the wages of war did not act as an incentive to those who considered military service as a way of bettering themselves, let alone of emerging with savings. But what of the perks of war: ransoms, loot, the semi-licensed leanings on civilians' credit and property? 'Hope is cup-bearer to war,' wrote George Gascoigne, himself an ex-serviceman. But in his disillusioned poem 'Dulce bellum inexpertis' – its title taken from Erasmus's 'War is a fine thing to those who know it not' – his chief protagonists, Haughty Harte, the man seeking honour and glory, and Greedy Minde, the recruit drawn by the prospect of loot, both find their expectations deceived.

The age in which campaigns were occasionally conducted with the deliberate intention to kill all prisoners seems to have ended with the repetition in 1499 of a Swiss order to grant no quarter, 'as the manner has been of our god-fearing ancestors'. The ransoming of prisoners (at a price roughly equivalent to their annual income from all sources) was, therefore, a possible bonus, though because the process could drag on for years, governments came to prefer straight exchanges which would get their own officers back in the field while a war was still in progress. And if evidence regarding money coming into the hands of ordinary soldiers or NCOs is thin, this is probably because the sums were moderate or because it seldom happened. Missile weapons, especially with the extended use of firearms, disabled ransomable men anonymously. Most captives were taken in group surrenders, when the pickings fell to officers, after negotiation with the commissaries who accompanied armies and who stood increasingly by the thesis that prisoners were not the personal property of the captor, and that the state, which had enabled the capture to take place, was entitled to a share of the proceeds. Prisoners of high rank were, in any case, claimed by government and the reward to the captor was filtered down through his captain and among the counter-claims of his colleagues. A wealthy prisoner had to be fed, housed and guarded; it could take months, even years before he could extract money through mortgages and loans or arrange an exchange with a captured enemy of equal value. La Noue, made prisoner in 1580, was offered immediate release if he agreed to be blinded. His refusal gave us his invaluable military memoirs, but at the cost of five years before he could get himself exchanged. The common soldier was neither in a position to conduct ransom negotiations nor to contest the reward that finally reached him. It is doubtful whether captures on the battlefield itself would yield the ordinary soldier more than lump sums amounting to at most three to five times his annual wage.

The prospect of loot, however, must certainly have acted as bait. After a victory in skirmish or battle there were spoils to be garnered: equipment, horses, the contents of baggage trains. In 'religious' wars theft could masquerade in the guise of iconoclasm. After a successful siege there was always looting, even though this was only formally permitted if the defenders had 'recalcitrantly' refused to surrender in its early stages. But there were rules and conventions intended to ensure that governments got the greater share of booty, especially what could contribute directly to the war effort – artillery, weapons, armour, horses and wagons, and coin – or commemorate it: captured drums, flags and standards. It was considered deplorable that some German recruiting captains in the 1520s were so desperate to attract men that they promised them anything they captured or looted. But the numerous codes published for proclamation in armies, and collected in books on the art of war, were quite impractical when dealing with the looting of personal possessions or property. The negotiations were full of fractions: so much to be reserved to government, so much to the commander-in-chief; such and such a proportion to volunteers serving without pay, another to men who had lost horses, others according to rank, nothing to men who had shown themselves cowards. The prayer suggested by Luther was more realistic: 'The booty and pay we will take as given to us unworthy men by God's goodness and grace, and we will thank him therefore from our hearts.' No regulations could check the soldier's instinct to conceal his pickings. His problem was how to turn them into cash. Perforce he turned, and lost, to the fences who battened on soldiers urgently wanting to turn clothes and chests and jewellery into money spendable on drink or dice. Or on savings? But men could not, in the gregarious peripateticism of army life, carry large sums with them until a campaign's end. There are only rare traces of bills of exchange safely wafting such gains to a soldier's home. He could desert; but there remained the problem of getting booty back home.

For the sixteenth century, M. M. Postan's comment on English evidence for the Hundred Years War still holds good: 'In the whole mass of . . . documentation bearing on the village land market I have found no indication that any substantial proportion, *indeed any proportion at all*, of the various buyers of land, engrossers of holdings, or recruits to the new "kulak" class, were returning soldiers.' The fool's-gold glint of plunder retained the perennial romance of something for nothing. Had not in 1527 Roman churches and palaces been stripped of their treasures? Had not the plunder of Antwerp in 1576 been estimated – even cautiously – at 20 million ducats? But no canny peasant proprietor or prospering artisan, wishing his sons to better themselves, recommended any other careers than the church, the law or the lower echelons of central or provincial officialdom. No literary work, however humbly pitched, risked the extravagant fiction of showing a man returning from the wars not poor and poxed but enriched.

Even for the nobility, war in itself was not looked to for profit. Guillaume du Bellay nearly ruined himself while holding a series of high commands under Francis I. Though both were salaried, the earl of Essex had to raise £28,500 to see himself through his commands, and Leicester's military career cost him some £40,000. These were punishing sums. They were invested in maintaining a dignified entourage, providing an openhanded hospitality, and offering gifts to captains who otherwise, given the tardy arrival of their pay, would have packed up for home: all in the hope of a continuing or an increasing royal approval off the battlefield.

For it was not in war that profit lay for the already powerful, but in those appointments at court or at the peaks of regional administration around which fees and favour clustered. Lesser men of birth could look – if they already had adequate means to maintain its status – for a knighthood for gallantry in the field. There were a few large fortunes made from ransoms and a division of spoils, chiefly among the pioneer German military entrepreneurs of the 1520s and 1530s, and during the French wars in Savoy–Piedmont. But even the tough life of a professional captain, moving from campaign to campaign, honoured and respected, was not one likely to be based primarily on the desire to accumulate savings; Monluc, in fifty years of service, amassed a tidy sum, Sir Roger Williams died in 1595 worth £2610. But both enjoyed spending money they could otherwise not have raised, more than saving it. As for the more humbly born, if they distinguished themselves and were lucky enough to be noticed, there could be an annuity or pension. When the chaplain in the play *Sir John Oldcastle* (1600) produces money for a dicing session with the troops, he says, 'I' faith . . . dost wonder how I come by gold? I wonder rather how poor soldiers should have gold, for Ile tell thee good fellow, we have every day tythes, offerings, chrisinings, weddings, buríalls: and you poore snakes come seldome to a bootie.' Emeric Crucé was probably looking on the bright side when he wrote in 1623 that 'for two soldiers who enrich themselves you will find fifty who gain nothing but wounds and incurable diseases'. And significant promotion from the ranks was, as we shall see, unusual. It was from business, law and leases, from pasture and arable lands, not from fields of battle that fortunes grew. There are not many exceptions to the rule that military profits accrued not to those who fought in wars but those who financed and supplied them. Only through the encomienda system in the New World, that mosaic of duties of protection and rights of exploitation within newly conquered lands, was it possible for men of all classes to better themselves notably and enduringly by combat. Otherwise, for common soldiers, 'profit' mostly meant a temporary eking out of the subsistence wage by bullying civilians and reneging on credit extensions from them or, with the encouragement of and a douceur to their captains, passing themselves off twice at the pay table and risking a noose if they were found out.

If civilians were not insulated from knowledge, however rough and ready, of the financially unpromising nature of military service, they were also aware, perhaps even exaggeratedly aware – for death-rolls grow in the telling by chroniclers or ex-soldiers – of its risks.

Precise casualty figures are few; a very small proportion of mid- or post-campaign muster lists survive, and fewer of these distinguish between the reasons for men not presenting themselves for pay: death in action, death from disease, incapacitating wounds, being made prisoner, desertion. Venice calculated that the wastage rate during its short campaign against Cremona in 1526 from death in action, wounds and disease was 222 per 1000. For Elizabeth's Lisbon and Brittany expeditions of 1589, 15,000 men went out and *c.* 6000 returned from the former, 50 per cent returned from the latter. Spanish losses from death or capture (officers only) at the battle of Nieuport in 1600 were reckoned at about one-half. La Noue was excluding the large category of deserters when he wrote that 'I am not so ignorant that I am unaware that it is the privilege of war normally to devour at least a quarter of those who haunt it. But when it devours four-fifths [he has the 1570s sieges of Maastricht and Haarlem particularly in mind], as it frequently does, is it not too greedy?' The interpretation of casualty figures becomes all the more disconcerting when we read of the 600 violent deaths (out of an unknown number of men serving) sustained by the Bavarian Federation in 1519: in almost equal thirds the causes were: killed in action, killed in brawls, and put to death for crimes. All that can be concluded is, perhaps, that for those who stayed with war, who marched among its episodes, were transported to it in hideously uncomfortable and underprovisioned vessels, slept in its siege trenches and stood up as targets on its battlefields, half died, the majority from bacteria rather than bullets. It was an age of actual or potential invalids. For the mature and well-nourished, hardened to their almost habitual infirmities, gout, stone, rheumatism and arthritis, the exertions and deprivations of war probably operated more fatally on their judgement than their persons; but for recruits escaping from undercaloried privation and finding wages too stripped to enable them to catch up, damp, sweat, cold and the swill of faeces no army regulation seemed able to keep at bay, took an even greater toll than they were to in the next great underpaid herdings, those of the age of industry. Pity forced the severely practical doctor Paré to a tone of sarcastic lyricism when he recalled the deaths among his Spanish patients as they slept in the snowy fields surrounding Metz in 1552. They *died*! – 'notwithstanding that each soldier had his field-bed, and a tester strewed with glittering stars, more bright than fine gold, and every day had white sheets and lodged at the signe of the moon'.

Few armies had men as widely competent both as physician and surgeon as was Paré. Great men brought their own physicians, and governments hired barber-surgeons either separately or along with large mercenary bands who had their own. One to every company of 150 men was the aim. It was seldom achieved, partly because doctors themselves fell sick; on occasion they too deserted, and during the always frantic search for reinforcements, replacement doctors could be overlooked. Nonetheless, it is likely that the majority of soldiers were more readily within reach of a trained medical man than they had been in their hamlet or farmstead homes.

The army, however, did not get the best. England's most famous military doctor, William Clowes, wrote in 1591 that incompetent surgeons caused more deaths than the enemy. But no doctor could then do much to check disease, as the epidemics of peace and the pathetic quack-worship of the times showed. It was not cynicism that led governments to call for few physicians and many barber-surgeons. In 1575 Luis de Requesens, governor-general in the Netherlands, reporting on his sick wrote to Philip II that 'most of the wounds come from pikes or blows, and they will soon heal, although there are also many with gunshot wounds, and they will die'. Nonetheless, medicine was better equipped to deal with wounds on the outside than with microbes on the inside of the body, and a host of men returning from the wars without an arm or with a wooden leg testified to its rough-and-ready ability to save lives; Pompeo Giustinian, one of the most redoubtable of late sixteenth-century commanders, owed his nickname, Iron Arm, to its skill. And without it Cervantes, who lost one hand at Lepanto, would not have been able to write *Don Quixote* with the other, or to claim – when mocked for his injuries by a rival author – that 'I would still rather have taken part in that prodigious action than be at present whole of my wounds without ever having fought there.'

But nothing could stop the deaths from dysentery, typhoid, 'spotted' and sweating fevers, that were, unlike the divinely appointed epidemics of peace, so obviously man-made. News of sickness in the Adriatic fleets in 1538 made Venice's recruiters despair of filling the reinforcement quotas. Word that Palmanova had become a vast hospital in 1616 led the inhabitants of the *terraferma* to present a plethora of excuses and refusals 'because they saw many returning sick and [knew] that the war, through disease and in other ways, had consumed a large proportion of them'. And it must be remembered that in a scarcely mechanized age industrial accidents were rare; this made the spectacle of the walking wounded, in addition to that of the debilitated, all the more disturbing.

There was substance in Giovanni Botero's observation that 'men usually avoid the dangers of war not so much for fear of death . . . but for fear of disablement and the misfortunes which are brought about by wounds and other accidents'. And he went on: 'If the ruler is able to assure his soldiers that not only will they be well treated if misfortune befalls them, but that their wives, sons, sisters or other relatives will be remembered if they are killed, then he will have done all that he can to induce them to face fire, bolts and death itself.'

Of course! Governments, made increasingly sensitive to the psychology of underdogs by the social dangers their growing numbers represented, could take the argument. But pensions and hospitals were costly, and neither central government nor local ratepayers were in a spending vein at a campaign's end. Elizabeth made a point of letting her 'love' for her soldiers be known. Proclamations from 1589 and a series of acts of parliament from 1593 expressed concern for the relief of disabled ex-soldiers by the parishes to which they returned. More is known of the objections to them than of their success. Henry IV was another monarch who broadcast his love of old soldiers; in 1606 one small hospice was founded for them in Paris. A single hospice for disabled or superannuated soldiers was founded by Philip II in Malines in 1585. It was no wonder that angry men pointed to the Turks who gave their veterans 'relief assured whereupon they need not go begging like our soldiers, robbing those they meet, and in fine trouble the hangman'. The ex-serviceman problem elicited fear as well as care, but not the cash for a solution.

There were, then, excellent reasons for not joining up. But if we only took account of them, armies would have to have been composed almost entirely of drifters and outcasts, and they were not. There were always men who positively wanted to join and others who at least yielded to pressure not too unwillingly, men who did not calculate their prospects in a rational manner.

Adventurousness, sometimes carried to the point of reckless mania in Spanish America, is, after all, a constant, and one not restricted to those soldiers of note whose acts of bravery and whose seeking out of danger in one theatre of war after another fitfully set the pages of sixteenth-century military memoir-writers aglow. So is restlessness, not just the sponsored trek of the apprentice's *Wanderjahr* or the roaming of desperation, but a desire for movement and change; demographic studies are showing how many men changed occupations or places or residence from choice, rather than need. The itch to change milieu led Elizabeth's government to express concern over the number of seamen who, to English service, preferred sailing in Dutch, Norwegian, Spanish, Italian and French vessels. In the same vein, Dutchmen, Germans, Greeks, African negroes and 'Indians' served as hands on English ships. It is difficult to track those whose temperamental impatience with things as they were took them abroad. Once there they become 'lost'. They escape the documentation of permits, property deals, marriages; muster lists often refer to them by nickname and place of enlistment rather than by father's name or – when they possessed them – surname; military justice was summary, its records scant; in a military society without notaries, deals, debts and 'wills' were recorded chiefly in soundless blows and tacit agreements.

Cultured men expressed nostalgia for that golden, pre-Saturnian age, when freedom did not have to be purchased with laws or a sense of responsibility. The dream was so bewitching as to wrestle early descriptions of native life in the Americas into the image of its own yearning. Vulgarized, nostalgias for an Age of Gold, an Earthly Paradise, were transmuted into a more resentfully shaped Land of Cockayne, where the repressors got their come-uppance. Boy-bishops, lords of misrule, carnival, charivari: all these tolerated aspects of popular holiday-making expressed the urge for escape from routines and hierarchies – and authorities' cautious acceptance of its force. These releases, these inversions of societal relationships had, however, strictly limited timetables. Might not armies have represented a more lasting release into an alternative society, one with its own enticing if hazardous rituals and which was actually institutionalized on the basis of that normally feared phenomenon, the crowd?

It is right to emphasize the satisfactions of communal living in civil society. But it did not suit everyone. And its restraints became intenser. Overpopulation brought the vagrancy laws and the poor-house. Reformation, and Catholicism's riposte with a stricter code of its own, brought more watchful eyes and sterner sentences in church courts. It is not just fanciful to see armies as representing for a while, and to some, a longed-for 'natural' life, unbourgeoisified and unclericized.

Clerics may have been better recruiters than they knew. Oh wicked soldiers, Thomas Becon chided; 'What dicing, carding, and all kinds of voluptuous riot is used among them! What drinking, quaffing, and superfluous banqueting do they use! . . . What whoredom is there committed among them! What maid escapeth undeflowered? What wife departeth unpolluted?' With tramping whores, bathhouses and brothels coming progressively under local government displeasure, and with marital sex made uncarefree by fear of conceptions that would break the poor man's budget, the constant iteration of complaints of the soldiery's promiscuity might have sounded as much like an invitation as a warning. And the connection between sexual attractiveness and violence that had helped to make chivalrous romances so popularizable was as lively as ever. 'All women', wrote a French author in 1543, 'mainly love men of action and turn above of all to those of war'; did not Venus herself turn from Phoebus, most beautiful of the gods, to Mars? And the sense that armies constituted a separate world emerges as strongly in the works of military reformers who sought to bring it nearer to the values of civil society as it does in sermons. Machiavelli advocated constant training, no looting, no gambling or women, regular harangues, the keeping back for disciplinary reasons of the soldiers' pay. But armies never became Genevas, and they owed some of their best men to the fact that they did not. When authors mourned that so many soldiers, of gentle as well as commoner birth, greeted peace by seeking another war rather than returning to their homes, they were commemorating the attractiveness of that alternative society to which men were drawn not by reason but, as Gascoigne put it, by the cup-bearer, hope. As with gold-strikes in nineteenth-century America, so with the hefty ransom or pillaged palace in the sixteenth: that fortune favoured a small minority was common knowledge, but the lure was there, and for those who sensed it, that was enough. A subsistence wage was the route, not the goal.

If the favoured recruiting grounds for mercenaries were regions where towns played an unusually small part in the productive economy, were native troops elsewhere also derived chiefly from the rural, rather than from the urban population? Given that only 10 per cent, at the most 15 per cent of the people of western Europe lived in towns of a size to distinguish the life lived within them from predominantly agricultural villages or hamlets, the statistical probability points firmly to the answer being yes; even more so when we take account of the 'urban peasants' who cared for the orchards and farms of townsmen, inside and outside the walls, the ex-rural unassimilables who were such obvious targets for urban recruitment, and those who had only recently found a niche for themselves. Swedish military commissioners were directed not only to enlist peasants but town journeymen because they were 'usually peasant lads who . . . have shown no stomach for farming and have therefore learnt a craft'.

While militias were enrolled almost exclusively in rural areas, surveys of potential manpower for war service applied only the criteria of age and fitness. But again, this meant a heavy concentration on the countryside. It had been from the countryside that the bulk of earlier armies had come in the retinues of landlord cavalrymen. And it is likely that this continued to be the case. Ruzante, the hero of the only realistic Italian play about war, Beolco's *Parlamento* (*c.* 1526), is a peasant. The delegation of much recruitment in Spain to seigneurial and provincial authorities led the duke of Alba to plead for more gentlemen volunteers to serve in Flanders, 'for there is nothing more important than to have this type of man in the army and not leave it to farm-hands and lackeys'. Similarly regretting for France the lack of well-born captains, Monluc complained that 'now the lowliest ox-team driver calls himself by this name'. And in 1621 Gustavus Adolphus ordered that 'since many will judge contemptuously of the infantry for its clothes' sake . . . therefore shall newly conscripted footsoldiers be enjoined . . . to provide themselves with proper clothes instead of their long smocks and peasant attire'. In England, Falstaff's Gloucestershire recruits, the rage expressed by Falconbridge in Thomas Heywood's *Edward IV* against his troops ('This dirty scum of rascal peasantry'), and the outbursts of Barnabe Rich (a professional captain) against armies composed of 'rogues, runnagats and peasants': these all point to Thomas Wilson's sober assessment in 1600 of English forces as being chiefly composed of copyholders and cottagers, some moderately prosperous, but others who are 'poore, and lyve cheefly upon labor, workeing by the day for meat and drinke and some small wages'.

It is true that surviving muster lists give towns as the place of origin of many, probably the majority of soldiers. But they do not specify that the men were born there. Against the statistical likelihood that most men came from rural occupations, and the literary evidence that takes this for granted, it is reasonable to assume that the towns cited were usually those whence conduct charges were to be calculated and where a recruiter had set up his standard and drum while his agents chivvied men thither from the surrounding farms and villages. An English order for the enrolment of naval recruits in 1602 called for the noting down of each man's name, appearance, and 'the place wherein he was impressed'. Or they were the provincial capitals which had been made responsible for filling a quota within their catchment area, as Palencia, in northern Spain, was in 1596 made responsible for 21 soldiers from the city itself, and 358 from the province it administered and which contained no town of any size. This may, indeed, be reasonably typical of the town-country origins of the native component in armies as a whole.

This did not make them, save in a very loose sense, 'peasant armies'. Machiavelli, who planned for a native army recruited entirely in the countryside, stressed the importance of including smiths, carpenters, farriers and masons. Excluding the nobility and men of gentle birth, the countryside contained farmers whose manner of living may have had much in common but whose holdings and revenues varied widely. Prosperous men were more likely to send their house-servants and labourers to fight than serve themselves. And not only were there artificers in the crafts named by Machiavelli, but cobblers, bricklayers, tailors (of a sort), hedgers and fencemakers, butchers and bakers, drovers and tanners and, in some areas, miners. All, like the greater number of propertyless labourers, the 'peasants' proper, were vulnerable to conditions that dried up spending power, to overcrowded hovels, to that rural boredom which caused tavern life to be a constant preoccupation for those responsible for law and order. They were vulnerable, therefore, either from volition or inertia, to the recruitment process.

Francis Bacon looked on rural manpower, as did Machiavelli, positively. Not for him men from the capitalized, specialized crafts of cities. 'It is certain, that sedentary and within-door arts, and delicate manufactures, that require rather the finger than the arm, have in their nature a contrariety to a military disposition.' Believing that 'generally all warlike people are a little idle, and love danger better than travail', and sharing a general prejudice that men worked less committedly in the country than in towns, he saw the best soldiers, apart from professionals, as coming from the country stock of 'tillers of the ground, free-servants [in gentle households], and handicraftsmen of strong and manly arts, as smiths, masons, carpenters &/c'.

Recourse to Bacon, yet another stay-at-home, is a reminder of how uncertainly the question, 'Who fought in wars?' can be answered from the official records of campaigns. And the same uncertainty dogs our enquiry into the sort of society-within-society that was formed by the men who came together to serve in garrisons and fight in wars.

5

The society of soldiers:
the professionals

As entrepreneurial captains came to play as large a part in raising and leading troops as did 'natural' local chieftains, as longer campaigns led to the snapping of more of the ties that connected the mores of field and village with those of battlefield and camp, and as permanent forces came into being, it becomes increasingly relevant to ask how far there emerged a notion of the soldiery as constituting a separate element within society.

We can expect affirmation from moralists who saw in those who embraced – in Erasmus's blanket phrase – 'the wicked life of the soldier' a broad and uncontroversial target. Those who heard or read denunciations of merchants as usurers, young women as Jezebels, youths as fornicators or peasants as tithe-dodgers, self-protectively sprinkled them with grains of salt; community life involved adjustment to one's own sins and allowance for those of others. But soldiers, who had put themselves outside the community, were fair game. Why are you so poor, Erasmus asks his soldier? 'Why, whatsoever I got from pay, plunder, sacrilege, rapine and theft was spent in wine, whores and gaming.'

Soldiers themselves did much to justify such typecasting, not only through their behaviour but by their appearance. In those countries where artists, first in Germany and Switzerland and then in the Netherlands, recorded soldiers with some degree of realism, they showed the sexually aggressive strut, the bulging codpiece, the suggestive sword-hilt, the mixture of tousled peasant hairstyle with flamboyant costume that marked them as defying civilian morals and the everyman-in-his-place social restrictions of the sumptuary laws. The author of the *Berner Chronik* (1503) criticized the ostrich-feather hats and slashed sleeves that Swiss mercenaries flaunted among their sober fellow citizens. Spanish civilians had a reputation for dressing with scrupulous decorum, but soldiers presenting petitions at court, and captains soliciting licences to recruit, bitterly complained of having to appear clad in black; an inventory of clothes belonging to soldiers who died in a Spanish hospital in the 1570s reveals an amazing range of multi-coloured tattered finery. Machiavelli noted that as soon as a man becomes a soldier he 'changes not only his clothing, but he adopts attitudes, manners, ways of speaking and bearing himself, quite at odds with those of civilian life'. And other Florentines noted the speed with which young men, when enrolled in the defence force against the Imperial army in 1528, let their beards sprout and hair flow (both criticized by martinets as giving purchase for an enemy's grasp); through this inversion of the tonsure they were signalling their entry into a separate way of life. And, like clerics, their faults focused attention on their difference from other men; from the later fifteenth century, anti-soldier attitudes swelled easily along the old grooves cut by centuries of anti-clericalism.

Freedom from the restraints of settled, civilian life: this was the Cockayne glamour that compensated for the dangers and hardships of soldiering. It was exaggerated, both by soldiers and those who generalized about them, as a defiance to conditions of service which meant that only in battles (infrequent arias within the long-drawn-out recitatives of war) were soldiers actually insulated from routine contacts with civilians. Niklaus Manuel, who as an artist repeatedly recorded the extravagant appearance of the Swiss *Reisläufer,* or mercenary, as a dramatist put in 1521 the following words into the mouth of one of them:

> If you pay us well
> We'll move against your enemy
> 'Til the very women and little children
> Cry 'Murder!'
> That is what we long for and rejoice in.
> It's no good to us when peace and calm rule.

Normally, in billets, in garrison, on the march, in camp, the soldier, as we shall see, was dependent on civilian support. This qualified his separateness. But a tension remained. Because they needed civilians, soldiers were open to exploitation by them. Hence the elaborate codes of prices for food, drink and lodgings (so much for a feather bed, so much for a flock mattress, so much for a straw palliasse) issued by governments to protect their soldiery. Because civilians needed the profit derived from filling the solder's belly, reclothing his bare back, satisfying his lusts and accepting his credit, they were exposed to his bullying and defaulting. Hence the gibbets erected in camps and behind siege-lines as reminders to soldiers that civilians were not to be abused. Another symbol of the divide between gun and trader's scales, sword and spade, was the successful insistence of soldiers that if called on to dig fortifications they should get extra pay in compensation for undertaking such demeaning, civilian work.

There emerged, then, a mental frontier between man of peace and man of war different in kind from the observation that had watched the peasant become temporary bowman, the landlord replace for a while falcon glove with gauntlet. The moralists helped shape it. Infantrymen, wrote Claude de Seyssel in 1515, are so 'out of key with everything that they can hardly believe themselves to be thought men of experience and courage unless they blaspheme the names of God, the Virgin and the saints'. Actual practice – war-locks, military legal codes, gibbets – flew pennants along it. The emergence of military memoirs, books devoted to the art of war, biographical compilations devoted to notable soldiers strewed literary laurels along it. Recognition that military experience was addictive and laudable (the key author here being the ex-soldier Brantôme, whose sense of personal failure and poverty at the close of his career did not dim his vision of the quest for risk and non-civilian camaraderie) romanticized it. It was endorsed by a new internationalism, no longer that of the knight-to-knight empathy that had led to the easy naturalization of French and Burgundian chivalric literature in (for instance) late medieval England and northern Italy, but a more hard-headed freemasonry of experts; men who crossed one another's lines of truce less to organize friendly jousts than to inspect and discuss the merits of field fortifications and types of artillery, men employable in major commands across national boundaries – Lombards by the grand dukes of Tuscany, Tuscans by the kings of France – because they were abreast of technical advances in what was coming rapidly in theory, if only haltingly in practice, to be looked on as a specialized and single-minded profession.

Within the literature of war, there emerged a new preoccupation with the soldier as an effective campaigner rather than as a brother-in-arms, a loyal retainer, a patriot, a loner, a grail-searcher or a stout yew-bender. Deepening interest in the achievements of non-Christian warriors, Romans and Greeks, gave respectability to a scrutiny that had far more of a socio-psychological timbre to it than that applied to any other occupation group. The individual's fighting capacity was considered in the light of climatic, family, religious, welfare and sexual contexts. As firearms made hand-to-hand combat rarer, and as the Roman legionary became a more persuasive model than the *preux chevalier*, a new ethic of service to the state and to obedient, disciplined mass enterprise, took over from the more individualistic ethic of chivalry. In the individual, what came to be valued was an unidealistic tenacity and willpower, the qualities praised by Vettori in the youthful Lorenzo de' Medici on his premature death in 1519. He was skilled in the planning of all military actions. He was a strong and feared disciplinarian. 'Day and night he kept his cuirass on, slept very little, ate and drank frugally, was moderate in his indulgence in sex.' Books on war also reacted to the bad impression many soldiers made by stressing the distinction between not only those who were swaggering and criminous and those who were not, but between those who put the pickings of war first and those who, while accepting a wage, saw that as incidental to a career of hazards cheerfully faced in a spirit of selfless service. 'Because the art of war was created for honourable purposes,' wrote Gerónimo de Urrea in 1576, 'valorous men are to be esteemed when they strive to realize them with honourable intention, but not when profit is the sole motive. . . . Those who expose themselves to risk and death only for the sake of a wage may be called good soldiers when they fully perform their duty, but never honourable and truly valorous ones.'

Soldiering remained a profession without a calculable career structure. The highest commands went, as we have seen, to nobles appointed because of their leading position in civilian life, or for their ability to recruit and then cover the arrears of pay of their men. Experience in war was not the test for many of these appointments. Louis XII appointed the twenty-three-year-old Gaston de Foix, duke of Nemours, to the supreme command in Italy; Philip II entrusted the largest army yet assembled, the force sent against Picardy in 1557, to his ally the twenty-eight-year-old Duke Emanuel Philibert of Savoy. For Venice, which always chose a non-native for the permanent supreme command, the criterion was not so much, or not only military competence but the number of his own subjects or dependants a candidate could raise in case of war. It was to be long after the close of this period that anyone expected commands-in-chief to go to men who had made a career of soldiering. More disheartening perhaps was the lack of a ladder of promotion within standing forces, and the absence of a correlation between such career structures as they did have and the appointments made to commands within a wartime army in the field.

Permanent forces began with only a captain- or governor-general whose appointment was for life and who was an 'officer' in the then current sense of being granted by government an authority which was also a possession and which, like a tenant's title to a piece of land, could be, with permission, leased or sold or passed on to an heir. Throughout the period the word 'officer' retained either this signification, which derived from medieval legal, fiscal or household appointments, or that of its alternative meaning, that of 'functionary'. In a military context, 'officer' usually meant NCO. Outside the Catholic church, with its hierarchy of pope, cardinal, archbishop, bishop, canon, priest and deacon, there was, after all, no parallel ladder of command: not among the doctors, nor among the lawyers, the only non-clerical professions that then existed. For administrative convenience other rankings came to be introduced, such as generals of infantry, cavalry and artillery. But it did not follow that in war the holders of these positions (which were not offices in the life-possession sense) would be given commands commensurate in size to their titles. To distinguish simple captaincies from the responsibility for garrisons containing more than one company (often only thirty to fifty men in peacetime), or for the defence establishments in whole provinces, colonels, military governors and regional marshals came to be appointed, and suitably remunerated. All the same, though the relationships between their stipends were various, there was no guarantee in war that the differential stature of their peacetime responsibilities would be respected.

How could they be? A fighting army was not just the men of a permanent force in action. Depending on the extent of the need to maintain a professional defence force, it comprised the rest of them within a much larger mass of allied contingents, mercenary bands and raw recruits. The command was arranged on an ad hominem basis as it became clear who was going to turn up. The temporary commands binding across the whole force, the offices of fieldmaster or sergeant-general (or major), were always offered to a man of tried experience, because these men were the essential choreographers of march, camp and combat formations. The other commands, whether of the horse or infantry as a whole, or of vanguard, main body or rearguard, or of units deployed separately as part of the strategic plan, were appointed from among those who brought the largest forces of their own. This process discriminated against but did not necessarily exclude men with long-service contracts within the permanent nucleus. Neither did it spell out

131

the precise degree of subordination between one general officer or commander of a large force and another. Just as there was no uniform or complete hierarchy off the field, there was no defined one on it, though the ultimate authority of the commander-in-chief was always, save in cases where there were awkwardly large allied contingents, spelled out in his commission.

Universal, this ad hoc dealing out of the cards of command could lead to the prolongation of contract negotiations or, far more rarely, to contests for precedence within councils of war. But it was accepted as normal, and it cannot be shown to have meant that the leadership of armies was worse than in the ordered, professional hierarchies of the future. It was based, after all, on the reality that still governed all notions of authority; power lay with personal control over numbers: as with landlord-magnate and tenants, so with a military leader and his troops. That parallel had been too close to be lightly discarded. And though bureaucracies were nurturing men's careers based only on talent confirmed by experience, the instinct of rulers to give them titles and land to explain, as it were, their power, remained incorrigible. Cosmopolitan, specialized in function: as far as leadership was concerned, armies were still seen as the claws expanding naturally from the tensed body politic as a whole. Command structure was the least modernizable of the elements of armed force.

On campaign, moreover, the honour of a seat at the commander-in-chief's table or a voice in the war councils he convened was not restricted to the higher command. Experience received its due here, and the captain who in one campaign held a colonelcy and in the next was restricted to the command of his own company, might in this way expect to be treated on equal terms in both.

While the lack of any calculable route to promotion in foreign campaigns probably did not deter men from pursuing a military life, its absence in the permanent garrison forces undoubtedly did. The chief infantry commands, those of military governor in large cities or in frontier zones where defence had to be coordinated between scattered garrisons, tended to go by favour to those who had friends at court. Cavalry commands resembled a second aspect of contemporary administration in general: they were frequently passed from father to son, elder brother to younger brother. The subordinate captains, with little hope of bettering themselves, were not of high calibre. The first to be turned off on demobilization, rather than seek another campaign they opted for the poor pay and lacklustre prestige of peacetime soldiering as at least preferable to the civilian niche they had quitted in the first place. Steady and competent some of them must have been, though civilian authorities and general officers on their occasional tours of inspection seldom found much, if anything, to praise about them or their men; Venice even had to institute viva voce examinations before retaining captains paid off from the wars of 1571–3 who applied for positions in garrisons. And it is rare to find any commendation of the deeds of those of them who were transferred back to campaign armies on a renewal of war. As for the men, promotion through the ranks to a captaincy seems rare indeed; on a captain's death his troops were transferred to another company; when the command did pass to one of his own men it was to the lieutenant who had helped raise them in the first place.

The tone of garrison life varied according to the size of the force – not all were like the seldom-inspected fortress on the Tuscan border where the garrison was found to include men so aged or infirm they could only hobble about their duties. But the scorn expressed by the fiery poet-freelance Luigi da Porto for his opposite numbers in Venice's permanent corps represents the view of those who saw the appeal of soldiering only in terms of action. He complained in 1510 about his transfer to Friuli: 'Because it means leaving the splendid sort of warfare we have in the Veronese, where I can play my part in actions of real importance, and going instead to a theatre where there are few troops, most of them in garrison and thus, I fear, given up to greed, idleness and self-indulgence, the mortal enemies of the martial spirit.' But he was soon relishing the 'marvellous skirmishes' that were a chief feature of guerrilla warfare in Friuli.

The inaction of garrison life was not, of course, complete. Citadels had to be guarded, ramparts patrolled, parties sent out to search ditch and glacis at dawn and dusk to see that no spies or other suspicious strangers had concealed themselves there. In many garrison towns the guard of gates, the searching through streets and alleys after curfew and the maintenance of patrols outside such key buildings as armoury, grainstore or town hall were matters of police and in the hands of men employed by the civic council. The military watches could be called on to supplement them. For most of the time, however, garrison duties involved, on a rota system, little more than keeping awake, walking up and down, and remembering the watchword of the night. There were no manoeuvres to help men keep abreast of their trade's practice, very scant evidence of drill, much evidence that gunpowder was too expensive to waste on regular exercises in marksmanship.

So there was much idleness. To be paid to be idle for much of the time was, of course, part of the Cockayne dream of peasant or apprentice, even if a Da Porto could not equate it with soldiering. Garrison regulations naturally expected the worst from human nature. Their repetitiveness, however, does suggest some of the abiding truths about it. Those of 1542 for Berwick, where the garrison was meant to be very much on its toes to detect Scottish incursions by land or sea, prescribed penalties (varying from pay stoppages to terms of imprisonment and death) for sleeping on watch, absence without leave, incompletion of a tour of 'skowring' or inspection, dodging turns of duty, counterfeiting the keys of the storehouse, failing to wear 'uniform' on watch, gambling for money rather than for drink 'except it be within the 20 days of Christmas', letting dogs go unleashed by day or allowing them to roam at night, leaving a post before the end of the watch, not having equipment or, worse, stealing a companion's to conceal the fact (one of the frequent consequences of pawning to settle gambling debts).

Apart from these not unexpected frailties, the military tone and effectiveness suffered from three major failings. One was an abuse of the leave system. Peacetime leave for cavalry company commanders was always generous because their social position meant that they frequently had property, and hence administrative and legal affairs to deal with at home. On request, their three-month annual leave could stretch to six. Infantry governors could seldom plead such a reason, but their normal monthly leave of seven to ten days could, again, be stretched, as could the three to four of their captain-deputy, as long as the leave periods did not overlap. For the men there were no leave provisions, but they could be absent if they could convince the clerk of the watch that they had found effective substitutes. Naturally, these regulations were abused. Drake's raid on Corunna in 1589 owed its success to the fact that most of the garrison, 'as it happens in time of peace, had left their quarters and their arms and were scattered all over the country'.

The second was corruption among paymasters and captains and the infrequency of governmental inspections to check it. The result was that soldiers found their pay being docked or diverted into the pockets of officers' pages and servants, or even to their civilian relations. It was this grievance that led men of the Spanish royal guard to desert or, in 1520, cross over to the forces of the Comuneros they were meant to be suppressing.

The third failing was the counterpart of this: going native on the spot, blending, through cohabitation or marriage and a second, civilian job, so thoroughly into the social fabric of the garrison town that the soldier was subsumed into the civilian. Some of Henry VIII's garrison of Tournai were married there within a year of its conquest in 1512. The Berwick regulations routinely penalized the second job. So did those for Zara in 1570, but with a shrug of acceptance: no man was to take a second full-time occupation as inn- or shopkeeper that would conflict with his duties, but, given the inadequacy of his wage, a poor soldier might work part-time for a tradesman. Garrison troops slept in citadel or castle (where there was one) during their stints of watch there, but barracks only made a tentative appearance from the late sixteenth century. Quartered on civilians, soldiers shopped in their markets, struck up friendships with, and scrounged jobs from them. Most countries had regulations forbidding men to be stationed within easy reach of their own place of birth, and for the transfer of companies from one garrison to another every few years. But the former was defeated by the difficulty of obtaining recruits, and the latter by the administrative complication in pay and other records it caused. That familiar headache of military administrators, fraternization, has a long history.

The first fifty years of the *ordonnance*, or *gendarmerie*, companies may be taken as exemplifying the tendency of permanent forces to settle into a quasi-civilian state. We are dealing with an elite corps of heavy cavalrymen and the mounted men of their 'lance'. At first there is considerable evidence that to identify oneself or be referred to by others as 'archer of the ordinance' or 'man-at-arms of the ordinance' was a source of pride, indicating a sense of special status within the social group indicated by family name and, in the case of most of the latter, aristocratic title. Many companies had the high morale which came from their comprising relatives and neighbours. Some, led by the wealthiest officers, set themselves standards of equipment and military exercises that gave them the status of crack units within the force as a whole. Thereafter, even though called to order for the successive campaigns of Louis XI and Charles VIII, by the early sixteenth century peace had eroded this *esprit de corps*. Inadequate wages, garrison duties in remote frontier towns, evidence that it was almost impossible for an archer to become a lieutenant, let alone a captain, and that commands were increasingly being absorbed into the crown's system of patronage: these led to the abuse of the leave regulations, early retirements, neglect of training, even a decrease in the employment of those nicknames, *noms de guerre*, through which men of the *ordonnance* had proudly distinguished themselves from civilians. Later, with their steady employment in the early civil wars, thanks to casualties and the transfer of officers to commands of new levies, promotions – from archer to man-at-arms and from man-at-arms to lieutenant or even captain – and rewards of offices at court or of local lieutenant-governorships, made career soldiering with the *gendarmerie* for a while an important source of social mobility for the lesser aristocracy. After a generation, however, this slowed. The heavy cavalry were needed less. The new officers abused their power; they would 'pillage and ravage the poor people' as they buccaneered through the countryside 'followed by an infinite number of *filles de joie*'. The possibility of promotion was suspected as a motive for prolonging rather than settling conflicts. From the 1570s their numbers were cut and their contracts shortened. Meanwhile, the problem of maintaining military morale in peacetime had been posed. And it remained unsolved. It was only in those Spanish garrisons in Milan and the kingdom of Naples whence men were regularly drafted for service in the Netherlands that the military, coached in the disciplines necessary for war, were clearly distinct from their civilian neighbours. In the garrison towns of Spain itself, and in the *presidios* of north Africa, it was a very different story.

The only bodies within permanent establishments that consistently retained their smartness were princely guards. Like other members of royal households, they were equipped and fed as well as receiving a wage. Elaborately bonneted and tunicked, equipped with weapons expensively proclaiming the prince's taste, they were in one respect simply part of the court furniture. But they were regularly drilled, and to watch their parades and evolutions was an entertainment offered to guests of a militant turn of mind. They were also a working corps, providing instructors for militia companies and escorts for royal baggage trains as well as patrols guarding the parks, walls and corridors of their masters' residences. And in war some provided the ruler's escort and others were deputed to stiffen bodies of new recruits. Their numbers, given the modest dimensions of permanent forces as a whole, were quite large. In 1476 the duke of Burgundy employed over 2000 soldiers (including eight companies of English archers). In 1481 Queen Isabella's household force contained 1100 men-at-arms and 130 light horse. In 1511 Louis XII maintained between 700 and

900 men capable of riding into battle with him. In 1523 Francis I had 720. After 1600, Henry IV employed 2550: 1950 French, 500 Swiss and – a tradition dating from the reign of Louis XI – 100 Scots. Of these forces, which looked back to the old practice of retaining, but whose numbers took account both of the dispersed nature of permanent troops now monarchs no longer left frontier defence to local magnates, the smallest was that of socially fairly stable and sea-girt England. Established by Henry VII, and including by 1549 the previously separated guard of the Tower of London, the Yeomen of the Guard were only about 150-strong under Elizabeth. In times of domestic or foreign crisis they were supplemented by the temporary enrolment of ex-servicemen as 'extraordinary' yeomen. Henry VIII took 600 yeomen on his expedition against Tournai; in the anxious year 1550 the young Edward was given a supplement of 300. But the yeomen, like the other English bodyguard units, the gentlemen pensioners, or 'the gentlemen called the new men-at-arms' who flicker up from the sources in 1547, have been little studied. Neither have the larger forces maintained in other countries, save for the papal Swiss Guard. Yet it is surely through gossip among their aristocratic commanders and combat veterans, commanders returning at a campaign's end, visiting professionals of many nations, court officers with military responsibilities or interests and, indeed, martial rulers themselves, that the ideas were swapped that helped to cosmopolitanize the changes in establishments, weaponry, methods of fortification and tactical aspirations that made up the military reformation. Proposals centuries later to emerge from staff colleges were then discussed in princely anterooms and at the mess tables of the officers of personal guards.

On the whole, then, it was not among the permanent establishments that soldiers felt or were looked on as notably separate from the manners and values of the rest of society. Those images of 'the soldier' that moralists added to those of the usurer, the pluralist, the social climber and the Jew, that link arms with monarch, bishop, judge, merchant and peasant in the Dance of Death or heartlessly cast lots at the foot of the Cross, come not from the ceremonious military accoutrements of courts, blending colourfully with their colleagues, pages, grooms, huntsmen, mewkeepers; nor from the majority of garrison troops, part police, part tradesmen – one rowdy group among many others which so circumscribed the outdoors freedom of decent, especially female citizens. They come from those who habitually sought not just soldiering but war.

This category of soldiers by vocation excludes those from all walks of life who, to escape from debt or taste adventure, or to tread water until they had resolved their true vocation, served abroad for months, as did John Donne in 1596 or, for a few years, the philosopher René Descartes, who served as a volunteer in 1617 with Prince Maurice and again in 1619–21 under Duke Maximilian of Bavaria. The casualness with which men could take themselves off to an army emerges clearly from Cervantes's story 'The little gipsy'. The ravishing fifteen-year-old Preciosa will only agree to marry or become the mistress of her suitor, a young aristocrat, if he will join her encampment for a trial period. He agrees: 'I will leave my family under pretext of going to Flanders.' It also excludes those ardent young men who went to war as though to a tournament, travelling at their own expense with a servant or two to seek adventure and renown. Known as adventurers or voluntaries in England, *soldati di fortuna* to the Italians, *soldats de fortune* to the French and *aventureros* to the Spanish, these youths of gentle or aristocratic birth were much prized by commanders for their gallantry and cheapness. 'I have at all times', wrote Sir John Smythe in 1587, 'served as an adventurer at mine own charges without procuring of any charge [i.e. a company of his own] or pay, making choice to do so because I wanted [to] be free and at liberty in all actions to accompany the lieutenant-general and the masters of the camp general and other such principal officers.' At a time when formal military training was rudimentary, thanks to their prior knowledge of sword and horse and the missile weapons of the hunt, and their habituation to shouting orders at their father's tenantry, contact with an army quickly made effective soldiers of them. But campaigning was only an instant within their careers. Either they returned home when the rains of late autumn spoiled the liveliest of the play or, by becoming addicted, stayed on to join the larger and socially far more various sector of long-serving freelances who served for pay and made of war a long-term avocation. The men in this last category, together with mercenaries, complete the range of professional military society and dominate its image.

Neither is easily defined. In the fifteenth century the 'free lance' was just that: a man who because his company of cavalry 'lances' had been disbanded, was leaderless, free to offer his services elsewhere. *Lanze spezzate*, broken-off lances, the Italians called them, welcoming them into the personal guards allocated to senior officers and their civilian counterparts, the military proveditors and commissioners. As with changes in the composition of armies their origins came to vary, the category broadened to include infantrymen and light cavalry and absorbed those who simply sought service as individuals in order to begin and follow a military vocation. The nomenclature broadened with their numbers: volunteers, 'private' soldiers, the Swiss *Freiharste, advanturiers* – floundering in a philological net of his own casting, Brantôme only becomes clear in his distinction between the last and the Spanish *adventureros*.

Part of the confusion arose because of the ease with which the war-seeking full-timer slid in and out of the ranks or commands of mercenary bands, themselves constituting, as we shall see, a sector difficult to define with precision. Another part reflected the belief that men from certain regions – Scotland, Gascony, Corsica, Switzerland, Saxony, the Romagna, Croatia–Dalmatia – were by nature such natural soldiers that they arrived in the spirit of volunteers, as vocational soldiers *in posse*.

The word 'vocational' sends us back to the distinction between garrison- and combat-oriented full-time military men. La Noue put it clearly. The latter, he wrote, 'who claim to be unable to live outside those parts where war is being waged . . . make of such a profession [soldiering], which should be occasional, a perpetual vocation'. And he translates a Spanish jingle 'which they often have on their lips:

War is my country,
My armour my home,
And in every season
Fighting is my life.'

He condemns such an attitude. It is natural for a young noble, 'spurred by an ardour to learn and to acquire reputation', to seek war. But the impulse should not become habitual. He should return to be useful to his country, raising a family (instead of fathering bastards on camp-followers) and following a profession in the law or the church, or joining one of the French commanderies of the Knights of Malta or the household of some great man, if he cannot support himself. And if he must maintain his interest in soldiering, then he should seek a position within the permanent establishment.

He reflects the conservative view previously expressed by Raymond, sieur de Fourquevaux in his *Instructions pour les faits de la guerre*. Men should be prepared to fight at the command of a sovereign, but to follow war as a roving volunteer was against their country's interest and, if they were slain in action, at the peril of their souls. And this view was in turn linked to the distinction between 'good', or 'just' wars waged by the ruler in the true interest of his country, and 'bad' wars – those not so waged, or those waged by others in which (unless it were a crusade) the service of foreigners could not be covered by the rightness of a cause not their own. This was no idle distinction. Having promised quarter to the Dutch troops defending Haarlem when it surrendered in 1573, Alba had the 2300 foreign troops in the garrison executed on the grounds that they were not fighting at the express command of their governments. Just as there were good and bad wars, so there were – to the many who thought in this vein – good and bad soldiers. The infection of the image of the full-time combat soldier by this belief was all the more titillating for the knowledge that these 'bad' soldiers were generally the best. And what of 'sans reproche' Bayard? Presented as the model of the good soldier, his eulogist, Jacques de Mailles, does not conceal the fact that when billeted away from home he was in the habit of calling for a girl to round off his tavern evenings. War-seekers like Bayard did still trail some of the romance of knight-errantry along their thoroughly professional careers. Many of them were, moreover, men of at least some substance, with property to support them in retirement, even if it became heavily mortgaged to ransom brokers. In spite of the generally unencouraging financial prospects of soldiering we have noted, there were cases of common soldiers acquiring well-paid commands and long-term contracts, most frequently through service with the artillery and by turning themselves into engineers and advisers on fortifications. But what of the run-of-the-mill vocational soldier? Men like Thomas Churchyard who, ruefully commenting on thirty years' campaigning interspersed with unsuccessful attempts to reintegrate himself into civilian life, confessed that

> My shues wear made of running leather suer,
> And boern I was about the world to roem,
> To see the warres.

If governments were unable to deal with demobilized men 'militarized' in manner by a single campaign, they could not offer a welcome to the far less assimilable wounded or retired professional without home or fortune. The 'bad' soldier promised to be bad citizen; another factor that coloured the image projected on them by civilians. Such men have no voices that reach us clearly. Some of their commanders speak indignantly on their behalf, as did Sir Roger Williams. Some rulers tried to keep them at bay by more or less inventing military work for them, as did Henry IV after the 1598 Peace of Vervins: leaving three regiments on pay in Holland and diverting some 5000 men under the duke of Mercoeur to serve the Emperor Rudolph II against the Turks.

The reputation of men who lived for war was decreasingly steadied by that of those father-figure magnates and their families who faithfully shouldered the burden of one after another of their rulers' wars, Talbots for England, Condés for France, Figueroas for Spain. The type did not die out. Son of a distinguished soldier, the future military leader of the Huguenot party, Henri de Rohan was coached in horsemanship, fencing, mathematics (for an understanding of fortifications) and ancient and recent military history before seeing action on behalf of Henry IV against the Spanish army in France at the age of sixteen, and having his horse shot under him two years later at the 1597 siege of Amiens. With the peace of 1598 he set off on a military grand tour of Germany, Italy, Austria, Holland and England, inspecting battlefields, fortifications and arsenals. Later he rounded off his self-education with a period of service under Maurice. Such men, save sometimes in their adventurous youth, fought only when needed, and for their own countries. All the same, they gave a reassuring tone to the pursuit of war as a career by others.

Lesser aristocratic blood still sought foreign war and settled into its gait. Sometimes with an elder's blessing; Antoine de Baissey's father (who died in the early 1470s), recognizing his son's avocation, simply cautioned him against entering the service of a *minor* foreign prince. After serving the duke of Burgundy he then – in a manner unclear – learned German. He ended up as his country's chief negotiator with and, in the early Wars of Italy, leader of France's Swiss mercenary allies. Sometimes with a ruler's endorsement; Robert de Balsac, after eleven years in French service, itched to serve elsewhere. In 1464 Louis XI wrote to Duke Francesco Sforza of Milan recommending him as his 'well loved servant, Robert de Balsac, Esquire' who had 'a strong desire to see the world and engage in deeds of war'. Sometimes after protest against the norms of home; Sir William Carew's son Peter, a persistent truant at his local grammar school in Exeter, and later pronounced by his teacher at the recently founded St Paul's in

London to be unable 'to smell a book, or to like of any learning', leapt at the chance to serve as a page abroad. After service in Italy on both sides, French and Imperial, he returned home – still only eighteen – with letters of high commendation in 1533, and began a career (with breaks abroad) in English service that led to his being given a cavalry captaincy in Henry VIII's Boulogne campaign of 1544 and by Protector Somerset the responsibility to quell the Cornish revolt of 1549. Sometimes against the general bias not to promote commoners; Nicholas Malby, a mere victualling clerk at the English outpost of Guisnes in 1547, gained experience with the enemy as a French light cavalryman that brought him, after returning to the fold with service in Ireland, the presidency of Connaught.

Governments which were not at war or in diplomatic crisis themselves were not averse to giving licences to travel to gain military experience, and were prepared to wink at evasions of what was in any case an unenforceable restriction. Bans on mercenary recruiting by hostile powers could be enforced because the activities of the recruiters were conspicuous. The movements of men of heraldic note could be monitored, because their style of life and the prominence of their contacts abroad enabled their progress to be reported by diplomatic agents, many of whom were little more than gossip-passing informers. That many slipped the port or frontier-post checks is known from pardons granted or the success of subsequent military careers. The establishment of permanent forces, slipshod as we have suggested that in the main they were, did not dim the need for men who by seeking experience beyond their own borders thereby became more useful in an emergency at home. Even Venice, which had the largest of permanent forces in Europe in comparison to its population, acceded, after the peninsular peace settlement of 1529, to requests for leave from subjects wishing to blood themselves elsewhere, and read sympathetically those claims for captaincies in times of mobilization from those who had, without permission, brought back testimonials from commanders in the 'schools of war' in northern or eastern Europe.

The survival of such records suggests, but only suggests, that numbers in the private sector of long-term military service were growing. So do the memoirs, narratives and treatises on war they wrote, sometimes in captivity, often in cramped retirement at home, sometimes helped into the light by their heirs as their only memorial. So do the compilations of military biographies that began with Paolo Giovio's *Eulogies of Famous Warriors* in 1551 and broadened through Thomas Churchyard's *A General Rehearsall of Warres* of *c.* 1579 and hit their stride with Brantôme's pell-mell *Discourse on the Colonels of Infantry of France*, composed in the 1590s, and its defiant reassurance that 'you, brave French soldiers who never quitted the pursuit of military honour, you shall never die!' So do the awkward moments when governments had to distribute commands between men competing for positions within their own country's forces whence the honours most relevant to the age of retirement could lie; such a choice confronted Elizabeth's advisers when three self-made soldiers of wide foreign experience offered their services for the 1590 Rouen expedition: Roger Williams, John Norris and Francis Vere. And so does the record of exile: the new political stability in Italy which forced men to seek their fortunes abroad instead of hanging around in other peninsular cities waiting for the clocks to be set back to pre-exile times; the enforced migrancies that followed the post-Reformation hardening of religious tests for tolerable careers at home. And so does the fact that armies were not only growing in size but becoming more aware of the need for career officers as captains and lieutenants, men who had learned to handle not only their weapons but themselves.

This awareness came at the time when the page system of preparing youths for war – a system anyway geared to heavy cavalry service – was breaking down. To take its place there were, from the 1530s, projects in England, Italy and France to create military academies where young men, while continuing with Latin and perhaps Greek and adding a modern language and some law or history, would receive formal instruction in the martial arts. None was realized until the court-based colleges of Tübingen and Kassel offered instruction, from 1589 and 1599 respectively, in weapons training, tactical evolutions and the theory of fortification and siegecraft. Others followed, all short-lived and, like the most famous of them, John of Nassau's 1617 *schola militaris* at Siegen in Westphalia, exclusive and attracting very small numbers. The same is true of the various riding and fencing academies that were set up from the 1560s, finishing schools for young men where they could learn what the page system – which in late fifteenth-century grandee households in Castile had included instruction from such men as the riding master Diego de Cárcamo and the famous master of fence Pablo de Peralta – no longer offered. The emphasis was very much on offering an outlet for valour that could be kept and later used, at home. The Venetian government's representative in Rovigo reported that the purpose of the riding academy set up there in 1565 was 'so that the [noble] youth of the city should be trained in the use of weapons and in horsemanship to the effect that this virtuous exercise should keep them from idleness and other, less honourable forms of activity, as well as make them ready to perform some service to the state when it is needed'. When Henry IV announced plans for a military school in Paris, the dedication to him in 1594 of a work of applied geometry (essential by then to the theory of fortification) praised the king for wishing 'to see revived and brought back to life those subjects so long dead in this kingdom, and which the gentlemen of France have been forced to seek out in foreign countries'.

The study of war itself as a 'subject' was, we have seen, one of the by-products of changes in weaponry, tactics and siegecraft. Among the woodcuts of that wonderful conspectus of the intellectual and practical education of an all-round, up-to-date, Christian emperor, the *Weisskunig* of Maximilian I, there is one showing him as a boy learning to joust with the aid of jointed wooden models. Assisted by the publication of books containing diagrams of military formations, the model soldier became a more ambitious educational aid. Do not bring up boys to play with wooden horses, dolls and toy carts, advised the old soldier Jean de Tavannes in the memoirs he concluded in 1596. Order instead six thousand models (in wood or pottery) of horsemen, arquebusiers and pikemen, also model cannon, castles and towns. 'With these little models you can carry out and explain how to draw up companies, squadrons, and main forces, and demonstrate the storming of breaches, charges, retreats, the posting of sentinels and watches . . . in such a way that by the age of ten . . . instead of having passed the time uselessly, they will have formed the habit of thinking of themselves as a soldier or a captain.' By the late sixteenth century metal toy soldiers were being moved about by veterans reliving past battles (at Siegen, cards representing tactical units – introduced around 1550 – were used in war games as more convenient). In 1616 Ben Jonson (who had served, though briefly, in the Netherlands) girded in his *The Devil Is an Ass* at the whole notion of learning how to fight out of engraved drill books (which were introduced from 1600) and toy soldiers. With reference to the training ground used by the London militia, he gets one of his characters to vent his spleen against a teaching-aid-taught soldier:

Get him the posture book, and's leaden men
To set upon a table, 'gainst his Mistress
Chance to come by, that he may draw her in,
And shew her Finsbury battells.

This scorn was only part of a wider and traditional bias against the idea that soldiering could be learned from cosy simulacra of the real thing. It is in Bandello's story of how Machiavelli, when given a chance to drill the troops of the great *condottiere* Giovanni de' Medici 'of the black bands', reduced them to total confusion; in the advice given in 1549 by Giovanni's friend Pietro Aretino to a young nobleman who was preparing himself for joining an army by a course of reading: 'you should study and consider things military in actual warfare and not in the classroom'; in Iago's contempt of Cassio as 'a great arithmetician . . . that never set a squadron in the field'; in Robert Barrett's captain – portrayed in 1598 – who before giving an order has to call to his boy 'hola sirra, where is my book?' and whose most frequent order is 'stand still until I have looked in my book!' It was to disarm such a prejudice that in the brochure advertising the Siegen academy, an old soldier, Octeranus, who has learned his craft the hard way by fighting in Poland, Sweden and Hungary, is set up to pour scorn on the very notion that 'warfare can be learned outside a war'. After watching the school's drills, manoeuvres and tactical card games he has, of course, to change his mind.

Books, toy soldiers, schools and academies all indicate, after the demise of the page system, the widening gap between increasingly complex warfare and preparation to take part in it. So does a growing emphasis on the *Kavalierstour*, the tour abroad, that is, during which a young aristocrat travelled not only to broaden his mind by acquaintance with other lands and other manners, but to acquire military knowledge if not actual experience, as Henri de Rohan did. By the early sixteenth century this included looking at princes' armouries and parks of artillery and, if this were allowed, their new fortifications. By the mid-century periods of residence in foreign capitals – Paris, Florence, Naples, Vienna – had as part of their point instruction in riding and swordsmanship from masters of international fame. By the century's end, the military component became wider still. The young counts of Nassau were regularly sent, after a humanist education from tutors at home, to a German court where the tradition continued of offering a military education to young local and visiting notables. After a further stage of learning the language of one of those countries whence the Netherlands drew so many private long-service captains, England, France or Italy, some completed the educational process by fighting briefly against the Turks in Hungary or enlisting for a while in the army of some prince-warrior like the duke of Savoy. In his comprehensive educational manual of 1607, *The Institution of a Young Noble Man*, John Cleland was clearly affected by this example. Given the English tradition that foreign travel was to gain wisdom, improve learning and polish manners rather than acquire a vocational qualification, his advice may have given some of his older readers considerable pause. 'When you are in Hungary,' he recommended, 'mark the forts, and if the Christian army be in the field, observe their order and fashion of martial exploits; enquire for the generals, coronels and number of soldiers of every nation; spare not to hazard yourself against God's enemie, for I would have you valiant and wise. . . . Come to Flanders, where you shall not spare to salute the Arch-duke and to see his forces, acquainting yourself with his Spanish captains, ever to learn some good observation in martial affairs. . . . This is the place where you may learn to be perfect in military discipline; there you shall be moved by example and encouragement to be valiant.' Then he equivocates; 'Yet I wish you not to be too rash in endangering your life and reputation where neither your death nor wounds can be either honourable or profitable.'

The literature dealing with the self-education of the would-be soldier was aimed especially at those who might be contemplating a long-service career in the freelance sector. Yet to fight, except against the Turk, for any country but one's own and its allies was morally wrong. Constantly meeting one another, now as friends, now as foes, in the 'schools' of war, a consciousness that they formed a separate order within the ranks of the military was enhanced by the stigma attached to them. United by an experience that had never before been so welcome, they were also united by a common grudge against two strains of thought that were developing within the civilian world: the growing emphasis on peace, which belittled the war-seeking individual, and the disapproval of men who fought for causes other than their countries' own. And the stigma was all the more isolating because of the ease with which they could be confused with mercenaries.

Except for the gentlemen volunteers, because all soldiers fought for pay, it was not receipt of a wage that made a man a 'mercenary', or indifference to the faith or cause he served in arms, but the size of the unit that comprised him (commonly between 600 and 4000) and his dependence not on a political authority but on a contractor who had negotiated his own bargain with government. The border between private, freelance soldiers and true mercenaries, but for this definition, would be unclear. The French men-at-arms who fought as individuals or small groups in the 1470s and 1480s for the parties contesting the episcopal power around Liège fought in a mercenary spirit but through local ties. Though most private captains bargained their own way from war to war, the rank and file tended to become absorbed into the bands of large-scale military contractors. Any private/mercenary distinction becomes blurred still more by such cases as that of Sir Francis Vere who, after a long career as a private captain, turned up in Venice offering to raise 2000 men for the republic's War of Gradisca. It is not surprising that the 'private' became contaminated by that of the 'mercenary' image. This, in defiance of much evidence to the contrary – of loyalty, disregard of danger and of mildness off the battlefield – was of men connected to the values of society only by the desire to get rich. Greedy, pitiless, godless, cruel, brave but roisteringly self-indulgent, drawn from the dregs of a society against whose restraints they revenged themselves through theft, rape, pillage and intimidation: the image was shaped not only by the peace-seeking, patriotic strains we have noticed, but by fear and snobbery. Fear because their ranks did include criminals; snobbery because many of these men, braggartizing it in their slashed silks and soiled velvets, were of humble origin; men, as Bayard put it, not fit to consort with: shoemakers, bakers, peasants. In itself, humble origin was far too common among soldiers to give rise to comment. It was the fact that entering the military life on a strictly business basis could lead to topsy-turvy fortune-making that galled. Martin Schwarz, who brought 2000 Swiss and Germans to the service of Richard III's sister Margaret, and was killed in the challenge to Henry VII at the battle of Stoke-on-Trent, had started out as a shoemaker in Augsburg. One of Francis I's chief sources of *Landsknecht* mercenaries was Sebastian Vogesberger, originally a baker. The extremely successful military entrepreneur Antoine, baron de la Garde, came from a peasant family. The abnormality of such careers led mercenaries to be associated with the outrage that was felt towards those other beating-the-system renegades from decent values, the Jews.

Though supported by some of their careers and much of their behaviour, the bias of peacemakers and patriots obscures the variety which makes it hazardous to present the mercenary as a type, whether as commander or man. In fifteenth-century Italy, where the rival powers were almost entirely dependent on mercenaries, the roll-call of great *condottieri* (leaders of mercenary cavalry) was beginning to close. Niccolò Piccinino, a butcher's son, died in 1444, a year after the baker's son Gattamelata, whose equestrian monument by Donatello is not so much a portrait as a commemoration of the whole forceful breed. In 1466 died Francesco Sforza, himself the son of a *condottiere*, the last example of a hired lance who used his following to seize political power. In 1476, after twenty years of retirement in his lavish and brilliant court at Malpaga, Bartolomeo Colleoni died, leaving 100,000 ducats to his employer, Venice, with a stipulation in his will that led to the commissioning of that second great commemoration of men as remarkable for strength of mind as of arms, Verrocchio's equestrian statue of him.

His retirement followed the conclusion in 1454–5 of the non-aggression pact signed by Milan, Florence, Venice and Naples, which, though punctuated by small wars, held up during forty years of unprecedented calm in the peninsula. Without annual campaigning to support them, the self-made *condottiere* careers were no longer possible; the supply of troops was left to rulers for whom mercenary service was a profitable side-line, as it was for the dukes of Urbino and the marquises of Ferrara and Mantua, and to those rural magnates, especially those of the Papal States, with warrior traditions reaching back over generations and who could easily, when the opportunity of war occurred, call up contingents based on their own and their relations' tenants.

At the same time that in Italy the entrepreneurial mercenary leader was becoming rare, in Germany men of his stamp were becoming more conspicuous than ever before, urged into war-as-a-business by the need for troops, and especially for infantry, caused by France's internal and external wars, Burgundy's battle-quarrels with the Swiss, and the inter-city conflicts and the succession struggles for local political or ecclesiastical power which flourished within Maximilian's ill-controlled empire. It was then that the three types of military contractor emerged that were to dominate central European mercenary recruitment throughout the following century. The first continued the tradition that had enriched those soldiers, such as Sir John Hawkwood, who had brought fortune-seeking troops with them into Italy during pauses – the 1350 Peace of Brétigny in Hawkwood's case – in the Hundred Years War:

companies, armed gangs, if you like, linked by contract to a captain (the word covered the command of units running into thousands) who displayed his wares in the military market and, if there were no quick offer to buy, could use them to force a bargain on a reluctant purchaser. The second was the man who, secure in the control of his own dependants, and shrewd in his estimation of restlessness within the civilian employment pool, negotiated a contract first and then raised and led the men to fulfil it. This remained the commonest type of military entrepreneur. It was essential that he had status enough to imply the ready fulfilment of his promises – and the checking of his credentials in this respect occupied much of the time of a would-be belligerent's diplomatic agents. The third was the most purely entrepreneurial, and as yet (he would come into his own during the Thirty Years War hunger for men) the rarest: the contractor who negotiated for the delivery to a purchaser of a package of men he would lead not in person – save, perhaps, to the mustering point – but through his deputy.

Large forces could be raised on the human commodity market. Franz van Sickingen, the knight who played a prominent role during the competition for troops during the early stage of Reformation tension, could deliver a whole army: up to 3000 cavalry 'lances' and 12,000 infantry. In 1599 Venice paid a retainer to Duke Charles of Lorraine's son, the count of Vaudemont, for a force of no fewer than 26,000 men, though a sense of realism came to prevail and it was never asked for. And large fortunes could be made. Combat entrepreneurs like Georg von Frundsberg in the 1520s and Sebastian Schertlin von Burtenbach, who died in 1577, made sums out of men not far below those made by contemporary merchant bankers like the Fuggers and Welsers out of silver ingots, bales of cloth and the interest on loans to princes – and with the same assiduous attention to the margins of their outlays and profits.

For the men they raised, to be treated as a commodity was not to be treated inhumanly. Mercenary troops would not serve for less than the going rate in the armies they joined; on the other hand, employer-governments would not pay much more for the convenience of having soldiers produced en masse. The contractor's main profits arose from retainers, annuities, grants of land, gifts of plate and gold collars, and kick-backs from subordinate captains. The men, in spite of the usual corruption which rubbed some of the contract wage away on every hand that touched it, if they did not receive more than their non-mercenary comrades-in-arms, at least received the same more regularly, because their colonels could threaten mutiny or withdrawal on their behalf. Better paid, then better fed: so they had a greater chance of withstanding hardship and throwing off disease. Moreover, the contracts under which they were raised allowed for a higher proportion of NCOs, drummers and fifers (signal givers as well as morale raisers), surgeons, priests, and clerks to keep the company books. There must have been defalcations here. All the same, the desertion rate was lower than among native soldiers. And mercenary contracts, as we have noticed, could sometimes protect men from particularly arduous – digging fortifications – or hazardous – assaulting breaches – aspects of their occupation.

How far such stipulations represented a contractor's wish to keep his capital of manpower as intact as possible, and how far they were the result of representations made to him by his agents (men with their ears still closer to the ground) to the effect that what recruits wanted was a wage, the possibility of windfalls and the probability of being left alive to enjoy them, can only be conjectured. It is difficult to see much of the lives and motives of mercenaries behind the screens of the entrepreneurial contract and the venom of moralists. The emergence of the Swiss, from the long-term contracts negotiated with the confederate cantons by Louis XI, as the pre-eminent infantry mercenaries in Europe, backed as they were known to be by governmental sanction and control over conditions of service, and given a sense of pride by a loose command structure which permitted an unusual freedom of expression on strategic and tactical matters from within the ranks, may well have communicated a firmer self-confidence within the increasingly reviled mercenary community as a whole. And when the reputation of the Swiss was dimmed by the defeat – Marignano in 1515 and Bicocca in 1522 – of armies in which they formed key elements, their glamour as sturdy, unshakable, non-prisoner-taking exterminators was transferred to the German *Landsknecht* companies. These, beneath the bracketing entrepreneur's contract, had their own elective and consultative practices which showed that the mercenary, though a hireling, was no mere chattel.

It was among the *Landsknechts*, and most consistently in the first third of the sixteenth century, that the passage from civilian into military society was spelled out most deliberately. In a ceremony owing something of its seriousness to Hussite and Swiss traditions and much of its symbolism to the surreptitious bondings of rebellious peasant groups, the process of mustering after recruitment was turned into a positive rite of initiation. The recruits entered the mustering ground through a temporary gateway formed by two halberds stuck in the ground with a pike laid across the blades to form a crossbar. They were then formally enrolled in the books of the 'regiment', allocated their weapon and given their first pay, minus the appropriate deductions. They were then formed into a ring while the disciplinary code was read. To this they had to swear by raising a hand with two fingers extended. Thereafter they were in a world which allowed for considerable personal eccentricity and an unusual degree of closeness between captain and men, but which was controlled with great ferocity. Absences were checked through an unusually strict system of leave passports. A gallows not only marked every mustering centre and stopping place but was used as an 'off-limits' symbol, on the doors of houses exempt from billeting, for example. And when a man's behaviour, by cowardice or in other ways, had impugned a company's honour, he was judged not by the forms of law we shall turn to in the next chapter, but by *Speissgericht*, spear-law. After defending himself among all his colleagues the decision – which could only be death or total acquittal – was given by a show of hands. The death sentence could then be carried out (though it is unclear how frequently it was) by the running of that gauntlet that allowed every man to strike at the criminal as he tried to dash between their files.

From the 1530s the pre-eminent roles played by Swiss and *Landsknechts*, both in the image and practice of the mercenary world, were dissipated among the more cosmopolitan cast that included Scots, Walloons, Savoyards, Corsicans and Italians. Because the Swiss confederation had become determinedly neutralist, such Swiss as were recruited could not proudly distinguish themselves as heretofore by marching under their cantonal banners. With Charles V's ban on recruiting, save by his own agents, in Germany, such units as the entrepreneurs could bring together lacked the local band of brothers, or proto-trade union solidarity of earlier contingents. Because the need for greater numbers, coinciding with the fall in the purchasing power of the military wage, overtook the ability or wish of men to go to war from the traditional recruiting grounds, it became rarer to find mercenary contingents that had not picked up hitch-hikers of other nationalities to make up their strength. And with the increase (as it seems) in the proportion of mercenaries who joined on a short-term basis, briefly to holiday with possibly profitable violence and impress their neighbours, transference from the private sector into the long-serving mercenary bands becomes more frequent.

All that can be suggested with any confidence is that the separateness of military from civilian society becomes more pronounced as we look from permanent forces and princely guards towards those private and mercenary sectors whose identities become progressively confused. But what is missing from this scale of distancing is the experience of military service itself.

6

The society of soldiers:
conditions of service

When a country mobilized for war, some of the permanent force was held back to form, with militia draftees, a defence force; few wars were fought against an adversary who lacked allies, part of whose land or naval forces could make diversionary counter-moves. Similarly, units from princely guards were retained to stiffen key garrison towns or to form the escorts of civilian administrative or liaison officials. When to these abstentions from immediate combat duty we add the presence in the field of novice volunteers among the category of freelance soldiers, the quite high proportion of first-timers who turned up in mercenary bands, and above all, the bands of raw native recruits, we get armies comprising a high proportion – at times, it seems probable, a majority – of men who had never fought before. This was particularly true of the opening stages of a campaign. In the 'schools', whether of Granada or the Netherlands, the proportion of tyros diminished year by year. All the same, as a result of disease, desertion and partial demobilizations to save money during the winter, the need for replacements made it always an important one.

Given the tendency of long-service troops, save for the professional freelance or mercenary, to blend into civilian life, soldiers never so much formed a separate society as when at war. The surface obviousness of the remark conceals a real problem. How was it that so large a proportion of inexperienced, often unwilling men, scantily, if at all committed to a cause and given little or no preliminary training, could be turned into adequate, on occasion conspicuously brave combat soldiers? Commanders might be cautious about exposing new troops to the initial shock of combat, and become more wary and Fabian in their strategy because of them, but it was a rare battle or siege that was decided by the flight of those who from inexperience simply could not cope with the enduring fears and occasional challenges of war. The French defeat of the Italian League at Fornovo in 1495 was caused by panic and indiscipline, but it was the mercenary heavy cavalry who withdrew when the initial odds turned against them, and the well-tried light Balkan cavalry who could not resist breaking away from the battle to pillage the baggage train of Charles VIII. The inadequacies of the subordinate command structure prevented the methodical distribution of raw troops among hardened ones. What process of militarization made them, after the mere formality of being named as a muster list and issued with conduct money, into effective members of that society of soldiers recognized by civilians as being so different from their own?

Ironically, civilians themselves contributed directly to that process. Battles were dramas without an audience. But they were rare, if climactic, performances within a life of marching, camping, patrolling, idling that was enclosed and catered for by a supporting cast – victuallers, hauliers, armourers, harnessmakers, clerks and miscellaneous camp-followers – whose presence helped to define the separateness of the soldier's role. It was as the central characters within an itinerant mass larger than the population of the great majority of European towns that new recruits came to see themselves as part of a special segment of society, escorted towards the uniquely hazardous tasks that they alone could carry out.

In peacetime, depending on the size and variety of the permanent force, civilian military administration was pared to a minimum. Save for the creation of the permanent Spanish Council of War there was nothing resembling a war ministry; military policy was decided by a ruler in council and carried out through each country's general-purpose executive body, the Privy Council in England, the College in Venice (where, exceptionally, two members had specific responsibility for the condition and payment of the land forces). Venice was also exceptional in retaining a professional soldier as head of its military establishment in peace, charged with carrying out tours of inspection. Elsewhere, efficiency experts were called in from time to time, as when in 1548 Migliorino Ubaldini was contracted 'to perfect the Scots in the knowledge of arms and to organize the defence of the realm', but overall responsibility for garrisons, militias and fortification works joined the other political and administrative chores of the French regional *gouverneurs*, the Spanish *gobernadores generales*, the English lords lieutenant, the Tuscan *capitani* and *podestà*. Pay flowed from standing charges on local tax and toll revenue and was disbursed and checked against muster lists by local officials as a paid extra to their normal functions. Titular grandee offices, master of the horse, grand marshal, though involving an advisory role, did not imply any professional responsibility for the cavalry or for the administration of justice in suits arising from conflicts between soldiers and civilians. Positions with a military flavour, the captaincy or castellanship of frontier towns, for instance, as often as not concealed a favour to a court official, even to a cleric or cultivated lawyer who had deserved well of the crown. Full-time peace forces were administered by part-time officials and sinecurists, or their substitutes.

The only exception was the artillery service, with its master (usually a nobleman) and its corps of gunfounders, carriage and gunpowder makers and other craftsmen, master-gunners, purchase and inventory clerks and treasurer. This was the one branch of the military establishment that universally heeded that so often quoted tag: in peace prepare for war. Even fortifications – and most countries employed a few full-time military engineers as well as calling in foreign specialists – were usually designed and constructed, as in the English 'King's Works', through the organization that built and maintained royal palaces and parks. The exceptions here were France, but only when, under the ex-artillerist Sully, a distinction was made between *bâtiments* and *fortifications* and was strengthened by his attaching to the latter a number of cartographers to enable the strategic-defensive state of the country to be evaluated more accurately than hitherto; and Venice, where a separate, permanent organization with its own staff and earmarked budget was set up in 1542 under the proveditors of fortresses.

Inefficient the running of military affairs in peace certainly was. The cause was not only parsimony and the desire to make any institution a source of patronage, but a function of distance. The smaller the political unit the more efficiently administered and readily mobilizable the force, as in the Rhine Palatinate of the later fifteenth century, with its regular attention to the armament and mustering of its resources of cavalry and infantry by nobles appointed by the elector who carried out periodical reviews, or Savoy in the later sixteenth.

The process of mobilization and getting a campaign under way not only placed an enormous strain on shoestring and largely part-time military administrations, but involved their supplementation by men drawn from other branches of the bureaucracy or from landed leisure or law practice. Political commissioners – part watchdog, part colleague – were appointed to advise commanders-in-chief or those in command of large detached units. Scores of men of substantial but lesser weight were deputed to assist in coordinating the defence of strategic towns or frontier outposts that might be in danger, and to liaise with, and keep a wary financial and political eye on, mercenary bands; thus sixteen commissaries and controllers were appointed to eight companies of German infantry amounting to 2490 men when they joined the French army in 1548. Under a paymaster-general an instant financial sub-bureaucracy was created to pass on coin brought by baggage train, or exchanged for bills of exchange on local bankers, to army quarters and thence to captains and their clerks. A smaller sub-bureaucracy of lawyers was run up to assist the marshal and his deputies, advise the officer members of military courts and offer guidance on the interpretation of military codes by provosts and their henchmen.

Largest of all were the ad hoc civilian organizations that were required to keep an army equipped, provided with transport, and fed.

As far as the artillery was concerned, the officers and some of the master-gunners came from the peacetime establishment, the rest of the master-gunners, and all their ranker colleagues, from the part-time artillery schools which, as we shall see, were organized on the lines of a militia. But these men were only the heart of a far larger support corps. Getting an artillery train on the move required horses to drag the carriages, wagons (and more horses) to transport powder, ball and implements (ladles, swabs, blocks and tackle and the like), draymen and grooms, stable- and route-masters, not to mention wheelwrights, carpenters, blacksmiths and a mass of labourers, or pioneers, to handle the guns into position, settle them back after recoil, and fill gabions or throw up embankments to protect them when in siege positions, as well as to use their weight when a carriage overturned or ground its wheels deep into the mud. The Milanese artillery train of sixteen large cannon in 1472 needed 227 carts and 1044 oxen to move guns and equipment. A French estimate of the late sixteenth century allowed for 1500 pioneers among the 1860 men (additional to establishment) needed to move and service a siege train of fourteen large- and sixteen medium-calibre guns. Just how crucial their muscle power was can be seen from accounts of Charles VIII's withdrawal from Italy in 1495. He was faced by the need to transport thirty-seven guns, fourteen of which were of large calibre, across the Apeninnes from Pontremoli, in northern Tuscany. That city had been, against his orders, sacked by his Swiss mercenaries in an atrocious, berserk act of vengeance for forty colleagues who had been killed there when the French were forcing their way south in the previous year. The king's own pioneer gang had been dissipated. Local resentment prevented the enrolment of others. He struck a bargain: the Swiss would be pardoned if they manhandled the guns over the mule track that crossed the mountains. In rope teams of 200 they aided the horses to haul the guns up the pass and braked them down the still steeper northern descent, urged on by the veteran commander, Louis de la Tremouille, who in a rare, intimate glance, is shown shirt-sleeved and with a floppy hat protecting his sun-scorched face and spectacles, shouting encouragement. But mountain passes aside, it was horsepower that moved guns. Another estimate put the number needed to haul a 1554 Spanish artillery train of fifty guns across the flat Netherlands at 4777. Such estimates, imprecisely documented as they are, at least suggest the scale on which armies became surrounded with a service element.

The presence of artillery also determined the time recruits spent getting used to the conditions of the march. On average, guns halved the distance – normally twelve miles – troops marched in a day. Much depended on the weather. During the War of Siena the same commander, travelling with guns, achieved nine miles a day on an expedition enjoying dry weather, only three and a third on another that followed weeks of rain. But even without artillery – which for this reason was often sent ahead, if possible by river – the pace of an army on the move was determined by wagon wheels, and the length of the day's march by the time required to harness and load, then to stable or hobble, unload and feed.

Wagons and carts were needed not only for such essentials as ammunition, portable flour mills and baker's ovens, or items such as the seventy hulls to make boat-bridges at river crossings carried with the army Charles V sent to invade France in 1544, but personal baggage. 'The first man to call the baggage of an army "impedimenta"', noted Guicciardini in the 1520s, 'could not have found a better name. And whoever coined the phrase that says such a thing "is more trouble than moving camp" was very right. It is an endless task to get everything in a camp organized so that it can move.'

As armour grew heavier in the late fifteenth century it became unusual to wear it on the march unless an ambush or other attack were anticipated. The habit of the aristocratic campaigner to eat from his own silver served by his own domestic servants, sleep in his own bed in his own pavilion died hard. The 'lance' was a small household, and it carried household goods with it. All this went into wagons, as, later, did the pikeman's corselet and the heavy musket. Then there was accumulated bric-à-brac and looted provisions. By 1515 Seyssel was complaining of all ranks that 'so many animals and men are needed to carry food and baggage that . . . they cumber the combatants and sometimes bring the army to a halt. Besides, there always has to be a great band to guard [the baggage train] . . . and sometimes the men-at-arms, fearing to lose their possessions, quit their ranks to protect them, or instead of fighting, their footmen are put in charge.' A century later, during the 1610 campaign of Maurice of Nassau (that great reformer!), 129 out of 942 wagons were used to transport the possessions of his own staff. In 1602 Maurice's army of 24,000 men needed 3000 wagons. And a wagon usually required two drivers and four horses. To put this demand for horseflesh in proportion, we can compare the report of Henry VIII's ambassador in 1526 that stabling for 22,500 horses and mules had been provided at Bordeaux for the reception of Francis I's itinerant court. But princes and important courtiers had large establishments of horses of their own. Practically all the beasts, carts and carters with armies were commandeered, leaving peasant plots uncultivated, produce unhauled to market. Though paid for their services, a whole swathe of civilian society was cut off from their normal and – to judge from a chorus of protest – more profitable livelihoods, as tribute to a society of soldiers many of whom, only months ago, had been peasants themselves.

We have seen that Charles VIII's plans for feeding the 20,000 troops he led against Brittany envisaged a further 28,000 who would also have to be fed. Though the number of great nobles taking an extensive entourage of servants and secretaries and messengers with them dropped, and though the dwindling number of men-at-arms meant that fewer 'mechanics' were needed to service their elaborate armour, the number of camp attendants underwent no dramatic decline. Another French food order, that of Henry II when joining the League of Lutheran Princes against Charles V, anticipated that his 50,000 troops would be accompanied by not many fewer non-combatants. Even in garrisons, where many services were provided by townspeople, the servants of officers and lieutenants and even of some NCOs added at least 15 per cent to the strength; the instinct to have a scivvy being as strong among badly paid soldiers as it was in the dismal tenements of nineteenth-century factory hands. So the baggage train came to be further encumbered with the camp-followers' clothes, firewood, pots and pans, tradesmen's and pawnbrokers' stalls and portable counters, and laundresses' cauldrons. It was wholly exceptional that Alba, planning to take 16,000 troops from Italy to the Netherlands in 1567, should only allow for 6150 non-combatants.

Much of the wagon space, much of the civilian bustle in camp or at halting points on the march, was caused by the need to supply the walking city with food. At 90,000 to 100,000, Henry II's army and its followers contained more stomachs than Milan and scarcely fewer than London.

Provisioning was, therefore, a major problem. No army set out with the intention of living off the land. Some, in extremity, did. All, at times, stole food or bullied the locals into giving it up at below-market prices or on 'credit'. Equally, perhaps, soldiers were told lies about the availability of foodstuffs or overcharged. There were a few times when armies waged war as deliberately against crops as against men. But military policy was to bring food to armies, not to scatter them in search of it. And as they grew in numbers self-help became ever more impractical. Milan reached up into the foothills of the Alps for its meat, far along the Po for its grain and wine. London was kept alive by carters, drovers and shipmasters plying a communications network covering hundreds of square miles. No moving city could reproduce these patiently accumulated systems. Food was the fuel of armies. And mutiny and desertion followed any serious breakdown in its supply.

To prevent this, a new system was developed. Broadly speaking, it can be described as a shift from exploiting late medieval rights of purveyance – the pre-empting of local foodstuffs from a multitude of producers to supply itinerant royal courts – and attempting to apply them abroad, to relying on contracts with individual merchants who commanded produce networks of their own and who could elaborate them to ensure massive deliveries, and who had capital enough to bridge at need the all too common time gap between purchase and government payment.

Too little is known about such merchants, their profits (encouraged by freedom from tolls wherever rulers could control them) or their losses (they had to engage to sell at prices no higher than those on the local market), to follow them into their counting houses and chart their subsequent fortunes or losses. Sent in advance, Charles

VIII's commissaries of victuals arranged with Italian merchants to accumulate food stores on his army's march to Rome, and on to Naples. England only came to rely primarily on monopolistic contracts when campaigns in Ireland became annual events. Spain, though using contractors to bring food to the halting points on the 'Spanish Road' between Milan and the Netherlands, relied on purveyance at home and local markets in the Netherlands until the 1580s. French monarchs preferred to rely on purveyance when fighting at or near to home, or on food supplied by allies, to a heavy dependence on the contract system, which was only wholeheartedly adopted late in the sixteenth century.

The move from public- to private-sector provisioning made little ascertainable difference to the troops. Save on regularly used military corridors like the Spanish Road, marches were subject to delays and changes of direction which could mean that the contractors' stocks were either not reached or, when they were, were in poor condition. Under the direction of a commissary-general, the civilian victualling commissaries had to work as hard as ever checking and supplementing rations and supervising the endless task of producing their essential component, the 'military loaf' of 24 ounces; no wonder inventors busied themselves with portable baking ovens, and mills geared to the axles of wagons so that grain could be ground while the army was on the move. Provision trains were still necessary – more horses, carts and carters – to transport an emergency food stock. And the private sutler, even though his role was restricted by reliance on the great contractors for most of an army's grain, salt fish, cheese, wine and beer, remained ubiquitous, not only topping up these basic, keeping commodities, but hawking fresh meat and fish, fowls, eggs and butter to whoever could afford to haggle for them.

The civilian penumbra that now trailed before and after armies, now surrounded and penetrated them as far as provosts and camp-marshals with their subordinate quartermasters would allow, was by no means simply a male one. If it had been, the duties of the *Trossmeister*, or official responsible for the transport and conduct of non-combatants (a post most regularly filled by the pragmatic Germans) would have been less arduous. In *Utopia*, where regard for morale in war was uppermost, 'if the women are anxious to accompany their husbands on military service, not only do they not forbid them but actually encourage them and incite them by expressions of praise . . . they are placed alongside their husbands on the battle front. . . . The result is that when it comes to hand-to-hand fighting, if the enemy stands his ground, the battle is long and anguished and ends with mutual extermination.' The passage was designed to be at thought-provoking odds with actual practice. The presence of wives was often prohibited, never encouraged, but, especially in garrisons or long-term camp or siege-line, inevitable. The snag, to authority, was the definition of 'wife'. With no marriage lines to brandish, and with the unlikelihood that real wives would have been removed from caring for a home, the chances were that 'wives' were actual, or potential whores. At a time without barbed wire or adequately trained military police, wives or 'wives' could not be kept from contact with their mates. Besides, they cooked, mended, laundered, helped tend the sick and, whatever their status, did something to keep their men out of worse mischief.

Military codes seldom distinguished between wives and prostitutes. Both, by making an army more or less sexually self-sufficient, could relieve a command from coping too constantly with the dangerous relations with the neighbourhood that followed the pestering and rape with which the soldiery, on solid evidence, was to be associated. This consideration it was that led Philip II's veteran commander Sancho de Londoño to conclude that 'it would be dangerous not to have them'. Moralists like Michel d'Amboise in 1543 could decry any sexual activity for soldiers on active service as 'reducing both bodily strength and courage', but his Remember Capua! train of preaching (with its reference to the effeminating of Hannibal's troops by the resourceful women of that sultry land) did not ring true to men who knew their men. Governments might try to keep this enemy at bay by legislation. All whores approaching the army will have their noses slit, ran a Venetian proclamation of 1514. In 1513 an English broadsheet proclaimed that 'no man bring with him any manner of women over the sea, upon pain of forfeiture of their goods to the marshal and their bodies to be imprisoned, there to remain at the King's will. And that no man hold no woman within his lodging beyond the sea, upon pain of imprisonment and loss of a month's wage. And that no common woman presume to come within the King's host, nor nigh the same by the space of three miles, upon pain if any so be taken to be burned upon the right cheek.' Only months after a similar prohibition of 1544, the council with Henry VIII at the siege of Boulogne was complaining to the council with the Queen in London that the camp was 'troubled with a sort of light women which daily do repair out of England hither'.

Vain ordinances such as these were gestures less towards morality than discipline. Charles the Bold's military ordinance of 1473 forbade men to bring women of their own. But each company of one hundred lances was allowed up to thirty in common. Charles VIII in 1484 similarly forbade men to bring girls of their own, adding that they must not offer horses to ride on to the common army prostitutes.

Given the tolerance shown by religious and civil authorities towards prostitution, though preferably in known brothels or licensed red-light districts, and the recognized treks of whores, some in the most pathetic and desperate state of poverty, to trade fairs, pilgrimage centres, harvest homes and vintage celebrations, to insulate them from a crowd of soldiers was as unnatural as it was impossible. La Noue expressed his amazement when the first, and most puritan, Huguenot army of 1562 not only tried to stop blaspheming but voluntarily kept women from haunting the camp. He congratulated their leader, Coligny. 'Very fine,' was the reply, 'provided that it lasts. . . . As an old infantry colonel I cannot but remember the proverb, "Young hermits may become old devils." We smiled at his saying,' La Noue went on, 'but it was only too true.'

It was also true that by then municipal regulations, infected by Reform of both religious brands, was squeezing the purchase of sex into ever more guilt-ridden alleys and states of mind. But that very fact gave added distinction to the licence that had to be permitted to soldiers. Spanish Netherlands army orders of the 1550s to 1570s demonstrated, it is true, the official change from the days of Charles the Bold: only five to eight whores permitted per company of two hundred men. By an order of 1596 they were down to three, and were subject to regular medical inspection. In 1590 the Dutch Articles of War laid down that 'all common whores shall for the first offence be shamefully driven from the camp, and for the second offence, being found in the camp, shall be heavily flogged and banished'. But there is no evidence suggesting that sexual licence became any the less a badge of distinction for the soldier.

Descriptions in such broad strokes of army society as an officially catered-for crowd, obscure much that was saddening and flavourless about military life. One example may count for many. After the greater part of Henry VIII's army had returned to England after the capture of Boulogne, the war continued in a minor key of raids and skirmishes. When in January 1545 the earl of Surrey called out the garrisons of Calais and Guisnes to intercept a French force coming to the relief of Etaples, the Welsh chronicler Elis Gruffydd, himself serving as a common soldier, explained their sullen response. 'This was for lack of food which was eatable and which would have strengthened them, and for lack of money to buy such food, for there was not a penny in the pockets of the common soldiers, because the English had not been paid for nine months. So they had to take what they could from the king's storehouses, where it had been kept too long. The bread was hard and baked with corn and meal which had lost its taste and savour, and the salt beef stank when it was lifted out of the brine. The butter was of many colours and the cheese dry and hard, and this was the best they could get from the king's stores, which made most of the soldiers miserable and reckless.' Not surprisingly, the interception was a humiliating failure.

It is, all the same, worth having emphasized the social atmosphere of the military environment, as its conditioning power was at least as pervasive as that of more technical 'isolating' factors, such as uniform, training and drill.

Deriving from the liveries worn by the dependants of a prince or noble, and necessitated by the need to distinguish friend from foe and – especially as smoke came to drift ever more thickly over battlefields – unit from unit, uniforms, or, more accurately, uniform markings, were universal but only patchily standardized.

From the second half of the fifteenth century French infantry sported on their tunics the badge of their city (a lion for Lyon) or the name of their province, and the custom whereby royal guards wore the colour of the sovereign – violet and grey for Charles VIII, yellow and red for his successor, Louis XII – was extended through mass clothing orders to part at least of the regional levies. In more general use was the white cross, tacked on to a tunic or painted on a breastplate or shield. Similarly, the English used the red cross, the Bretons (while they retained their independence) the black, and the men of Lorraine their barred cross, the Burgundians the red St Andrew's cross. The need to identify units more precisely than through the banners and pennants of aristocratic captains and the distinctive *banneroles* attached to their helmets was precociously recognized in Charles the Bold's cavalry ordinance of 1473; heads of squadrons were to wear *banneroles* with their captain's badge and 'large gold letters reading C, CC, CCC, CCCC according to the squadron' while subordinate section leaders were to add 'I, II, III, IV respectively, inscribed beneath the C of the squadron'. In the same spirit, Machiavelli wanted each infantry company to be identified by a coloured banner and, within it, each corporal (head of ten) to have a number painted on his helmet, each man a number on his shield.

Both his and Charles's recommendations were an overreaction to a grasp of the new importance of tactical units within the older 'host' or 'battle' formations. Both had permanent forces in mind that could stand still to be counted. But in the flux of mobilization men turned up in what they had been issued with locally or chose to wear of their own; and replacement tunics and hose, in spite of government recommendations (that a body of German infantry engaged in 1544 by Henry VIII should arrive clad in blue decorated with a border of 'three fingers broad of red', for instance) were at the mercy of what dyed stuffs contractors happened to have in stock; dyes which, at cut-price, must in any case have leached out after the first few soapless boilings and poundings. Throughout the period, wartime 'uniform' chiefly signified the tacked-on cross or armband. It was not only in the interest of visibility that after-daylight raids were literally *camisades*: 'Sent yesternight', the military governor of Boulogne reported to Henry VIII on 16 July 1545, 'young Cotton, Spencer, Bowes and William app Roberts, each with 100 men with their shirts uppermost that they might know each other, over the water at low ebb opposite the Picards' camp to cut betwixt them and their ordnance.' The anonymity of armour in any case militated against distinctive uniform. So did the absence of permanent regiments. It was only with the skimping of the former and the emergence of the latter in the later seventeenth century that uniforms came to be a clear divider of unit from unit – or side from side – in the field, or soldier from civilian when off duty, save as a matter of style. Group loyalty, and its contribution to combat morale, owed more to the unit's standard, focus of oaths of loyalty, and held aloft by an ensign-bearer paid to do little more than defend it with his life.

Neither was training an activity that methodically transformed recruit into soldier. Save, perhaps, in those Spanish garrisons in Italy which received newly raised men and sent them up to Flanders, there was no formal preparation for battle by 'the army'. Even among the *Landsknechts* the handling of weapons and formation drill were left to the inclination of individual captains. Thomas Audley drew on his experience of Henry VIII's later campaigns in France when he explained that an ex-soldier was of little use in training the militia because he had learned nothing himself on active service. And why was this? 'Because his captain is as ignorant as he . . . I wish . . . that captains would be as ready to take pains to train their men as they be ready at the payday to take pains to tell money, for it is a grievous pain to set a battle with untrained men.' It was noted as something remarkable of Leicester that, in 1589, 'His Lordship findinge want of experience in many of the souldiers, thought yt fitt to drawe forth some squadrons both of horse and foot not so much to fight as to practice them and make them more apt and ready to be commanded.' A similar note is struck in a 1595 commendation of Maurice of Nassau because he 'did move a third part of the men out of the entrenchments on to the field and did place, change, turn, wheel, break and reform, close and separate them in various battle-orders, in order to accustom the men to hold their files and ranks . . . which exercise would be very serviceable in time of need'. Andrea Palladio, whose hobby was military reform, complained in his 1575 edition of Caesar's *Commentaries* that military leaders, though recognizing the new relevance of the drills and tactical formations of the ancients, said that nothing could be done about it because of the impossibility of training the sort of men who comprised modern armies. The great architect saw this as mere defeatism. 'I myself,' he wrote, 'being with some gentlemen [including the classical scholar Francesco Patrizi] experienced in military affairs, to satisfy them I took certain galley oarsmen and pioneers who were on the spot and put them through every possible drill and military exercise without producing the least stumbling or confusion. So it would be far easier to introduce the practices and regulations of the ancients than many think.' His friend Valerio Chieregato, as a colonel of militia, was in a position to carry out this experiment on a larger scale, teaching 'my own evolutions', he reported to the doge in 1573, to 6600 men 'without all the shouts, curses, threats and blows and other untoward excesses that are customarily used today'.

Legislation setting up permanent forces made no reference to training. Neither did any legal code published to regulate an army's conduct on campaign, nor any contract with mercenary bands. The sixteenth law in the eighteenth *titulo* of the medieval Castilian Second *Partida*, with its pious but impractical references to such formations as the hedge, the wedge and the circle, had no progeny. It was, indeed, only with respect to militias that training was mentioned in legislation, sometimes with a fair degree of detail. But Chieregato's remark suggests the brusque and hugger-mugger way in which this was carried out. Training periods, in any case short because of communities' reluctance to pay militiamen's food and travel allowances, were largely occupied with checking muster lists and arms. Reports on them to central government dwell rather on numbers, equipment and 'warlike' appearance than on drills and evolutions performed; it was felt perhaps to be illogical to concentrate a concern for training on the branch of the military least likely to see actual fighting.

There was, of course, a theoretical belief in the importance of training, especially as military weapons came to differ from those used in hunting, competitive recreations and self-defence. It was strengthened by the admiration for the training and tactics of the Romans which had led to the reading in French, Spanish, English and Burgundian aristocratic military circles of translations of such authors as Vegetius, Frontinus, Livy, Caesar and Sallust from the middle of the fifteenth century, strengthened in the following one by the growing interest in Aelianus Tacticus and the diagrams that accompanied his work, and in Polybius's description of the military practices of the Greeks. This back-to-the-ancients fad was not simply the preserve of cultivated warriors and scholars. An observer of Henry VIII's army's march into Scotland in October 1545 noted that it kept such array 'that if Vegecius Frontinus [sic] were present' he could not have bettered its procedures. But even when practical drill handbooks began tentatively to appear from the 1560s (such as Henry Barrett's unpublished *A brief booke unto private captaynes*) and in some quantity from 1600 (Sir Clement Edmonds's *The maner of our moderne training, or tacticke practise* of that year, Jacob de Gheyn's widely copied *Wapenhandelinghe van roers, musquetten ende spiessen* of 1607), there is little evidence that men were prepared by formal weapons-instruction and drill, let alone by manoeuvres, for combat. The responsibility, burked by captains, was ultimately that of the *maestro di campo* or field-marshal, but one of the keenest and most knowledgeable of them, Londoño, wrote bitterly that such a rank 'carries less authority today than did that of a simple captain in our ancestors' time'.

Again, it was well enough known how a smart unit should comport itself. In 1521 Battista della Valle's handbook, *Vallo: libro continente appertenentie ad capitani*, described how the pikeman should support his weapon: blade uppermost, with his left hand snug to the shoulder so that the elbow jutted well forward and with the butt pointing precisely down towards his left foot. 'And thus with every man in the same file. And each of them in the formation must heed the drum with slow but vigorous strides, each keeping pace and moving the same leg at the same time, and not wavering either in rank or file; and performing thus, I conclude that such a formation will give much pleasure to the cultivated and informed observer.' This last phrase gives away the significance of much of the preoccupation with marching in step, drill comportment and tactical exercises (his book concludes with a veritable firework display of diagrams of bizarre and complex formations) that haunted the burgeoning literature of war. Outside the tiny military academies, training of this sort was an aspect of pageantry, not of war. Parades, balletlike evolutions, rehearsed mock-combats; these were entertainments performed by guards units for the delectation of visiting dignitaries. Their relationship to service conditions was on a par with that of Leonardo's procession inventions – 'flying machines' and 'tanks' – to practical means of transport.

Drummers, together with fifers, certainly went to war. Though most readily traceable through contracts with Swiss and German mercenaries, they were in all armies. Used not to keep the troops in step save on parade, but to provide diversion on the march, they were primarily engaged to transmit the sound orders (move off, assume battle order, charge, halt, retire) that supplemented the mimed commands semaphored by sergeants' manipulation of their halberds. Together with trumpets, which appeared to have been used less to bray out battle orders than to wake men up and call them to listen to proclamations in camp, they formed a military music – criticized by Budé as too effective in arousing blood-lust – that formed part of the conditioning by atmosphere and milieu that was so much more important than uniform or training in inducting the recruit into preparedness for his specific task.

How otherwise can the transformation process described by Brantôme be explained? 'What I find so remarkable', he wrote, 'about these infantrymen, is that you can see young men emerging from villages, from labouring jobs and workshops, from forges and stables, from being domestic servants and from several other similarly base and inferior positions, and hardly have they spent a while among the infantry [on active service] than you see them all at once warlike and prepared.'

Space itself was a factor. The scarcely documented, tom-tomlike communication network that kept relatives that had scattered in search of work or betterment in some sort of touch through itinerant pedlars, clerics on official or more dubious wanderings, gossip at fairs and at crowd-gathering stages on princely progresses, failed to reach armies, incalculably on the move or temporarily moored across distant frontiers and not granting any home leave to the common soldier. The story of Martin Guerre, a Basque settler in Languedoc, is an instance. When local humiliation, rubbing on some deep vagrant whim, made him leave wife and family to soak his mood in the bustle and anonymity of an army, he passed into a zone of silence so prolonged that an ex-comrade, posing as Martin, was years later able to move into his property and his wife's bed. Years more passed before the impostor was ousted (and hanged for his deception) by the return of the real, and by now peg-legged Martin. Martin's silence had been voluntary. But posts were for governments and the rich. Not even the constant fall-out of deserters and walking wounded necessarily brought news within reach of radii that would relay it home. Voluntarily or not, the soldier passed a check-point of talk and messages that left him the more dependent on the military society he joined beyond it.

One last separating influence of that society may be mentioned. On leaving the civilian world the recruit also left the dense patterning of its laws.

We need not be concerned with jurisdictional debate that went on far above the soldier's head: the questioning of how far rulers could delegate legal powers to commanders-in-chief in their role as royal lieutenants; the validity of the notion that there should be a separate form of justice for soldiers because there was one for clergy and for merchants; the challenges to the competence of military courts of appeal (those of marshal, constable or war council, depending on the country concerned) to try cases between soldiers and civilians; the shifting of emphasis within the zone of military law itself between these somewhat remote organs and the day-to-day sentences, which included maiming and death, of on-the-spot courts martial and the even less formal judicial bodies summoned by provosts – officials ever more desperate to give teeth to campaign codes while periods in strategic camp or siege-lines grew longer and longer, and thus the theoretical distinctions between civilian and military crimes narrower and narrower.

These issues were of little concern to the recruit, who was greeted by proclamations and, from the 1540s, printed hand-outs, to the effect that he would be hanged if he deserted, fined if he gambled, imprisoned if he failed either to bury his excrement or go well outside the limit of the lines to relieve himself; lists of rules to be read or listened to, and, when reception in camp or the town chosen as a *place d'armes* was orderly, sworn to, that had a completeness and a direct personal application which sharply distinguished them from a vaguer awareness of civilian laws.

It was not that soldiers escaped the law but that they moved into a judicial world in some respects more tolerant (thieving from civilians), in all cases more summary in its execution. Cases concerning ransoms, points of honour in quarrels between commanders, suits brought by civilian authorities against the military: these were likely, after a preliminary hearing by court martial (senior officers, usually advised by a professional lawyer), to be passed up to central, 'political' courts. It was the proclaimed or published campaign code, or Articles of War, that determined the rules of the soldier's world. There was much that was traditional and international in these codes. All strove to prevent disobedience, desertion, taking unauthorized leave, changing sides, sleeping on watch, betraying the password, selling arms, brawls, blasphemy, the alienation of civilians, conspiracy, the ill-treatment of victuallers, contesting the harbingers' choice of lodgings.

From the early sixteenth century military leaders took an increasing interest in one another's codes. Coligny's published Articles of 1551 were based on those of Guillaume du Bellay, proclaimed in 1537 when he was Francis I's lieutenant in Piedmont, and on the 1545 code of Giovanni Caraccioli, prince of Melfi; both of these incorporated material from Ferdinand of Hungary's code of 1526. In 1590 Elizabeth instructed the earl of Essex to devise for the Rouen campaign a code based alike on Leicester's and that of his adversary the duke of Parma. In the same year the first code actually passed as permanent legislation by central government was published by the States General of the Dutch United Provinces. Based, again, on Leicester's personal code of 1585, it came to be copied by other governments and thus promoted ad hoc rules to the status of international convention.

The Dutch code, in spite of its eighty-two Articles, accepted its incompleteness: 'All other abuses and derelictions, not specified in this ordinance, shall be punished in accordance with the Decrees, Laws and Customs of War.' For over a century, however, codes had been becoming more elaborate and more specific in naming penalties: fines, stripping of rank or privileges, imprisonment, death by hanging or (for officers) either beheading or – towards the end of the period – execution by firing squad. Armed with clearer instructions, the provost's courts of summary justice became correspondingly more powerful at the expense of courts martial, the assembly of which could be subject to long delays, and of appeals to the 'political' military tribunals. Rough justice, with its gibbets and armed posses, gave an edge to rule-breaking much sharper within armies than outside them.

In this chapter we have been concerned with describing a process of militarization primarily dependent on an ambience sufficiently different from life outside army concentrations to justify cautious reference to 'the society of soldiers'. The drawbacks of that society, quite apart from the higher incidence of disease, maiming and death, are as important as are its Cockayne aspects in establishing that difference. The swift savagery of military justice (though the chopped-off hand and wrenched-out tongue were not imposed on men paid to fight and pass on orders) was one such drawback. It was compounded by the disciplinary powers granted by convention to captains. Just what these were, apart from fines and demotions, is unclear. There were complaints from Spanish units in the Netherlands of arbitrary floggings. The Dutch code recognized the soldier's dependence that placed his pay and promotion within his captain's discretion, and Article 65 was aimed at checking its abuse. 'If any soldier shall have committed a fault or misdeed, his captain shall be required (on pain of being suspended from his position for three months) to place the man in the hands of the general, or the commander of the quarter [in camp], who with the captains, lieutenants and ensigns present, shall give judgment according to the evidence that he shall take for this purpose, following this Ordinance and Articles of War.'

The code also attempted to deal – for every military regulation, whether against blasphemy, drunkenness or slipping through the lines in search of a woman or a clutch of eggs, was a stable-door tribute to what was fundamentally incorrigible – with those other abuses practised by captains: underpayment, cooking the muster book, bribing men to leave other companies to join their own. Of these, only the first was against the interest of the common soldier. Among the many abuses and corruptions that hurt him – inadequate supplies of food or their soaring prices, the career insecurity that arose from captains' desire, on partial winter demobilization, to dismiss the best men (who were paid extra from his bonus fund) first; contract clothes that shrank and shoes whose soles dissolved – the worst was the non-arrival of pay. As Leicester wrote to Francis Walsingham from the Netherlands: 'There was no soldier yet able to buy himself a pair of hose, and it is too great shame to see how they go, and it kills their hearts to be seen among men.' Hedgingly, the Articles faced this issue, too. 'No one', it ran, 'shall create an uproar because of this, nor make mutinous speeches, nor try to force his captain to make payments nor any the less perform and truly hold his marches and guards. But he shall content himself with a reasonable partial pay until the money arrives or can arrive, doing everything that good soldiers and cavalrymen are responsible to do, and anyone who shall do anything to the contrary or participates in such action, shall be punished with death.' Death was also the penalty for holding any 'common meeting or assembly . . . whether to demand money or anything else'.

The almost chronic inability of governments to produce pay on time meant that from among those who did not desert because of it, there was constantly the threat of mutinies; and governments were well aware that these were primarily caused by themselves. Apart from the early *Landsknecht* bands, and the national pride that was strengthened among the Swiss by the knowledge that they were, for three generations at least, universally regarded with a special fear and respect, and the *esprit de corps* that developed within the long-service Spanish tercios in the Netherlands, nothing so fused a sense of solidarity among soldiers off the battlefield as mutiny. When orders came from Henry VIII to reduce the strength of the Tournai garrison in 1515, the men demonstrated in front of the governor's house chanting 'All! All! All!' until they were promised that the order would be rescinded; just as previously they had all shouted 'Money! Money! Money!' until being assured that pay would be forthcoming. Among Spanish armies in the Netherlands there were forty-six mutinies between 1572 and 1607, some lasting a full year, the procedure becoming practically institutionalized, with forces up to 4000-strong occupying some strong-point, appointing a leader, drawing up their own stringent Articles of conduct and punishment, levying a reasoned subsistence charge on citizens and neighbouring villages, forming, in fact, a self-disciplined military force stripped of those officers who did not wish to be tarred with the mutinous brush and of any higher command or government commissaries. If circumstances made it necessary, these self-made unofficial units would fight the common enemy, and with an order, bravery and success that both smacked of the Bohemian Taborite 'heretic' forces of the 1420s and those of the German Peasant Wars of 1524–6, and pointed towards the revolutionary armies of the distant future.

Their purpose, however, was not revolution but blackmail.

There was nothing ideological about their aims. Pay on time, food in sufficiency and at a fair price, provision for the sick or wounded, punishments that were not too casually, arbitrarily cruel: mutineers protested against the failure of authority to protect working conditions, not against social systems or war aims. Military protest movements could be rich in insult, as when one of the striking Spanish soldiers during the Neapolitan campaign of 1501 shouted at their normally highly respected commander, Gonzalo de Cordoba, who was explaining that he was not responsible for their arrears of pay, 'Sell your daughter and you'll find the money!' They could be sullen go-slows, as when the 1512 English expeditionary force in Spain had to be shipped home again without striking into Guyenne. They could turn berserk, as during the aftermath of the sack of Rome in 1527 or the almost equally ghastly Spanish sack of Antwerp in 1576. They could bring small wars to an end, affect strategic plans; to more conjectural effect, news (and veterans) of them could influence insurrectionary impulses – also chiefly caused by poverty, food shortages and judicial arbitrariness – at home. Indeed, because of the conservatism of their demands, and what was by and large the moderation of their conduct, mutinies have been likened to popular revolts among civilians similarly emboldened to lash out when on the brink of being forced over the edge of tolerable existence.

Linked as they were by the absence of an ideological flywheel and by the dominance of local issues that produced local reactions (for mutinies developed in single garrisons or scattered units rather than in armies as a whole), the heterogeneity of social, occupational and national origin of soldiers' protests did distinguish mutiny, as did its armament and its ability to squeeze a tourniquet against the arteries of governmental policy, from the protests of civilians. Army service followed a separation from civilian society that generated its own risky brand of defiance. It is only from this assumption that we can understand why large numbers of men, not only individual daredevils, attained the morale that enabled them to fight, and fight again; watching the vanquished returning from the field of Marignano in 1515, some missing a limb, others carried on their companions' backs, an onlooker was reminded of the stricken souls in Dante's *Inferno*.

To follow soldiers as they filed off from camp and billets, leaving behind the civilian providers of services and the support host of camp-followers for the isolating uncertainty of a battle site, is to become progressively more uneasy about the status of the evidence that might suggest conclusions about combat morale. That with so many undertrained men an army was not automatically an efficient fighting force was assumed. The need for something that could compensate for the lack of a shared sense of caste destiny, something that might link raw groups and professional bands with a scattering of battle adrenalin was taken for granted by a convention – the eve-of-combat harangue – whose use is difficult to assess but which was clearly assumed to be if not routinely essential, at least likely to be supportive.

'Fellow soldiers,' Monluc represented himself as saying in 1544 to his unit before they moved against the opposing *Landsknechts* at Cerisoles, 'let us now fight bravely, and if we win the battle we gain a greater renown than any of our men ever did before. History records that up to now, every time the French fought the Germans hand to hand, the Germans got the victory. To prove that we are better men than our own ancestors we must fight with double courage to over-come them, or to die – and to make them recognize the kind of men we are!' Then he added: 'Gentlemen, it may be that there are not many here who have ever been in battle before. So let me tell you that if we take our pikes by the butt, and fight at the full pike's length, we shall be defeated. . . . You must grasp your pike in the middle, as the Swiss do, and run at full speed into the midst of them; and you will see how staggered they will be.'

Within the context of his down-to-earth memoirs the exhortation, especially its change of direction, rings true. But did he actually speak it?

Machiavelli, constantly alert to the importance of morale, had roundly endorsed the importance of the pep-talk. 'Many things may prove the ruin of an army if the general does not frequently harangue his men: for by that he may dispel their fear, inflame their courage, confirm their resolutions, point out the snares that are laid for them, promise them rewards, inform them of danger and the way to escape it, rebuke, entreat, threaten, reproach and encourage.' But he was, if not a classical scholar, a do-it-yourself humanist. Vegetius, whom he followed enthusiastically, had laid down that 'a general can encourage and animate his troops by suitable exhortations and harangues. . . . He should employ every argument capable of exciting rage, hatred and indignation against their adversaries in the minds of his soldiers.' Cicero, in one of his Philippics, justified his oration by saying, 'I shall act as commanders commonly act when the line is in battle array; although they may see their soldiers absolutely prepared for battle, they nonetheless exhort them.' Unexpectedly attacked by the Nervii, Caesar explains in his *Commentaries* that he 'had everything to do at one moment: the flag to raise as signal of a general call to arms, the trumpet to sound, the troops to recall from entrenching, the men to bring in who had gone somewhat farther afield in search of material . . . the line to form, the troops to harangue, the signal to give. . . . Caesar gave the necessary commands, and then went in a chance direction to harangue the troops, and came to the Tenth Legion. His harangue was no more than a charge to bear in mind their ancient valour, to be free from fear, and bravely to withstand the onslaught of the enemy. Then, as the enemy were no farther off than the range of a missile, he gave the signal to engage. He started off at once in the other direction to give a like harangue, and found them already fighting.' With such evidence buttressed by the reports of harangues in the works of such constantly cited historians as Livy, Sallust and Quintus Curtius, it is not surprising that they turn up in well-read medieval chroniclers like William of Malmesbury and Henry of Huntingdon, that Christine de Pisan in her reformist paraphrase of Vegetius of 1408–9 should give a sample harangue to be delivered by the commander to 'all the captains of the host', or that a century later not only Machiavelli and Erasmus but Seyssel should all, within a few years of one another, independently dwell on the importance of the spoken word in toning up morale. The harangue, as the last author put it, 'puts great heart into a whole army, to the point of making them courageous as lions where hitherto they had been as frightened as sheep'. Writing in 1528 the history of his own times, Francesco Vettori explained that in his accounts of battles he had missed out the harangues in the interest of saving space in what was, as its title claimed, no more than a *Sommario della istoria d'Italia*. In 1557 there appeared the first collection of harangues, the *Orationi militari* edited by Remigio Nannini. François de Belleforest's *Harangues militaires* of 1573 contained no fewer than 1434 pages of them.

All the same . . . given the Renaissance fascination with the techniques, and assumptions about the power, of rhetoric, and the imitativeness of historians together with their belief that history should provide models of behaviour as well as be true: were harangues actually given? Louis Le Roy bitterly regretted that the custom had lapsed in France, 'whence it has followed that many kings and great lords are poorly followed and supported in war'. Really? We do not have to answer this doubt by reference to military treatises, almost all of which, published or unpublished, take the usefulness of the pep-talk for granted and frequently offer models for adaptation. In 1513 Venice's commander-in-chief, Bartolomeo Alviano, is reliably reported as having tried to animate the shaken conglomerate of his last-ditch army by telling them how right they were to hate the foreign enemy, 'barbarians, the pillagers and incendiaries [they had set fire to Mestre, on the very margin of the Venetian lagoon] of Italy'; how they would be not only paid their arrears in full but in this extremity could keep the whole of any loot they took and kill prisoners if they wished; how, if he had offended anyone since he took over the command he regretted it, and would share every danger with those he knew would demonstrate their native bravery. In 1545 Elis Gruffydd reproached the earl of Surrey with failing to encourage his men 'with tender, kindly, godly words'. Michel de Castelnau reported how, at a crucial moment during the 1562 siege of Rouen the duke of Guise stood before the breach before calling his men to assault it 'and harangued the captains and soldiers . . . and I was present'.

It is not to be imagined that Guise was as eloquent before his breach as was Shakespeare's Henry V before his on the London stage. Nor, perhaps, can any fully reported harangue be trusted to have avoided subsequent embellishment. The model speeches do, however, suggest the themes commanders could have touched on: our own strength compared to the enemy's weakness; our own superiority as a people as opposed to the craven/vainglorious/bestial/godless foe; remember the great martial tradition of your forefathers; your wives and children depend on you to protect their lives and innocence; remember the loyalty you owe your ruler; your leaders will share every risk with you and, as eyewitnesses or receivers of reports, will make sure that your deeds of heroism do not go unrewarded; God is on our side. Some added cogency is given to this repertory of motifs by the differing emphasis given to them as the period proceeds. From the Reformation onwards the theme of the just cause which God will surely aid becomes more prominent, while as wars became more expensive and governments more anxious to recoup some of their cost, decreasing stress is placed on the plunder that will fall to the troops themselves. Reflecting the humanist cult of fame as well as the increasing documentation of war by historians, memoir-writers and compilers of military anecdotes, added emphasis is given to the immortal memory that would enshrine gallant deeds and heroic deaths.

Further verisimilitude is given not only by clear indications that (in an age of motley language components in an army and without loud-hailers) such speeches, though aimed at the whole force, were in fact delivered to a meeting of subordinate commanders who would then pass on the substance to their men, but also by a telling piece of counter-evidence. Luigi da Porto observed that when Gaston de Foix was poised for his attack on the city of Brescia in 1512, his captains begged him that before ordering the attack he should 'comfort the army [the assault group] by speaking to them. He answered that little or no weight could be given to any commander's words in such a situation. For no address or allocution could be delivered with sufficient eloquence to make timid and effeminate men fiery and courageous in a day, or help those who did not know how to handle sword or pike or couch a lance ready and able to do so.'

De Foix's youthful haughtiness, his organizational pragmatism and chilly impersonal recklessness make him, perhaps, a case apart. Few other commanders, given the composition of their forces, could have been unaware of the effect of reassurance given even to experienced men by 'a little touch of Harry in the night'.

It was also recognized that men could join up in a spirit of excitement that soon wore off unless they were got on the move within a few days. Thanks to shoe-leather transport, delays caused by allies and the settling of mercenary contracts, getting an army together was a slow business. But the recruit thus had time to be conditioned by military society before facing action. It was recognized, too, that morale improved the further men were serving away from their homes. In armies of mixed national components, patriotic pride affected morale. Commanders threatened to decamp if 'their' contingent was not given a conspicuous place of danger in the vanguard, or in the first wave of a siege assault (at Gournay in 1591 the French and English contingents had to have separate breaches opened for them by the artillery). It is difficult to bring into focus either the religious feelings of individuals or the eve-of-battle role of the clergy. Both faiths preached the need for penitence before men ran the hazard of meeting their maker. Catholic chaplains, unable to hear the confessions of large numbers, granted mass absolutions, though pointing out that these would only be valid if each man had strictly examined his own conscience. Such absolutions were popularly believed to 'last' during months of scattered skirmishes, ambushes, the scores of priestless actions that made up the death texture of campaigns, regardless of a man's intervening behaviour. But outside Machiavelli's nostalgia for the gods-supported battle spirit of the Romans there is little in the literature of war that connects religion with morale, no advocacy of a priest's as opposed to a commander's harangue. Though in the rich clerical literature justifying any tolerably 'just' war, there were cautions that to fight in an unjust one was to imperil the soul, there was no counter-balancing assurance that to die in battle, even against the infidel, was to increase, let alone guarantee, salvation. More general comfort for fearful men came from tobacco, increasingly in use from the 1560s, and, for those who could afford it, brandy; the rum ration still lay in the future.

In one of the period's rare extended comments on the nature of morale, Jean de Bueil, in his *Le Jouvencel* of *c.* 1466, invoked God's approval of the warrior's trade but explained motivation in terms of comradeship and battle fervour.

'I believe that God favours those who risk their lives by their readiness to make war to bring the wicked, the oppressors, the conquerors, the proud and all those who deny true equity, to justice. War . . . is a proper and useful career for young men, for which they are respected both by God and man. You love your comrade so much in war. When you see that your quarrel is just and your blood is fighting well, tears rise to your eyes. A great sweet feeling of love and pity fills your heart on seeing your friend so valiantly exposing his body to execute and accomplish the command of our Creator. And then you prepare to go and live or die with him, and for love not to abandon him. And out of that there arises such a delectation, that he who has not tasted it is not fit to say what a delight it is. Do you think that a man who does that fears death? Not at all: for he feels strengthened, he is so elated that he does not know where he is. Truly he is afraid of nothing.'

Stilted, aristocratic as it is, the passage illumines the atmosphere of such moments as that in which the rebels closed in on Norwich during the Norfolk rising of 1549 with arrows sticking out of their bodies which they tugged out and handed to their own archers to shoot back, while they pressed on, yelling, to the walls; or that in which the overconfident tercios forced their commanders to commit them to being massacred at the battle of Heiligerlee in 1568.

Thomas Coningsby's journal of his participation in the siege of Rouen in 1591 shows war as an adventure which quickly imposes its own rules of endurance and risk. 'This evening there are pickaxes and spades brought us to entrench our selves, which we are doing . . . we here are well and eat and drink that we can get, and lie upon the straw, and for many of us never better in our healths in all our lives and many times less contented.' He relishes the diversions of siege-line life: challenges to single combat; skirmishes 'where the people of the town stood upon the bulwarks of the town and beheld it as though it had been a triumph of sport; there were slain some on both sides'; doughty boozing bouts with the Swiss 'where there was drinking to the healths of others till some of them were sick or asleep'; talk of women with men like a mercenary captain who 'if he speak three words one of them is of that sex'. Both deeds of individual daring – the night-time reconnoitring the breadth of a moat illuminated by flaming bales of straw dropped by the defenders, for instance, as well as massed advances against shot and pike, emerged from the atmosphere generated among the society of soldiers on the eve of action. Asked to comment on the lacklustre morale of Elizabeth's forces when invasion still seemed possible after the pushing of the Armada up into the North Sea, Sir Francis Drake had written reassuringly 'that the threatening of the enemy will put a great part of their weakness from her Majesty's good subjects, and no doubt but they will fight valiantly'. Coningsby's experience bears this out: 'It was a world to see how men that were before dull with daunts, sickness, and discontentation, pulled up their hearts, and grew into a wonderful hope.'

Again, that cup-bearer! The nearer the historian tries to move towards the mood of combat in this period, the less secure he must feel. Fear and its assuagement by the trustfulness of male psychological bondings; the challenging contempt of veterans; the hardships which produce a dogged base-line over which mere endurance generates a sense of exhausted pride; the on-your-mettle flashes of communication between units and comrades: these can all be suspected but only clearly grasped, from diaries, letters home and autobiographies, after the time we are dealing with. Their sharedness, their intensity, depends, moreover, on the nature, at any moment, of the society of soldiers from which they grow. When that congregation can only be defined with considerable reserve, the psychological, emotional meaning of war's central rites must be doubly veiled. It was in the midst of battles, and with reference to them, that Montaigne noted that 'the fortunes of more than halfe the world, for want of a register, stirre not from their place, and vanish away without continuance'.

7

The direct impact of war on civilians

Larger, ill-disciplined armies, extended campaigning seasons, prolonged sieges: the brush-strokes of war in the sixteenth century were broader than formerly, and probably leached out more widely into the fabric of civilian society. Compared with the spasmodic nature of the Hundred Years War, the Wars of Italy and the Netherlands were almost unremitting molestations of normal life. Guicciardini noted in the 1530s the changed impact of war on civilians who, especially after 1509, 'saw nothing but scenes of infinite slaughter, plunder and destruction of multitudes of towns and cities, attended with the licentiousness of soldiers no less destructive to friends than foes'. And as a Dutch popular ballad of the 1580s put it:

> Our fathers were in their time
> Also chastised by war's strong rod.
> But never endured its punishment for so long a time,
> Nor suffered so much ill as we unfortunates do.

There was a similar difference in intensity and scale between the French civil wars and those of the Roses. It was overall damage to life and property that forced Bodin to conclude that 'the only way to maintain the community is to make war [abroad] and to invent an enemy if there is not one to hand'.

Worse was to come with the even larger and still poorly controlled and supplied armies of the Thirty Years War of 1618–48, and their need to exploit non-combatants as the source of food, shelter and criminous or sexual diversion. But what there was was bad enough. Towards the end of the sixteenth century wolf packs, symbols of the breakdown of civilization, were reported as attacking the starving peasantry of the southern Netherlands and Brittany. Of course contemporaries exaggerated. It was in an unwonted mood of optimism that La Noue remarked that 'France is so populous and so fertile that what the war has damaged in one

179

year is restored in two'. Little credence can be given to the pioneer statistician of war casualties, Nicholas Froumenteau, who in 1581 recorded the destruction by fire of 252 villages, the death of 765,200 civilians (out of a population which had by then reached about 16 million), 12,300 rapes; war does not hold out a clean slate to such ineluctables as fire, death and ravishment. But soberer figures give a gaunt picture of what happened in areas most directly and consistently hit by war. The population of Pavia fell from 16,000 in 1500 to less than 7000 in 1529 when there were 'chyldren kreyeng abowt the streates for bred, and yet dying for hungre'. That of the Dutch textile centre Hondschoote fell from 18,000 in the 1560s to 385 in 1584. 'The voice of the poor peasant cries out to God, recorded the Estates of Flanders in 1604, and with reason. Not just a life-or-death reason; it was emigration, precautionary or forced, that accounted for by far the greatest part of local population losses. This could lead not only to survival but occasionally to a better livelihood elsewhere. But the impact of war registered on emotion as well as on life and limb. Any estimate of war's impact on civilians must allow for the effects of flight, humiliation, privation and fear. These are all the more to be borne in mind because populations generally picked up again on the return of peace as refugees returned and new immigrants arrived (Hondschoote was almost as prosperous by 1620 as it had been before the wars engulfed it), because statistically, deaths caused directly by war are scarcely discernible amidst the still rising tide of population figures as a whole, and because the great majority were not caused directly by sack or pillage or casual brutality but through a conspiracy between war and those more impersonal and far more effective killers, epidemic disease and famine.

In the seven years between 1567 and 1574 some 43,000 men left Castile to fight in the Netherlands; perhaps a quarter were to die there. The Castilian outbreak of bubonic plague in 1598–1602 caused 600,000 deaths over those four years. Plague bred fastest in overcrowded, insanitary cities. There is no clear evidence that it was fostered by the comparable concentrations of men in camp or siege-line, but diseases like influenza, dysentery and hepatitis certainly were, and they were passed, through marketing and billeting contacts and the wandering of deserters, into a civilian bloodstream often too weak to resist them. It has been estimated that the diseases spread in 1627–8 by a French army of 6000, as they marched and camped between La Rochelle and Montferrat, led to the deaths of over 1 million civilians.

Too weak because undernourished. It was by exacerbating existing food shortages that war won its most pathetic trophies. It won them partly by engrossing foodstuffs for military hordes whose presence upset the local balance of production and consumption even in a good year. These increases were not limited to a war zone, but could affect, for example, the local price of the residue of salt beef and grain that had been bought in bulk in Naples for shipment to the Netherlands; the feeding of a garrison in Flanders could thus break the budget of a peasant in Calabria. Hunger riots in the English counties of Hampshire, Gloucester and Suffolk followed their stripping of grain for the army in Ireland and meat for the Netherlands expeditionary force. And meanwhile wars had to be paid for by increased personal taxation and by heavier tolls and sales taxes on the transport and purchase of essential commodities: wine, grain, meat, cloth, firewood, salt. Tax collectors, customs men, clerks of the market: these were the officers of war's financial alter ego and, though unarmed (if sometimes supported by armed guards), they contributed to its casualty lists.

Prices rose, too, because of 'unofficial' shortages caused by the devastation of the countryside by armies fanning out from the march or marauding from camp, as well as by the loss of the age's only fertilizer, manure, after the driving off of livestock to provide armies with meat on the hoof. When epidemics eased, reduced numbers could set to in unspoiled fields and intact workshops: war left proportionately greater numbers to face capital damage that made recovery a more painful process. Meanwhile purchasing power was falling, especially in towns, as a result of the loss of artisan jobs that followed the interruption of trade: underemployment was another 'normal' problem intensified by war. Through its effect on prices and purchasing power, bullet war's connection with social war (bread riots, peasant insurrections) had never been closer. The sense of shock expressed by contemporaries when Englishmen came to blows with one another during the Wars of the Roses was out of proportion to the scale of actual military campaigns, which amounted to sixty-one weeks over a period of thirty years, but the battles gave publicity to long-familiar non-war-related miseries and resentments: hunger and joblessness, haves and have-nots. The peasant revolt which convulsed Inner Austria in 1515 was triggered by the extra taxation Maximilian I had been imposing to fund his anti-Venetian wars. But the peasants' list of complaints only mentioned the underlying grievances that were goaded into violent expression: the misappropriation of tax revenue by its collectors, excessive labour services, unreasonable fines imposed by local courts, falsified scales and measures in markets, debasement of the coinage so that the kreutzer no longer bought the same amount of food as it had in the past, limitations by landlords on the traditional rights of the peasantry to fish, hunt and collect wood. If there was so little challenge to a ruler's right to go to war, or considered protest against war as such, this was because war, for all its dramatic apparatus, was experienced as a last straw on the burden of familiar forms of deprivation.

Much of the suffering inflicted by the soldiery on non-combatants arose from the inability of civilian society to deal with large numbers of men on the move. Even mass pilgrimages, which provided the only comparable concentrations of transients needing to be fed and housed, were regarded fearfully, and led to outbreaks of violence at their destination, Compostela or Rome. Yet pilgrims were, in theory at least, meek and peaceable folk, representing one of the best instincts of the populations through which they moved; moreover, their routes, goals and timetables were – in contrast to the peregrinations of armies – regular and could be anticipated well in advance. The military routes which most resembled pilgrim ways, the Dauphiné corridor used by French armies en route to or returning from Italy in the first half of the sixteenth century, the 'Spanish Road' between Savoy and Luxembourg used by troops going to the Netherlands in the second half, both led to military-civilian friction, although we have seen that food stores were accumulated in advance at their stopping points and the legal and financial modes for settling claims to compensation for theft and damage had been carefully elaborated.

No system, however ingenious or responsible, could protect a breadline community from an artificial population surge. The legal situation was clear: anything soldiers took that had not been bought in advance by the army's commissary service, whether food or drink, straw or firewood, should have been paid for. In the ordinances of war issued by Henry VII in 1487 at the start of his campaign against Lambert Simnel, he forbade any soldier to 'presume to take any manner of victual, horse meat, or man's meat, without paying therefor the reasonable price thereof assigned by the clerk of the market or other king's officer therefor ordained, upon pain of death'. His billeting order was similarly designed to protect civilians: so that 'no manner of person or persons, whatsoever they be, take upon them to lodge themselves nor take no manner of lodging nor haborage but such as shall be assigned unto him or them by the King's harbinger, nor dislodge no man, nor change no lodging after that to be assigned, without advice and assent of the said harbinger, upon pain of imprisonment and to be punished at the will of our said sovereign lord'.

Similar ordinances were proclaimed for armies of all nationalities throughout the century, it being in no commander's interest, save when deliberately scorching the earth or when entirely deprived of cash or credit, to alienate the population who possessed the rations and roofs to keep his army fed, reasonably comfortable and, in poor weather, fit. Implementing them was another matter.

The 'reasonable price' of foodstuffs could be maintained in camp or town by victualling officers when distributing bulk supplies earmarked for troops; and if the latter could not pay, they might be given credit. But official purchases were seldom adequate, especially when foul weather or sickness delayed the march. So additional 'official' purchases on the spot created shortages which raised prices for civilian consumers (producers, if they could organize transport fast enough, could make good short-term profits), and private transactions might be made clamorous, often violent, by the discrepancy between official and 'free' prices which no clerk of the market could control, particularly when the 'purchasers' had already gambled and drunk themselves out of credit with their captains and shopped with threats and blows rather than money. Even when the army had moved on, scarcity prices continued to oppress the poor because of the aftermath of crop destruction and beast-stealing caused by its troops and camp-followers when on the road. The cutting of fruit trees and timber for fires and shelters along the line of march also added its mite of interest to the cost of living.

These generalizations seem applicable to the period as a whole, though each campaign had its own timbre of civilian-soldier relationships. Relations varied within single campaigns. The main force of Henry VIII's French invasion of 1544, directed against Boulogne, in great measure owed its success, and, in the main, its acceptance by locals, to efficient victualling, whereas the division sent against Montreuil, not only because of poor official victualling failed to achieve its object, but left the countryside stripped and destitute: when a woman, begging for bread, was offered money by a soldier, her reply was 'God in heaven, what should I do with money, or anything else but bread, and only a little of that, so that we can eat it now, because we do not dare to store it for fear of the wild men.'

The abuse of billeting could lead to bullying, sexual crime and theft, and though householders were entitled to compensation via tax rebates from regional authorities, damage and loss weighed all the heavier on poor householders because of the delays in receiving it: five years in a Venetian case settled in 1613, eight in a claim submitted by villagers in Lorraine in 1587. But at least problems arising from lodging troops in wartime were restricted to the line of march, whereas the less immediately dramatic consequences of victualling reached out far into civilian society.

Naturally, civilian interests were brushed aside when making military decisions. That this was taken for granted is shown by a conversation overheard near the Calais Pale between two Frenchmen during the truce period between England and France. This would be a good time to attack Calais, said one of them. 'And even in one night we may burn all that country and destroy them, even to the hard gates of the said town; and so, their victuals destroyed, it was not possible for them to continue one half year's space without yielding of themselves.'

Of the most shocking aspect of war's direct impact on civilians, a deliberate scorched-earth policy, there are few early modern examples. In 1483, in a desperate attempt to complete the conquest of Granada, some 30,000 men were raised in Castile to destroy crops there. But as this was a crusade against the infidel, no moral problem was raised. In 1536, to counter Charles V's invasion of Provence, Francis I ordered the evacuation of Aix and the destruction of mills, stocks of wood, grain, salt and wine, the filling in of wells, and the driving off of farm animals from the land southward towards Marseilles; peasant resistance was brushed aside by the military, who then withdrew. The stratagem worked. Unable to force a fight, or supply his men, Charles was forced to retreat. From at least 1522 English commanders tried to bring the Scots to heel and forsake their French allies by burning farms and villages; in 1544 Edinburgh, Leith and other towns were attacked in this blackmail vein and the earl of Surrey reassured Henry VIII that they had been 'well burnt'. English armies employed artificial famine again as a weapon against the Irish from 1593, and were answered in kind. Sir Arthur Chichester's report to Mountjoy of a punitive raid along Lough Neagh is not untypical: 'We have killed, burnt and spoiled all along the lough within four miles of Dungannon, . . . in which journeys we have killed above one hundred people of all sorts, besides such as were burnt, how many I know not. We spare none of what quality or sex soever, and it has bred much terror in the people, who heard not a drum nor saw not a fire there for a long time.' Most notorious was Alba's encouragement of sack and massacre at Malines, Utrecht, Zutphen and Naarden in 1572. He considered this justified when dealing with rebels and heretics, though, as he wrote to Philip, 'God grant that the rest will learn from it and that it will not be necessary to . . . go from town to town with the army of Your Majesty.' These were the horrors that prompted an Antwerp merchant to comment that 'the wars in these provinces are the worst that have ever been', and – to little strategic effect – launched the Black Legend that the Spaniards were as bestially cruel in the Old as they had been to the Indians in the New World.

If such examples of destruction as a deliberate policy were unusual, the firebrand remained a valid symbol of war. To burn a farm or village which, together with its animals, had been evacuated on the news of an army's approach, was a regular outlet for baffled appetite; anticipating it was part of the agonizing calculation whether to flee or take a chance with the mood or discipline of a military unit. Burning as a threat to extort food or money was so common that, at least in Germany, a certificate known as the *Brandschatzung* was issued to houseowners who had paid 'fire tax' to protect their homes, and they were safe as long as they could display it and soldiers were not too desperate to ignore it. The same system was used, on a quasi-official basis, by the Spanish in the Netherlands between 1578 and 1591 and officially by the Dutch themselves in 1590. According to their Articles of War published in that year, 'No one may do anything or cause anything to be done against any persons, cities, countrysides, villages, castles, harbours or other properties which are provided with safeguard certificates or other security from the Generality, on pain of death.' How far 'contributions', as this stand-and-deliver form of war taxation came to be known, were viewed as illegitimate extortion or a form of payment welcome for the protection given by the certificate-receipt, depended on the political sympathies of those paying. On the whole it did mitigate the violence from individual soldiers or units from which civilians could never be entirely safe, though villagers still took the precaution of forming *Huisliedengilde*, self-defence groups supplied with weapons by the military authorities (aware that they might have to be used against terrorizing soldiers of their own) but otherwise unsupervised.

They were never safe largely because the behaviour of soldiers was incalculable but also because of the uncertainty in the minds of their officers as to the status of non-combatants. Military codes, which saw the persecution of non-combatants as, rather like gambling and wenching, a threat to military discipline, were protective, especially as far as a ruler's own taxpayers were concerned: 'Soldiers travelling within the queen's majesty's realm or dominions may not slay any cattle or fowl, take anything to another appertaining to use the same as his own, [or] start out of the way to fight, quarrel or defraud,' as a handbook for English captains of 1562 repeated. But for lawyers or legally minded laymen the issue was not so straightforward. In his *Discourse of War* of 1558, Ascanio Centorio wrote that as improved fortifications have slowed the pace of war, it was best to lay waste the countryside and rely on fear and starvation rather than assault. And – the firebrand motif again – he justified this harsh advice on the grounds that 'it is much better for the people to suffer from a single act of incendiarism, however drastic, than from the many fires that are the consequence of a long-drawn-out campaign'. Something of the background whence this sentiment emerged can be grasped from a conversation the great Spanish jurist, Francisco de Vitoria, who died in 1546, had with a member of Charles V's Royal Council about the standing of those who have no say either in the planning or the waging of a war. The councillor 'thought it expedient for the proper waging of a war that everyone should be killed'. Vitoria's own qualification was, 'firstly, that everyone able to bear arms should be considered dangerous and must be assumed to be defending the enemy king; they may therefore be killed unless the opposite is clearly true, i.e., unless it is obvious that they are harmless. I believe, secondly, that when it is essential for victory it is lawful to kill the innocent.' He instances the bombardment of a town. Once the town had surrendered, however, 'one must not kill the innocent on purpose when it is possible to separate them from the guilty'. And in another work he wrote that it was wrong to kill 'harmless country people and the rest of the peaceful non-combatants who are presumed innocent unless the opposite is proved'. But who, in the heat of danger, rage or vengefulness, would stop to distinguish the innocent: could anyone, save children, be absolved from guilt when they might have offered succour to one of their own side or refused it – by hiding produce or running away – to your own? 'Grown women who march with the enemy', wrote a later theologian and jurist, also a Spaniard, Luis de Molina, 'or are beside them in a besieged town are usually not free from blame, but are as a rule helping the enemy. For this reason they are not to be considered as having the same degree of innocence as children, though it is safer [to one's conscience] to leave them alive when their guilt is not established.'

En route to the acceptance of the idea that there could be an internationally accepted law of war, such opinions are worth quoting because they play an intellectualizing light over the practical assumptions *jus in bello* had to come to terms with, in this case that anyone who was not for you was potentially against you. Campaign codes offered redress through martial courts. But, especially when an army was in enemy territory, they were seldom prepared to listen to civilian pleas unless the plaintiff carried political or financial weight or raised an issue which, by leading to the making of an example of a soldier, could improve security or protect supplies – in the cases, for instance, of a soldier slipping against orders out of camp and becoming involved in a tavern brawl, or of an assault on a sutler bringing food to camp. For crimes committed by troops on the move civilians had little hope of redress. Though armies moved at foot pace, the law moved far more slowly. And as armies now perched and now moved on in the continually redesigned jigsaws of civilian-military interlockings, there were basic uncertainties of jurisdiction that encouraged the settlement of conflicts by violence rather than by due process.

Save, then, when an army was quartered in its own country, or crucially dependent on fair relations with civilians when campaigning abroad, the non-combatant was at the mercy of the soldier's mood and need.

'They say there is no satisfaction to be made for what is done in war, for all things are lawful there,' says the soldier in one of Erasmus's *Colloquies*.

'You mean by the law of arms, I suppose?' the author's spokesman asks.

'You are right.'

'But the law is the highest injustice. It was not the love of your country, but the love of booty that made you a soldier.'

'I confess so, and I believe very few go into the army with any better design.'

Slanted as Erasmus's colloquies always are, there is little doubt that soldiers, almost as soon as they had ceased to be civilians, thought of the latter as fair game. In a letter written from the Netherlands in 1575 a German officer in Spanish service boasted that 'when we have devoured everything in one place, we travel further, we gobble and guzzle at the farmer's expense'; a Utrecht chronicler may, then, be trusted when he wrote (of the previous year) that the troops were 'robbing and plundering as if the peasants were enemies'. An earlier example is typical of the period as a whole. In November 1494 Charles VIII, Florence's ally, was in the city waiting for reinforcements before moving on to Naples. 'This morning', Luca Landucci wrote of the 27th, 'more of the troops from Romagna reached Dicomano, and were quartered there, about twenty horses being put into my place. I left my son Benedetto there, and they nearly slew him several times, though he paid them proper respect, as I had impressed on him. It was at great cost to us. . . . 29th November. The rest of the King's troops which were in Romagna went past here, coming from San Godenzo to Dicomano and to the Ponte a Sieve, and then going along the upper valley of the Arno, doing much damage. At Corello they slew about eleven men, and took others prisoners and placed ransoms upon them; ruining all the country like a flame of fire. The wall of my house at Dicomano was broken, and also all the locks, whilst my farm was entered forcibly and suffered not a little, the wine and corn being consumed, and any household goods to which they took a fancy being carried off. Those whom they slew at Corello were certain old men who had come to receive them, but there was a misunderstanding. It is true that at first certain young men had come out and tried to force them back, but these old men caused the others to desist; these brutes of Frenchmen, however, struck them on the head and left them lying dead in the fields; and they committed cruelties on all sides. 30th November. Nothing else was spoken of but these cruelties.'

And because non-combatants were conditioned to believe the worst of soldiers, such stories lost nothing in the telling. In 1501 Landucci reported of Cesare Borgia's troops that as they moved from the Romagna against Florence (which he was treating as an enemy) his men had forced a girl to have intercourse with her brother, while 'some others, finding a young husband and wife, bound the husband to a pillar, and in his presence dishonoured the woman shamefully'. Compared with the plain story of violence in a district near at hand and in which he had property of his own, this is hearsay. But not necessarily baseless: there is documentary evidence throughout the period to show that the folklore of atrocity was based on the reality of crime. The difficulty is, rather, to establish the extra incidence war induced in crimes which were familiar enough in peacetime and which in many cases were committed by men who were already hardened criminals or perverts before enlistment (like the Neapolitan soldier who set up a children's brothel in Valencia for homosexuals when in garrison there). Some of them had, after all, been expressly offered pardons in return for their service.

Armies which were regularly paid and supervised by responsible officers could live on reasonably amicable terms with civilians. Two main factors caused the breakdown in this always tense symbiosis. One was peculiar to civil wars in which public conflict was used as an excuse for paying off private scores: abducting a previously unobtainable bride, slaying a rival who could now be dubbed an enemy or traitor or heretic, forcibly occupying a coveted property. Not for nothing had Henry VII after Bosworth warned the disbanding armies to 'pick no quarrels for old or new matters' on pain of death. The second was far more general and had, at least to begin with, little to do with any pyschological or cultural distinction between combatants and non-combatants: arrears of what were in any case most frugally adequate wages. Of the Spanish occupying forces in Naples in 1504, cut off from supplies of cash, Guicciardini noted that 'Ever since the times of [classical] antiquity, in which military discipline was severely imposed, the soldiery had always been licentious and burdensome to the people, yet they never gave themselves up to all manner of disorders, but lived for the most part on their pay . . . the Spaniards in Italy were the first that presumed to maintain themselves wholly on the substance of the people.' And he grimly, and rightly, added: 'This was the beginning of a corruption which soon spread.' It reached its peak in those frequent mutinies by Spanish units in the Netherlands when pay was in arrears and commissary stores barren. It would be difficult, however, to show that it was a corruption actively relished by the majority of men or their commanders. Asking for money for his troops from the *parlement* at Aix, the Catholic League commander, Carcès, proudly said that hitherto 'I have never fattened myself at the expense of the countryside.' 'It is deplorable', wrote Brantôme, 'that our soldiers dedicate themselves to pillage rather than to honourable feats, but it is all due to their not being paid', though he added that inadequate discipline imposed by their officers was also to blame.

That self-help at non-combatants' expense became an easily accepted habit, both for men and their officers, was eased – and here a cultural dimension can be legitimately invoked – by the assumption that peasants were scum; 'peasants', that is, in the sense of smallholders and rural wage-earners of all occupations. The view was fitfully challenged by a few clerics, humanitarian intellectuals, exceptional landlords and the handful of writers who chose to exalt pastoral simplicities as a shepherd's crook with which to beat the corrupt morals and manners of the cities. Political thinkers recognized that if pushed too far by taxation or lack of access to legal redress they could threaten the stability of the state. Authors – like Machiavelli in his short story *Belfagor* – could grant them a native cunning. Don Quixote lavished an exasperated affection on Sancho Panza. Artists had to accept that Christ's birth was revealed to shepherds. But in general the middle and upper ranks of the rural classes and practically all townsmen despised the peasant. From the German Peasants' Revolt to a frantic worms' turning against the exactions of the troops of the United Provinces at Overijssel in 1580, no educated voice was raised save in a chorus of censorious contempt. Soldiers, therefore, whatever their background, found it natural to see their own military society as having in the peasantry an endemic secondary antagonist. As in times of dearth the peasant hated the engrosser of food, so when in arrears of wages the soldier hated the non-risk-taking peasant with his smug little store of wine and grain, his chickens and his pig. With this image in mind, greed led quickly to inhumanity. Within the revolt against central government of the Comuneros was a vicious minor theme of town militias versus their supposed allies in the countryside. A Comunero quartermaster noted that 'The troops were living off the villagers without paying them anything', and that if a family had no food left to give them they calmly proceeded to take their extra clothing and household items and pawn them. And this contempt for the rural population was all the more revealing because it followed decades during which the billeting system for the permanent royal guard had revealed the same antipathy. After their extortion of food without payment in 1498, a petition was sent from Zebriliego begging to be relieved of this burden because 'previous quartering of troops had almost destroyed the villages'. Bullied by travelling bands of recruits who were hardly yet soldiers, beaten up and pillaged by troops scattering outwards from armies in search of food and loot, however humble, robbed and tortured by the gangs who used war as a cover for brigandage, it is difficult not to assume that some real sense of inferiority held peasants, when not outnumbered, from striking back. Most had weapons or scythes and pitchforks that could be used as such; many, as militiamen, had pikes and arquebuses. Certainly they could be pitiless when they came across troops who were disarmed or exhausted, and there were sufficient atrocities perpetrated against soldiers to make the threat of a 'peasants' revenge' another component of civilian-military animosity. On the other hand, rumours of counter-atrocities were probably still more terrifying. So many of Coligny's men – presumably stragglers – were set upon and killed by peasants as he crossed the Dordogne in 1569 that he sent back a force 'to teach them a lesson for their cruelties and slaughterings' which cut them down in the fields: in one phase of this anti-civilian campaign 260 were herded into the Château de la Chapelle Faucher, kept locked up for a day and then killed. 'I have often heard him confess to being repelled by acts of cruelty,' noted Brantôme, 'but he had to bend his nature in the interest of public order.'

Up to now we have been tracing aspects of war's impact on civilians in terms of armies in camp or billets or on the march. But the most drastic and direct civilian confrontation with the military was the siege. Outside the walls the effect on the peasant and village economy was literally devastating if the operation were a prolonged one; many lasted several months, some for years. The Spanish siege of Ostend, for instance, started on 15 July 1601 and ended with its capture on 25 September 1604. However effective was the organization of long-distance supply trains, the hordes in the siege-lines and perimeter base camps always needed more. They took animals and fowl first because the trains only brought salt meat; then came grain, finally straw from thatch and wood from any farm buildings not used for billets; for sieges, from that of Pavia in 1524–5 and Florence in 1529–30, to those of Metz in 1552–3 and of Haarlem in 1572–3, came to follow a logistic rather than a seasonal calendar, and cold nights were more dangerous to the troops than the besieged's raiding parties.

Inside the walls there was, by contrast, a necessary collaboration between the populace and their garrison. Armed to defend their families and property, citizen patrols could keep the proclivity of troops to break into shops as supplies ran short within bounds; indeed, there seem to have been almost as many cases of citizens profiteering at their fellows' expense. The lives of the professional soldiers depended on the support on the ramparts of all males capable of bearing arms, and also on the labour of women in repairing breaches and building secondary lines of defence behind sections of the wall that had been made vulnerable by bombardment. In Charles the Bold's unsuccessful siege of Beauvais in 1472 the women's contribution was such as to prompt Louis XI to exempt them from the sumptuary laws (a particularly relevant form of decoration). Women of all ranks toiled with spades and wheelbarrows during the Imperialist siege of Marseilles in 1524. During the eighteen-month siege of Siena in 1552–3 every girl and woman, noble and common, between twelve and fifty was registered, issued with baskets and shovels or picks and organized into district labour gangs, pledged on pain of death to drop their household tasks and hasten to the walls when the order was shouted through the streets. By thus helping to protect their lives, civilians were also putting them at risk. To a conquering siege-army there was little distinction between a soldier who fired a shot and the men and women who plied a spade against them.

It is difficult to estimate how many civilians in sieges were killed by enemy action, either in repelling assaults or through cannon and (from the last third of the sixteenth century) mortar fire. Clearer, because recorded in wails of protest and claims for compensation, was the destruction of suburbs for one and a half or two miles to ensure a clear field of sight and fire from the walls: monasteries, farms, mills, orchards, all had to go. But everyone suffered financially. Even if food convoys could occasionally break through the lines (brought over the snow by sled to Haarlem), shortages forced prices up; 'Give us bread or peace!' an armed throng chanted at the military governor of Rouen during the winter siege of 1591–2. In this case the garrison was still well fed enough to agree to charge and break it up, but only too often the military and civic authorities had anticipated such protests by reducing the number of 'useless mouths'.

In 1495, when Novara, occupied by Charles VIII's lieutenant Louis d'Orléans, was besieged by its dispossessed owner Lodovico Sforza, duke of Milan, a diarist recorded that 'the people began to eat bran bread because food was very scarce, and for this reason the duke of Orléans drove out all those of the populace who were poor and useless'. When Coligny's defence of St Quentin in 1557 was reaching crisis point he, again presumably with a divided conscience, expelled the 'useless mouths', children and the unfit. Nowhere is this logistic tactic so coolly and movingly described as in Monluc's account of what he had to do during the defence he conducted in Siena in 1553. He went to the chief civic council and announced, 'You must put the useless mouths out of town.' There was no protest. 'I thereupon created', he goes on, 'six commissaries to take a list of all the useless people. . . . The list of these useless people I do assure you amounted to 4400 or more, which of all the miseries and desolations that I have ever seen was the greatest my eyes ever yet beheld . . . and these poor wretches were to go through the enemy who beat them back again towards the city, the whole camp continuing night and day in arms to that only end: for that they drove them up to the very foot of the walls that they might the sooner consume the little bread we had left, and to see if the city out of compassion to those miserable creatures would revolt. But that prevailed nothing, though they lay eight days in this condition, when they had nothing to eat but herbs and grass, and above the one half of them perished. . . . There were a great many maids and handsome women, indeed, who found means to escape, the Spaniards by night stealing them into their quarters . . . and some strong and vigorous men also forced their way and escaped by night. But all those did not amount to the fourth part, and all the rest miserably perished.' 'These', he concluded, 'are the effects of war. We must of necessity sometimes be cruel to frustrate the designs of an enemy. God has need to be merciful to men of our trade who commit so many sins, and are the cause of many miseries and mischiefs.' The expulsion of the useless mouths did not save Siena.

Horrible as such expulsions were, and as were the sacks that too frequently celebrated the success of a final assault, the most consequential impact of siege warfare on citizens was oblique and insidious. Far more died from the effects of malnutrition and disease (intensification of endemic ones and others introduced by garrison reinforcements or a conquering army, almost always sick itself from the rigours of the siege) than from wounds. Some 13,000 died of starvation during Henry IV's siege of Paris in 1590. And the effects lingered, with siege deaths occurring long after a chronicler had closed his account.

As in the case of declarations of war, the use of the formal summons proclaimed by a herald demanding that a town yield had become intermittent. It was, indeed, observed by the English more frequently than by nations more habituated to war, as at Tournai in 1513 and as late as at Rouen in 1591, when the earl of Essex challenged the duke of Villars to settle the matter by single combat with the splendidly anachronistic challenge, 'The King's cause is more just than the League's, I am better than you, and my mistress is more beautiful.' Similarly with surrender terms. The conventions were known; stripped of heraldese, they meant that the longer a town held out the worse its surrender terms would be. But it was known still better that the actual terms were unlikely to be decided by medieval conventions, whether these specified the honours with which a departed garrison could step out bearing arms, beating drums and with banners fluttering into a six months' or a year's ban on fighting again for the same cause, or determined the size of indemnity a town would have to pay, or the number of hostages which would be held as guarantees until the occupation had settled, unchallenged, into routine.

Such matters were still written into surrenders negotiated in advance, usually with an 'if not relieved' within ten or fourteen days clause. Articles of War, like the Austrian one of 1527 and the Imperial code of 1570, forbade the sacking of cities which had surrendered – not from Christian charity but because the restoration of order immobilized the occupying troops after their orgy and still further complicated what was bound to be a provisioning crisis. In the same vein, 'unconditional' surrender terms, negotiated at a later stage in a siege, were usually followed by the holding for ransom, rather than the execution of men of station. (As for the rank and file, stripped to their shirts as a condition of egress, while they scattered for safety they had to run the gauntlet of those countrymen who had stuck to their holdings – often because pressed into labour as pioneers on entrenchments – and who were waiting to exact the peasants' revenge.) Nevertheless it was recognized that whatever followed a surrender was really determined by the mood of the entering troops, the hold over them of their officers, the army command's reliance, or not, on a cooperative municipal government, and, finally, on the decision whether order or terrorism would be better strategy given the situation in the war zone overall.

In practice, there was little distinction between what happened within a town that had negotiated surrender terms and one that had been stormed without such formalities. Of the factors listed above, the overwhelmingly determinant one was the mood of the occupying soldiery. When Shakespeare had Henry V shout up to the governor of Harfleur as he stood on the wall that he had better surrender because

'We may as bootless spend our vain command
Upon the enraged soldiers in their spoil
As send precepts to the Leviathan
To come ashore,'

he was echoing Raleigh's explanation of why he had not stayed in Cadiz after it had fallen to his expedition: 'For the fear I had to be shouldered in the press, and among the tumultuous, disordered soldiers, that, being then given to spoil and rapine, had no respect . . . all running headlong to the Sack.' The academic jurists recognized this. They made little of the difference between negotiated capitulations and walls stormed against defiant defenders. Sacks are deplorable, wrote Molina, not unrepresentatively, 'because of the slaughter and torture of innocent persons, the rape, adultery and violence used on women which soldiers usually commit in such circumstances, and because of the desecration of churches and other atrocities and injustices which generally occur. Despite this, in itself it is not unlawful. So, if it is considered necessary for the progress of the war . . . it is like burning down a city, which is sometimes permissible for good reason. On the other hand, when a city is given over for looting, the generals are bound to forbid such atrocities and injustices and prevent them as far as they reasonably can.' Intellectually this was sorry, hedging stuff. But it recognized what happens and tried to attach a fetter of conscience to it.

The conquerors' entry into a hard-fought-for city was, in any case, only too likely to develop into the military form of Carnival or All Fools' Day, a sudden, obscene release from arrears of pay, hardship and fear into the rituals of misrule, with the men giving, in effect, the orders which their officers and provosts were forced to accept. When the French, to avenge Francis I's capture at Pavia in 1525, sent another army into Lombardy two years later, its commander, Lautrec, gave orders when the city fell that at least the lives and honour of nuns and girls were to be respected; but the troops held back from no form of 'cruelty and acts of shame'. We have seen something of the barbarism which characterized the sack of Rome by the Imperial army in the same year. An English survivor of the sack of Antwerp in 1576, an orgy of sex and greed which led to the loss of 7000 lives, said, referring to the Last Judgement in the Sistine Chapel, that the bodies offered 'as many sundry shapes and formes of man's motion at time of death as ever Michael Angelo dyd portray in his tables of Doomesday'. When the Spanish troops stormed Maastricht in 1579 one-third of the city's men, women and children were slaughtered on the spot or died subsequently from the brutalities inflicted on them. Civilians suffered so appallingly in part because of the displacement on to them of the hatred that had grown between besiegers and the men of the defending garrison. If at the start of operations there were chivalrous challenges between the two sides, jousts and other forms of fraternization between cannonades, truces mutually agreed for the removal of corpses and the incapacitated, such amenities soon withered as the weeks of hardship lengthened and the death roll mounted. In the early stages at Rouen a man wounded in an assault might expect a rescue party to be allowed up to the wall. Later on he was more likely to be left to die or, as happened in one case, be dragged in and have cannon balls dropped on his stomach. At a siege's end the populace was exposed to a soldiery not only at the moment most symbolic of the impatience with convention and law which had prompted them to join up, and at the peak of their rancour against non-combatants in general, but at their most bitterly vengeful. It is tempting, moreover, but perhaps overfanciful, to conjecture that there was another impulse behind these orgies of hate (many of the savageries described by eyewitnesses went far beyond the sheer need to gratify sexual appetite or obtain loot), and to see the rape of the town as another form of the peasants' revenge, so many of the men in armies being, as we have seen, of peasant or village origin.

In terms of personal impact the burdens of war certainly afflicted the rural more than the urban population. Not only because of their larger numbers but because of their vulnerability to administrative pressure, the highly discriminatory process of impressment drew more unwilling recruits to war from the countryside than from the towns, where more men were able to pay for substitutes and where there was a greater argument for letting the able-bodied stay at home to pursue their crafts and defend their walls. As district or regional centres essential to the maintenance of a nation's economic, ecclesiastical and legal life, cities and large towns, while targets for war taxation, were also let off lightly relative to their size within the local population as a whole as far as the provision of the non-combatant labour needed for war was concerned. It was from hamlets and scattered farms that men were selected for service as pioneers, to accompany an army to dig its trenches and the defences surrounding its camps, to manhandle its guns (the campaign mortality among draught horses was up to 30 per cent) and tunnel its mines; from the country that carts and their drivers were impressed to form part of an army's baggage train. At the very times when cultivation for food was most crucially important, the labour force might be drastically reduced.

Peasant proprietors could share in the momentary boom in

demand for surplus produce if they had any that was not needed for their own subsistence, but the real advantages accrued to the town-based merchants whose agents bought their crops. Nearly all the profits to be derived from provisioning and manufacturing – food, clothing, armaments – were made by men who, even if they employed rural labour, lived, and had accumulated the necessary capital to win their contracts, in towns. We might add the fact that after rural 'conscripts' the next largest component of infantrymen in armies was recruited from those who had failed to integrate themselves into the economic life of the towns to which they had drifted and into whose gutters they had been pushed. This gives a wider social dimension to the 'peasants' revenge' aspect of the violence that followed a successful siege.

Turning from the impact of a war to the burdens that peacetime preparedness for the next one laid on civilians, there is a similar imbalance between the inconvenience and hardship caused to the inhabitants of the countryside and of towns. Billeting, always so vexatious an issue in war, had, thanks to the creation of standing forces, become a permanent one. The solution was the building of purpose-made barracks. But though Venice built lodgings for troops in some of its garrison towns from the 1570s and there was some move in this direction two decades later in the Netherlands, in the main the old practice of expecting civilians to house the troops engaged to protect them persisted. Most resented was the lodging, feeding and stabling of the cavalry, who only moved into towns for their annual or biennial musters. In theory the company clerks should have paid for everything consumed and at least a token rent for the use of beds and bedding and cooking and eating utensils. During the second half of the fifteenth century the reissuing in France of decree after decree to this effect showed the extent to which payment was dodged when the time came for the unit to clatter away and batten on another farmstead. Other legislation reveals the frequency with which companies demanded ransom from farmers or innkeepers in return for abstaining from their right to demand accommodation.

By the early sixteenth century individuals were compensated – at least in France and Italy – for loss from a special cavalry tax paid by a region as a whole; if this spread the burden, it also spread the resentment. 'To the devil with the King who burdens us with so many men-at-arms,' a French sufferer was drawn treasonously to exclaim, 'I would rather be a good Englishman than a Frenchman.' The problem in good measure came to solve itself as the numbers of cavalry maintained on a permanent basis declined, but another was posed by the growing numbers of infantry either in or on the move between garrison towns. With the enlargement of garrisons the violence that lawsuit after lawsuit reveals was increasingly transferred from the country to the town. But because compensation from the regional tax for supplies contributed by rural producers was administered, often to its own advantage, by the municipal government of the chief town, the pre-existing ill feeling between country and town worsened, as has been documented for mid-sixteenth-century Dauphiné. In general, indeed, permanent armies contributed to that source of tension. And among the grievances moving the south German peasants to revolt in 1525 was a military tax levied on them to compensate the townsmen of the Swabian League for the cash demanded in lieu of their personal service.

A more widely shared, if less consistently resented burden was militia service.

All governments in the fifteenth century had the right to call on the military service of their able-bodied secular subjects, though commonly this was not available abroad for more than forty days in a year. The first attempt to rationalize and improve the effectiveness of civilian service within a militia structure was the formation by Charles VII of the *francs-archers* – 'free', that is, from paying the *taille* and cavalry tax. Initially 8000, their numbers were doubled in 1466. Recruited throughout the regions subject to effective royal control by parishes, on a basis of roughly one man for every eighty 'hearths', they were to equip themselves (or be helped by the parish if they were too poor) with helmet, brigandine, sword and dagger, bow or crossbow. A small permanent command structure was appointed to supervise musters two or three times a year from groups of parishes and to command them in action. For though the training of these part-timers was minimal, it was envisaged that they would supplement professional forces in wartime as well as relieve garrison troops for service in the field. In this respect they were not a success. Freedom from the *taille* attracted volunteers from those prosperous enough otherwise to have to make substantial payments of this tax, farmers and shopkeepers, many of them with families to support which they were reluctant to leave. Socially, the *francs-archers* were a 'safe' force, but they were also an uncommonly settled and unmilitaristic one. This was the chief reason for the disbandment of the central organization in 1480, though parishes were charged with keeping the archers mobilizable as semi-trained men within the ad hoc rural bands that were still called up under older obligations, and the citizen forces which towns could be summoned to produce in order to patrol communication routes or frontiers in their vicinity.

Given the poor showing made by the archers when contingents of them did reluctantly join armies during the reconquest of Normandy and Louis XI's internal wars, it is not surprising that an attempt to create a similar national body was postponed until 1534. In that year Francis I set up an organization for the recruitment, on comparable lines, of a militia force of 60,000 men based on the whole circumference of border provinces. Divided into six legions – the name reflects the humanistic infection of military thinking – enlistment was 'voluntary', with exemption again from the *taille* and, to attract nobles to serve as officers, from feudal military obligations. The enlistment oath took account of long experience of those changes in demeanour even part-time soldiering produced; recruits had to swear to protect women, and to expect the death penalty if they stole, pillaged, burned houses, mutinied or deserted.

With Francis about to embark on yet another war of conquest in Italy with a thin treasury, the motive, while chiefly to secure frontiers from counterattack, also included the use of a proportion of the legionaries to lower the cost of relying on foreign mercenaries. And once more, after being put to the test in the Piedmont–Savoy campaign of 1536, the results were disappointing. France, with its slow communications and networks of interlocking and competing local administrations, was simply too big and too complex for such an organization to work, especially one with a large territorial hole in its middle. The full complement of men was never raised, even on paper. Preference for *taille*-exemption and the swagger of military garb counted more than the daily wage on leaving home – the same as that on which the professional soldier found it so difficult to live. The legionary bands came to be used only as frontier guards or garrison substitutes in their own localities. By the opening of the civil wars their organization was weak, even at provincial level, and in the wars themselves the leaders on both sides relied on ad hoc bodies of men rather than the uncertain loyalties concealed in the legionary muster lists.

After the *francs-archers* the next early attempt to organize civilian part-time military service on a country-wide basis occurred in Tuscany in 1505–6. When the French advanced on Florence in

1494 the urban militia was mobilized and some 10,000 men readied in the surrounding countryside. Dissatisfaction with their equipment and competence, coupled with a growing disillusion with the mercenaries the city was employing to retake the rebel city of Pisa, led to acceptance of a plan for a new, trained militia, and its implementation was left to Machiavelli, then secretary to the Ten of War and widely experienced in military administrative matters. It called for a force of, again, 10,000 men, all to be recruited in the countryside (for fear of adding more weapons to the problems of policing within Florence and its subject cities), grouped in companies of between 100 and 300 men under a professional soldier, at least 10 per cent of whom were to be armed with arquebuses. Training was to take place locally on major holidays (with the church's approval) and there were to be two provincial musters a year, largely as an administrative check on the system. Given the volatile political sympathies of the recruits and the venomous quality of inter-regional feuds, all had to take an oath to be faithful to Florence and to serve under the insignia of the Marzocco, the city's symbolic lion. Captains were to be moved from one locality to another each year lest they build up a loyalty to themselves that could be dangerous to the state. And to protect the unenrolled peasantry from harassment, boxes were placed in the main church of every mustering centre into which denunciations of any offence could be slipped anonymously. The incentive to serve was here not tax concession but a licence to bear military arms on ordinary occasions, even in cities, a concession granted by the authorities with some distrust.

As with the *francs-archers*, militiamen were envisaged as joining combat troops in action as well as acting as military maids of all work; at least this was true of those units judged most competent. Some did so serve without adverse criticism at Pisa, but for the majority mobilization was not only clogged by a straightforward wish not to risk their lives when the habit was well established that others should be paid – and not just, as they were, for the days of actual service – to do that for them, but by a reluctance to leave families and property vulnerable to the raids and counter-raids that were part of the passionate parochialism of country life. When the Medici returned in 1512 the militia was allowed to founder for lack of central control; they were 'republican', and the taking of Prato by the Medici's Spanish army had put their timorousness in lurid relief.

It was because of the 'republicanness' of the idea of military self-help that the Medici relied entirely on mercenaries and that on their second expulsion in 1527, a section of the extreme supporters of the restored republican regime was able to persuade a hesitant government to establish a militia in the city itself as well as to revive that of the rural *dominio*. The first civic enrolment was small, 2700, and carefully restricted to the most responsible class of citizens, men whose standing qualified them to sit on the Great Council, and their sons. Even so, their periods of training by professional officers were carefully supervised by commissioners appointed by the government; they were forbidden to carry arms when not on duty; and their solemn oath of loyalty to the present regime was sworn on the gospels in the presence of the regime's chief magistrate, the gonfalonier of justice. Even when Florence came under siege from the Imperial army it was only with considerable reluctance, and mainly out of distrust in Florence's mercenary defenders, that the number was increased by stages, and by admitting men of less standing, to 10,700. But by this time the militia had turned into the sort of civic defence force generated in any city under siege – with the notable difference that it was increasingly resented as prolonging the war under the banner of doctrinaire republicanism while the majority of Florentines, their spirits dashed by hunger and disease, would have preferred to surrender.

Not surprisingly, when in 1530 the surrender came and the Medici returned, this time to stay, the urban militia was disbanded. What took its place for the rest of the period was a reformed rural militia which, after the conquest of Siena and its territories, comprised 30,000 infantry, 2000 cavalry and a force of 12,000 pioneers who could be called up for roadmaking and drainage works as well as for labour on fortifications.

The other Italian state that had led in the rationalizing of peasant military obligations was Venice. After earlier local trials, a militia blueprint applicable to the whole of its mainland territory was issued in 1507. Almost at once its provisions were buried within the confusions of occupation and reconquest that followed the disaster of Agnadello. Re-established in 1528, and progressively re-modelled, the Venetian militia organization by the 1560s called for a military reserve of 20,000 men and a naval one of 10,000. As permission to carry arms remained the chief attraction to join, this meant that out of a rural population on the mainland of 200,000 secular adult males, one in seven was so trusted. In the 1570s, moreover, the nervousness in matters of defence felt by Italy's only truly independent power led to the enrolment of a reserve (*di rispetto*) militia which practically doubled its size. And in 1616, when Venice was at war with Austria in Friuli and fearing diversionary strikes from the north, something like 35,000 men in the region of Verona, half the able-bodied male population, were armed and enrolled in self-defence units: a peasant army twice the size of the republic's total professional force.

Because the very notion of militias implied the possession of arms and some training in their use (though all governments were very guarded in their issue of gunpowder), their establishment was a measure of a government's confidence in its people as well as in its bureaucratic ability to direct them. Loyalty was a factor that counted considerably more in their institution than the wish to save money (for the savings on professional recruits were slight thanks to militiamen's reluctance to fight other than as guerrillas in defence of their immediate homeland), or than the administrative convenience of having a centrally directed domestic force, one that could be mobilized more speedily than by invoking medieval feudal and municipal obligations which disuse had rendered so easily challengeable in law. Seen as a very rough and ready indicator of settled political maturity, the dates of the establishment of formal militias in other Italian states are at least suggestive: Urbino 1533, Ferrara 1560, Piedmont 1566; there were none in Milan or Naples, where Spanish rule remained insecure, nor in the states of the church with their local animosities and their fragile and often resented administrative structure. Similarly in England, the rationalization of native military service on the lines of a single, governmentally controlled militia in 1558, and the creation within it of select men to form 'trained bands' in 1573, was in marked contrast to the inability of the Spanish administration to pull provincial, feudal and municipal levies into a coherent whole despite repeated attempts to do so. In the German states, in spite of earlier blueprints for territorial or even pan-German trained reserves, distrust of rural insurgency postponed their implementation (in individual states) until the 1580s and 1590s. In Sweden, the difficulty of administering a regularly trained militia led to a preference for refining the machinery for securing recruits for combat service – the *utskrivning* system.

Overwhelmingly, then, militiamen were countrymen, agricultural labourers or smallholders or village craftsmen, volunteers in the sense that if they did not actually choose to enrol they were 'persuaded' to, not by the state but by their own community in its search to fill its quota. And the system brought them advantages. As with the *francs-archers*, in Italy there came to be exemption from the personal tax (the *estimo*) levied on every adult male. Varying from country to country, there were these or additional baits; beside permission to carry arms and the free provision of them, exemption from other labour services, preferential procedures in lawsuits with non-militiamen, travel and food allowances and a small daily wage when attending training sessions or musters, and compensation for loss of wages when these involved absence on working days; above all, perhaps, theoretical exemption – for it was not always observed – from wartime recruiting for service abroad. For many, militia status may have brought some increase in their standing in local eyes; they became, in a petty way, officials, their names preserved in provincial and central records as men potentially able to say, 'I have done the state some service.' But in professional eyes they remained cyphers, necessary to line coasts and walls and look like soldiers in defensive campaigns but all too often, as a Venetian administrator put it, 'like farmyard dogs, fearless of death in the yard, fleeing at the least alarm outside it', and liable to abuse the heady freedom from local restraint when they came together at musters. In England military gatherings of more than three hundred were forbidden unless the lord lieutenant was there in person; even smaller training sessions were to be watched by two justices of the peace or other 'grave and discreet persons'.

The impact on society of the militia system is not so much to be measured in terms of inconvenience to the individual (trainings were infrequent and were often cancelled if they conflicted with late harvests) or of risk, as of cash. The numbers involved were fairly large in relation to population. In 1591 it was reckoned that the English militia enrolment was as high as 91,400 at a time when the number of rural households was little more than 1 million. And the system – arms, allowances, wages, administration and professional instructors – had to be paid for. Government, naturally, passed the greater part of the expenditure to local authorities. Throughout western Europe methods of tax assessment led to the militia rate, chargeable to landholdings, falling more gravely on the country than on the towns, and on the poor rather than on the rich. Townsmen owning land in the country were charged only on their property in the parish of their domicile; the same was true of rural landlords of widely scattered holdings. The country communities who actually had to hand out arms and money to militiamen paid an unfair – and, as stacks of petitions witness, widely resented – proportion of the system's cost. And in countries where militia service carried exemption from taxes, part of whose total was normally held back for the defrayment of local expenses, the burden on non-members was all the greater. As so often, the impact of the military reformation fell most heavily on those least able to bear it.

Far less is known about a companion militia, that of the gunners. An example, but not a model, is provided by Venice where, from its beginning in the city in 1500, membership had risen by 1600 to 4700, shared between nineteen mainland towns. Venice's early start in the setting up of a *scuola* ('school' not only in the training sense, but that of a craft guild with religious and charitable roles) was doubtless due to its need for trained men to work the guns on naval and armed merchant galleys, but the system as it extended was used to provide part-time gunners to defend fortifications and join the army artillery service in war. Enrolment in this case was limited to townsmen. Because besides a licence to carry arms it also – earlier than the normal militia – carried with it exemption from personal taxation as its main attraction, the more prosperous citizens were excluded and a preference was shown for men who, when called up, would be able to put ancillary skills to use: carpenters, blacksmiths, bricklayers and masons. Registers of names show, however, that such men were in a minority, and were trained (under full-time professionals) alongside cobblers, grocers, even an occasional bonnetmaker or organist. As government grudged the expense of issuing gunpowder save in small quantities, practical training was seldom on guns larger than the falconet; the musket, or even the arquebus being most commonly used in the monthly competitions. It was probably only in Venice itself, where the 'scholars' had access to the proving grounds on the Lido used by the founders casting guns in the Arsenal, that the *bombardieri* were trained as gunners in the modern sense; the rest formed a variant on the 'trained band'; given preferential treatment if they wished to join a wartime artillery unit but normally looked on as stiffeners within units of the ordinary light-armed militia.

The same appears to be true elsewhere. In whatever tongue, 'artillery' meant the whole range of weapons. The Artillery Company of London, which traces its origin to a royal charter of 1537, came to be a privileged, self-financing element within the trained band organization; real gunners, whose training involved 'levelling brass pieces of great artillery against a butt of earth', worked not as amateur part-timers but as true apprentices to the heavy weapon establishment, the gunners of the Tower of London. The same is true of many towns in northern France and across the Netherlands, where alongside the late medieval guilds of 'shooters' (*Schutters*), equivalent bodies emerged composed of well-to-do merchants who met regularly for voluntary training and prepared themselves to lead self-defence units, while at the same time, as in London, enjoying the sociability and strut of playing at soldiers.

So while the introduction of new weapons – pike, arquebus and musket – led to the replacement of ad hoc levies in rural areas by militias, permanently organized and centrally administered, it led also to some reflection of this change in towns, though without replacing the traditional summons to arms binding on all adult males in time of emergency.

For civilian familiarity with weapons in peacetime was widespread. Not only were there intermittent self-defence needs caused by cross-frontier raids in border regions, piracy in coastal areas, brigandage in sparsely populated tracts of countryside. In a period of quick tempers, volatile social and political resentments and minute police forces, urban riots, especially in cities with large numbers of unemployed, or of unmarried, non-property-owning apprentices, could easily swamp the law-enforcement officials: the civic guard and the constables and watchmen of parishes. The urban calendar was punctuated with holidays – Shrove Tuesday, Midsummer Day, Christmas – traditionally associated with punch-ups in taverns, jeering attacks on brothels or the houses of unpopular ambassadors or alien communities, and roaming street gangs of hooligans whooping and smashing windows.

The situations which called for the possession of arms by householders covered, then, a wide range. In cities like Nuremberg, self-governing but constantly on guard against the itch to bring them to heel on the part of Imperial and local territorial chieftains, the possession of arms and some evidence of being able to use them was an unquestioned obligation. Many towns were like Exeter, where it was not so much preparedness for a royal summons to local military service that kept half the able-bodied males enrolled, provided with arms and paraded at an annual muster, as the fear of freebooters or foreign vessels seeking reprisals. In the case of London, or Paris, it was above all riot, with the possibility in times of food scarcity of its escalating into insurrection, that was the chief motive for householders possessing arms of their own, and for civic authorities having armouries to top up private equipment that was inadequate or out of date.

Whether in towns or villages, the possession of arms was accepted both as an aid to the mobilization of resistance in case of an invasion threat and as a complement to an undermanned law-enforcement organization. Naturally governments, central and local, plastered the potentiality of its abuse with regulations. Arms could only be kept by taxpaying householders and their servants; daggers and firearms could not be carried in streets or on country roads; no arms at all could be taken out of the house to fairs, markets or church services; important visitors, but not their escorts, could travel armed. The regulations varied, country by country, and were repeated to a degree which shows how widely they were ignored but also with a regularity which gave some attraction to the militiaman's exemption from at least some of them.

Only an intricate shading could do justice to the civilian's familiarity with or preparedness to use arms, which varied according to place and occasion in a way that permits no generalization – except one: that a nation with arms is not the same as a nation in arms. Their possession, whether rusty or burnished, was associated rather with peacekeeping and self-defence, than with state-directed military service in time of war. This is why governments edged their way, through organizing more formalized trained bands, towards reserves pledged to identify themselves – in theory, at least – with wider, political issues.

If gunpowder, through the skills required to make its weapons work, acted as a disciplinarian of the new civilian reserves of military manpower, it also increased, intermittently but far more disturbingly, their obligation to take part in public works ordered by governments. To withstand cannon fire and gunpowder mining, fortifications had to be radically modified: walls became far thicker; tall towers were replaced by wall-height bastions, massive solid gun platforms designed for guns to strike outwards against enemy batteries and along the walls and neighbouring flanks to deter mining or assault parties; and, depending on the nature of the ground, supporting outworks and ditch systems became far more elaborate than hitherto. These changes, whether expressed in the modernization of old fortifications or the creation of new ones, caused an unprecedented demand for straightforward manual labour. Though the walls and bastions might have an outer dressing of masonry and brick, the massive amounts of earth that had to be dug and piled represented the major work element. It was performed by peasants, and it was peasant carts and their drivers that were commandeered for transporting the mass of material needed to keep the construction site supplied with tools, stone, lime, sand and beams, as well as food for the work gangs, whose growth in size on major projects paralleled the growth of armies in major campaigns.

Montaigne's was a minority voice when he challenged the building of fortifications as being more likely to provoke than protect: 'Inclosure and fencing drawe on the enterprise; and distrust, the offence. . . . Our forefathers never dreamed on building of frontire townes or castles.' From 1536 Francis I protected his southern frontier by a string of fortified towns running from Piedmont to Provence. In 1539 Henry VIII ordered the construction of newly designed fortresses to defend the whole of the south coast from Kent to Cornwall. In 1545 it was the turn of France's north-east frontier where, among the remodelling of existing defence works, Francis commissioned the construction of two new fortified towns, Vitry-le-François and Villefranche-sur-Meuse. Spain meanwhile had begun a massive programme to protect the coasts of the kingdom of Naples and Sicily from Turkish attack, and started a new one beside the Pyrenees in the late sixteenth century, Venice one for the modernization of garrison towns throughout its empire on land and by sea, Tuscany one for the securing of frontiers and internal communication routes. Cosimo I also ordered the transformation of the sea-village of Livorno into a capacious fortified city and of Portoferraio into a bastioned Cosmopolis. The refashioning of Valetta after the withdrawal of the Turks from the siege of 1565, the frenzy of urban redesign that forced the Spanish campaigns in the Netherlands to be a series of sieges, Henry IV's avid attention to the protection of his frontiers and the wave – almost the fashion – for fortress construction that swept through the states of north-eastern Germany from the 1590s: all these are but some of the major reminders that in the first gunpowder era, war's impact must be seen in terms of picks and shovels as well as of guns.

Throughout Europe, governments had the power to impress labour for the defence of the realm. It was a power dangerous to focus attention on, so, as in the case of military recruiting, the buck was passed through the quota system to regional, and by them to local administrations, with safety-valves en route permitting the commutation of service for a money payment, and with some leeway allowed for petition and appeal. In this way impressment appeared once more in the guise of pressure from neighbours on those least able to protest. Transport to the site was paid, food provided and, at least in peacetime, a small daily wage; there were always those for whom this was better than nothing. When real volunteers or men persuadable by threat or the cajolement of bonus payments did not suffice – and the building season was also that of tillage and harvest – contractors were engaged to scour further and were paid a bounty for whomever they could round up. In consequence, some of the hardest labour that could be undertaken was carried out by many who were unfitted for it. In 1594, when work began on the new frontier fortress town of Palma in Friuli, 7000 labourers were called for. Something of the conditions in which they and their successors worked can be learned from a complaint from the governor in 1599 that during his three years on the site he had offered wages far above what was normal. But in spite of this many fled as soon as they saw the working conditions, 'terrified out of their wits and holding the name Palma in hatred.'

But the true social cost of fortifications is not only to be measured in hardship and sickness – crowded and insanitary work-sites could be as unhealthy as trenches or camps – but, yet again, also in terms of cash. No government could pay for more than a fraction of important new projects out of revenue nor in peacetime risk raising the whole of the cost from new taxation imposed on the country at large. Always a significant portion had to come – with the plea that they were, after all, paying for their own protection – from the local populations whose rural members were already providing the workforce, and suffering the inconveniences and losses caused by the commandeering of the carts that would normally ply between farm and market. The town-dweller lost the right to build on the firepower *cordon sanitaire* extending outwards from the new fortifications. But this, by increasing population pressure within them, led to higher rental and site values; there was, besides, an enhanced sense of protection, perhaps also of civic pride to be derived from becoming defensively up-to-date. And defences were a form of real estate, a wise capital investment, even if an unrealizable one. But neither financial nor psychological profit accrued to the populations who had provided the labour and helped to pay for them. And when an advancing army forced them to take refuge there, it was with the knowledge that they would be among the first to be thrown out as 'useless mouths'.

8

The indirect impact: war and the economy

When war came, what effect did the sudden expenditure of the unnaturally massive sums raised by taxation and loans have on individuals and the economy?

They were spent on interest charges, on transport, on bulk purchases of arms and clothing, on foodstuffs, and on wages. The concentration of men in armies, removed from their own environments in which barter, labour in exchange for goods, and small-scale credit and loan arrangements kept cash transactions to a minimum, meant that coin was used in wholly exceptional quantities. Mints took on extra hands; closely guarded mule trains laden with the bewildering variety of small silver or base-metal discs that soldiers demanded lest they be defrauded by the profit money-changers made from breaking down nobles, sovereigns, cruzados, livres, florins, guldens and ducats, were whipped ahead of artillery and baggage convoys; war-zone bankers, alerted by letters of credit, rounded up what surplus currency they could lay hands on and poured it into the sealed canvas bags the army paymasters needed if they were to quench the grumbles of troops threatened with being 'paid' in cloth or left entirely dependent on the commissariat.

What happened to this money? Much of it was 'lost'; it would be difficult to disprove estimates that between one-fifth and a quarter of the moneys credited to campaign expenditure never got through the networks of peculation stretched between cash raised and cash distributed through commissariat purchases and wages.

There were, perhaps, few examples of fraud on a grand scale, though the duke of Parma's military secretary in the Netherlands from 1580, Cosmo Masi, somehow was able to put 443,750 florins out at loan in 1596, and between 1599 and 1606 Elizabeth's treasurer-at-war in Ireland, Sir George Carey, was held to have embezzled over £150,000. But save among the patrician commissioners and paymasters employed by the German and Italian business-states who had a personal, or at least a class interest in the control of military investment, money raised for war was seen as arriving out of the non-combatant blue, as it were, without nagging personal moral commitment. And this state of mind was encouraged by the grandiloquent style of living maintained by noble commanders and by the knowledge that no government had the personnel or expertise to ensure the running of a cost-effective campaign.

There was an absence of adequate control over every aspect of military preparation and practice. Contracts for arms and uniforms and foodstuffs? Complaints abound about falsified quantities and quality. The provision of the most important war commodity of all, men? At every point in the recruiting process – enrolment, selection, transport, muster, equipment – there was the opportunity for bribes and fraud. Shots, cries, the trudge of marching feet: the sound most prominent in the economic historian's ears is that of the greasing of palms. War provided a massive subsidy to the self-interest of a host of petty peculators, a steady deflection of public money into improvements in the comforts or status of individuals.

At a time when opportunities for making a profit from ransom and plunder became restricted, and when governments tried, however incompetently, to keep profit margins on war industries and supply as low as possible, alongside manufacture and commerce, peculation has to be borne in mind as the elusive third man haunting any discussion of the economic consequences of war.

'Unproductive': this is the usual verdict on the war-bills of campaigns which so seldom led to the conquest of those new markets, raw materials and taxpayers that could return a profit on military enterprises. But save in the case of military prostitution – which itself could save women from depending on municipal charity – what coin, even when peculated or 'wasted', that changed hands might not induce a minute jolt in some service or productive energy? That soldiers drank a tavern dry was not unproductive to the brewing industry of the country concerned. What paymasters and captains stole, and what soldiers spent, was good for the local economy if not for that of the regions whence their purchasing power had been transferred; and this metallic sprinkling of theatres of war played a part in their reburgeoning when peace returned.

It is uncomfortable to draw attention to the speed with which war zones recovered; it appears to belittle the misery caused by hostilities. Something of the same inhibition applies when indicating gains made as a result of war by some regions at the expense of others: Valencia's long-lasting economic 'victory' over Barcelona, for instance, when the latter's commerce was virtually immobilized during the Catalonian revolt of 1462–72, or Amsterdam and its hinterland's pulling ahead of Antwerp during the wars of the Netherlands, or those German, Alsatian and English towns which at the same time benefited from militant religious persecution.

Both the long and the wide views of the economic consequences of wars must appear heartlessly at odds with the immediate impact on the civilians caught up in them. And both are denied even the justification of accurate analysis because of factors working within the economy which were not directly linked to war. The population of Amsterdam, for instance, was about 31,000 at the time of the 1576 sack of Antwerp and had trebled by the end of hostilities in 1609. But the prosperity which attracted settlers was only in part due to a war-induced shift in commercial and financial opportunities from one city to the other. Coincidentally with the war at home, and more than counterbalancing the heavy taxation imposed to pay for it, Dutch overseas trade was flourishing: across the Baltic for timber and grain, to Brazil for sugar, to the East Indies for spices, and in the Mediterranean. Most of the cargoes brought back were for almost instant re-export. And the Amsterdammers speedily became masters of the credit-raising, warehousing turnaround and price-fixing aspects of the entrepôt trade. Without the interruptions war brought to communications and its diversion of capital from commercial investment, Amsterdam's gains would doubtless have been still greater. The growth of the city, moreover, contrasted with the stagnation of the more vulnerable countryside. All the same, a contemporary could write of Amsterdam and its neighbour territories, that while 'it is known to all the world that whereas it is generally the nature of war to ruin the land and the people, these countries on the contrary have been notably improved thereby'.

Unglamorously supporting the transoceanic trade on which C. P. Hooft chiefly based his remark were army supply contracts and the multitude of small cash transactions made possible by troops' wages. It was the influx of money from Spain for wages and commissariat purchases that enabled Antwerp to retain a considerable level of prosperity (part of which had been lost, again for factors unconnected with war) in spite of the catastrophes that befell it, and at the war's end be in a position to recover much of its lost prominence.

To towns which did not act as commissary centres or benefit from the spending power of garrisons, the effect of broken communications, burdensome taxes, and the high price of foodstuffs caused by the desolation of their countryside, war could bring severe depressions even when violent occupation did not cause damage to homes and workshops. And it is unlikely that the demand for accommodation and the increased number of market transactions that resulted from transient influxes of refugees from the countryside formed any appreciable compensation. While no two cases were similar, it is probable that the greater the extent to which recovery depended on capital expenditure for raw materials the more slowly it was realized; non-industrial market towns recovered at the pace of the recultivated countryside around them. Even in the southern Netherlands, however, where thirty-seven years of almost continuous war up to 1609 led to the flight of two-thirds of the population from a number of the worst-hit towns, recovery began with peace. Whether market- or industry-based, the slowly self-redefining economic logic that had dictated the siting of towns almost guaranteed that they would re-establish themselves when given the chance, especially during a time of population growth. War did not leave behind the permanently deserted villages and stagnant towns that resulted from, for instance, the English substitution of pasture for tillage or the moving of clothworking processes to newly exploited sources of water power.

War could not destroy land's native fertility, but capital was needed for its recovery: for seed and root-stocks, for animals to provide additional fertilizer, for the rebuilding of cottages and byres, for wagons to replace those requisitioned and broken or never returned. Here, too, transactions based on wages or sutler's purchases that had allowed coin to be saved helped both landlords and peasant proprietors to restock and start again. As for the recruitment of agricultural labourers, this was not inevitably a matter of crucial importance to productivity; it was above all in the context of militia call-ups that communities raised the cry 'harvest in danger', and women and children could bridge at least part of that gap just as they could toil on the repair of fortifications. It is very unlikely, given the poor quality of recruits and the drifting home of deserters, that the land lost able-bodied and willing workers over a significantly lengthy period. It was enemy occupation, pillage, extortion and flight that led to land becoming temporarily derelict. Yet it was in areas traversed or occupied by armies that the cash transactions took place that facilitated recovery. Soldiers, of course, stole chickens, herded off goats, cows and horses, cut down fruit trees for fuel, saw apples and grapes as natural recompenses for their arduous trampings. In the main, however, on the road or in camp or billets they relied on topping up commissariat issues with purchases from peasants, camp-following sutlers or market stallholders. In these ways the troops' little discs found their way into so many hands that to apply the term 'waste' to the function of military wages is unrealistic if the context is not one of cash raised at home and spent abroad but of the impact of war on the economy as a whole. And it was by noting the recuperative capacity of war theatres as well as the generally adequate if grudging resilience of countries taxed to raise armies, that intelligent observers as well as statesmen were helped to view the phenomenon of war without faltering overmuch in their intellectual stride towards accepting the next one. Government bankruptcies were not directly related to gross national product, the income generated within all sectors of a national economy.

While some two-thirds of the cost of military consumables were spent in the agricultural as opposed to the manufacturing sector of the economy, wartime conglomerations of mouths needing to be fed did not lead to any attempts to increase agricultural productivity. Such attempts as there were – the cultivation of marginal lands in France and to a lesser degree in Spain, drainage and reclamation schemes in Italy and the Netherlands – were responses to population increase and profit-seeking that were independent of the demands of armies. The need for wood, heavy enough in peacetime for ship and house and implement making and for heating kitchen hearths and the furnaces and vats used in the metallurgical and 'chemical' industries (dyeing, brewing, soap and glass making) was greatly increased by war, with its myriad watch-lines and bivouacs and its earthen fortifications consolidated with stakes, and still more by preparing weapons for armies of increasing size. Less was consumed in hafts and butts and gun-carriages than in the preliminary smelting, casting and smithery called for by the arms trade. Put end to end, the arrows discharged by the Burgundian archers at the battle of Montlhéry in 1465 would have constituted a rod 40,000 metres long. But it took 409 sacks of charcoal to cast a large culverin in 1478; every time a gun of any sort fired it consumed ground charcoal that formed between 15 and 26 per cent of the composition (with saltpetre and sulphur) of gunpowder. Restrictions on the felling of forest trees became widespread from the mid-sixteenth century as rulers became more concerned about what came to be seen as a wood-energy crisis. Undoubtedly woodcutters and their haulage gangs became more numerous and ranged further afield into high and remote afforested zones, but how much further they were driven by war's needs on top of those of peace – a stout fishing craft, a quayside crane or the props in the tunnel of a mine could consume more than the making and mounting of the largest piece of artillery – it is impossible to say. In 1615 Edmund Howes, up-dating Stowe's *Annales*, wrote that 'such hath been the plenty of wood in England . . . that, within man's memory, it was held impossible to have any want of wood in England. But contrary to former imaginations such hath beene the great expense of timber for navigation, with infinite increase of building of houses, with the great expense of wood to make household furniture, caskes, and other vessels not to be numbered, and of carts, wagons and coaches, besides the extreame waste of wood in making iron, burning of brick and tile, that at this present . . . there is . . . a scarcitie of wood through the whole Kingdom.'

The same uncertainty applies to other raw materials called for by war. Wool, flax, cotton: soldiers, so often arriving in rags, needed clothing, needed, now campaigns were so prolonged, blankets; armour called for padding; guns needed match, wads and swabs; cavalry pennants, infantry ensigns, officers' tents – among all these stimuli to production only clothing (seldom, as we have seen, amounting to 'uniform') was really significant. It often called for bulk purchase. But how far this stimulated production as a whole depends on the impossible estimate of how far military service wore out clothes more speedily than the occupations whence the soldiers came. And leather? Marching wore out shoes. So did the peasant's diurnal trudge. Leather was needed for specialized cavalry saddlery and harness, for shield-coverings, quivers, scabbards. But there is no evidence that this sort of demand transformed a tanning industry already coping with the growing daily need for shoes, belts and pouches and with the luxury trade in stamped leather wall-hangings and hunting equipment.

With metallic resources one can tread on slightly firmer ground. This is especially true of copper. By itself, or mixed with zinc to make tougher brass, copper was already used by the mid-fifteenth century to make a wide variety of household utensils, wire for industrial wool combs, and church ornaments, especially candelabra. Mixed with tin, as bronze, it was used chiefly for bells but also for church doors, medallions and other small sculptural objects. It was the overtaking of iron by bronze as the most favoured metal for artillery that made the greatest new demand on the ore, and the bronze age period of gunpowder weaponry lasted until iron moved into the lead again in the early seventeenth century. It was, moreover, primarily the need for small change for military wages that led to the development of copper-based coinage: even silver-rich Spain introduced such a currency from 1599. Meanwhile, though no new industrial processes were introduced, the mining and manufacture of copper and its alloys employed a greatly enlarged workforce. The main centres of production were in central Europe, in the Tyrol, Hungary and the environs of Mansfeld in Thuringia. Here the crucial nature of copper for local armaments and to satisfy foreign demand (not only for guns: Venice re-exported large quantities of copper to the Levant and the Far East) led to monopolistic and cartel operations on the part of German bankers of unprecedented daring: in 1546 the Fugger company, working under Imperial licence, had copper worth a million florins warehoused for distribution in Antwerp alone. The case of England illustrates the demand. From 1530 a series of statutes forbade the export of the country's meagre supplies of ore. In the militant 1540s Henry VIII's agents, advised by his chief gunfounder, John Owen, were forced to buy Fugger copper in Antwerp and Brussels. From 1568 the monopolistic Company of Mines Royal was set up to exploit new domestic seams and in the following century was employing up to 4000 workers, men and women (as ore-washers), in the area of Keswick in Cumberland. By this time the country was self-sufficient, partly because improved iron-smelting procedures had encouraged England to anticipate the wider move to prefer cheaper guns made of iron. But though war supplies in England as elsewhere had dictated the nature of contracts negotiated by rulers – in virtue of their sovereign right to semi-precious ores as well as to gold and silver – with businessmen, they had never been considered in isolation from other areas of the market. As Robert Cecil in 1599 put the intention of the controllers of the Mines Royal: 'Their desire principally has been that Her Majesty and the Realm might be served with that commodity to make ordnance *and necessaries* rather than stand to the courtesy of strangers.'

With regard to the military raw material *par excellence*, iron and its derivative, steel, the peacetime-wartime balance of use is trickier to estimate. Even the humblest inventory might contain a cooking pot, a farm implement or weapon of iron or a pin. On the other hand, the price of iron was such that hardwoods were used even for such strain-bearing components as ploughshares and the gears of mills and winches. As in cooking, industrial procedures involving heat, like the boiling of brine or of fats for soap, used iron pans. But if a vessel or implement could be made of ceramic or wood it was. Though nails and angle-irons were available, even builders and shipwrights used wooden plugs as much as possible – and not simply with rust in mind; in boats save those of the largest size, the mass of iron in the anchors was probably as great as that distributed elsewhere.

Armour, weapon blades and points, artillery (in the bronze age mainly the clamping-points and wheelrims of gun-carriages) and its balls, and portable firearms: all increased demand. The mining of iron ore for armour and weaponry was not, however, exclusively linked to war itself. Hunting, chivalric sport (the joust and tournament), municipal policing and personal self-protection: the peacetime demand was constant. The needs of war, or, more specifically, of preparation for war, can be linked to a steady increase in mining from the mid-fifteenth century in the main ore-bearing regions of the Austrian and Lombard Alps, the Rhineland, around Guipúzcoa (near Bilbao) and Liège, and in the Kentish weald. They can be listed in a rough chronological order: early, massive iron cannon, whose overtaking by bronze guns coincided with the general substitution of iron for stone balls (contemporary sources estimated between 5500 and 10,000 fired against Padua in 1509 and 40,000 against Rhodes in 1522, 140,000 to 170,000 during the seventy-five days of the siege of Famagusta); the rapid extension of the use of handguns and, as a consequence, the more widespread use of breastplates rather than reinforced canvas jacks by infantry; the equipping of permanent forces recruited from men not bringing any, or the right sort of arms with them (the stockpiling of arms for new recruits for large armies led Venice, for instance, to aim for a reserve of 10,000 sets of equipment) and, still more demanding, the arming of militias; the increasingly routine use of iron guns on shipboard and for coastal defence as improved methods of production came to add greater strength to their cheapness – something like a quarter of the cost of bronze guns.

But while it is probably true that of the 100,000 or so tons produced in Europe annually by 1525 a considerable proportion was already war-related and, as it mounted, continued to be, and that thus war has to have a place in the explanation of Europe's supreme 'pre-industrial' commodity at every stage from the communities who mined it to the arms dealers who sold its products, the size of the proportion cannot be determined, any more than can its influence on methods of extraction or the technology of manufacture be assessed. For the demands of the domestic market also constantly rose. More printing presses, more distilleries, more clocks, the growing use first of special knives and then of forks at mealtimes all helped account for increased demand for iron. Improved forced-draught furnaces bettered its purity while requiring less fuel. More ingenious methods of draining and pumping enhanced the depth to which seams could be exploited. With iron and steel easier to come by, and at a cost that lagged slightly behind the rise in that of other commodities, the permanence of their products led at last to increasing demand.

Indeed, the only raw material exclusively exploited for war was saltpetre, the chief ingredient in gunpowder. (Even sulphur, the third ingredient, was used for medicinal as well as incendiary purposes.) Saltpetre was found naturally in the soil in certain parts of Europe, notably in France and Lombardy, but locations were patchy and laborious to prospect, so a greater reliance was placed on earth that had become saturated with urine and faeces, animal or human: sheepfolds, cattleyards, stables, dovecotes, earth closets and other domestic areas that had, in the course of time, become saturated with nitrate-laden nightsoil. Both feudal landlords and rulers were quick to see the importance of refining such deposits and claiming rights over them modelled on those claimed for metallic ones. By the second generation of the sixteenth century the digging of saltpetre out of the earth, its refining into crystallized potassium nitrate and its marketing to state-owned gunpowder manufactories or for export, had developed into closely supervised monopolies. Even if these were leased to agents, the 'saltpetremen' who arrived with a shovel and a licence to dig and excavate and commandeer labour and transport to the refineries were government agents, and constituted the most resented of those forces – tax collectors, harbingers, purveyors and recruiters – sent by the state to invade the 'liberties' of subjects in the name of the defence of the realm. They came with powers to excavate stables and cellars, sheds and pigeon lofts, and to set up temporary refineries without paying rent for the land they occupied. They were meant to replace the nitrogenous soil with earth if their work imperilled the foundations of walls, and they were not interested in manure itself but only its leaching. So in theory they did no capital damage. But the firm wording of the licences, the exemptions granted the property of exceptionally important subjects, the petitions of protest, all support other evidence that their invasions were widely resented. The extent of their intrusiveness is shown by the justification offered by English saltpetremen in 1628 for their digging under churches: 'The women piss in their seats, which causes excellent saltpetre.'

Thus, apart from the peacetime necessities, alum, coal, stone, and the sand, clay and lime needed for bricks (though the construction industry itself was stimulated by the remaking of fortifications), the extraction of raw materials was, if to an incalculable extent, influenced overall by the needs of war – lead for bullets and the proving shot of cannon might be added to its use in pipes and roofing. How extensive, then, was war's contribution to the industrial, manufacturing component within western Europe's economy when these materials were made into saleable objects?

As the population grew, for all the checks imposed upon it by disease, famine and the lowered resistance to natural calamities caused by war itself, sheer numbers offered some stimulus to traditional crafts; more people had to be clothed and shod, housed and provided with the tools to make a living. But as food prices rose in roughly the same proportion, the purchasing power of the 'new' population was low. There was also a slightly disproportionate increase in the number of town- as opposed to country-dwellers, caused as much by immigration as by an up-turn in the urban birth and survival rates. But, again, the greater part of this increase was constituted by men and women unable to purchase more than what was essential to keep body and soul together, and not always so much.

It was the few whose purchases of land, whose building of villas, palaces and town houses and whose patronage, in their furnishing, of the decorative arts, revealed the extent to which the economy was prospering. The increase in the demand for sheet glass, for instance, does not simply demonstrate that less fear of violence from street or field encouraged larger windows but that there was more money available for glazing rather than for oiled paper. Yet the parallel record of bankruptcies, property sales and mortgages suggests that expenditure on luxuries, the chief stimulus to innovation and an important sustainer of volume in manufacture, was still quite modest compared with the capacity of manufacturing procedures to produce still more. It is against this background that the additional military purchases of rulers and municipal governments – who via taxation could, unlike other individuals, spend money they had neither inherited nor earned – must be seen.

It is impossible to assess the role of the arms trade within the manufacturing economy as a whole if it is fastidiously seen simply as an aberrant form of conspicuous expenditure, as of all forms of display the most wasteful. There was nothing novel about the armaments industry, though its capacity from the mid-fifteenth century was progressively increased. And military hardware was, after all, hardware. Gunpowder went up in smoke. And economically this was its best feature: it had to be replaced. Ammunition, on the other hand, once lead and iron overtook the wood of arrows, crossbow quarrels and the frangible stone of cannon shot, could be dug out and recycled. Cannon themselves locked up large quantities of capital. They were used less frequently than their civilian counterparts, church bells or the anchors of large vessels. But like town walls, which have escaped the head-shaking of economic historians, they could on occasion save far more capital than had gone into them. To deplore expenditure on artillery is like deploring that on fire extinguishers, which are bought in the hope that they will not have to be used. Navies required more guns in relation to seamen than did armies in relation to soldiers. But cannon lasted. In 1605 the Spanish *San Agustin* sailed from Panama with one dated 1522 and two founded in 1500. In spite of a numerically increased demand, plus the added stimulus of the supersession of old designs by newer ones, the productivity of the cannon industry was actually hampered by the lasting usefulness of its own products. And apart from the salving of ball from siege and battlefield and the gouging out of lead shot from the timber frames to which militia targets were attached, guns were melted and recast when outmoded. Similarly, the markets for armour, though refreshed by the introduction of new styles and heavier plate proofed against shot, and for handweapons by innovations like musket, carbine and pistol, were limited by the sturdiness of the product. Much recycling occurred through troops pawning their equipment (though pawnbrokers were forbidden to accept it) or losing it by confiscation at the end of a campaign during which they had not been able to pay for it in full. Some was reclaimed from the dead by official search parties or scavengers. That part of this equipment passed into civilian hands had little effect on the arms industry. Geared up for war, it was already geared for peace, and soldiers, as we have seen, were expected to bring their own weapons with them. The leaving of armour in wills and the ease with which it could be hired from armourer-costumiers, adds a caution to any notion that a newly raised army was altogether a newly equipped one. And though bulk orders for arms or pieces of armour feature as the most challenging demands that were made on any industry, the impression (it is no more) is that they were never fulfilled in number or quality: a topping-up through a hasty scouring of the secondhand market being necessarily accepted by governments during the process of mobilization.

An estimate of the exceptional, tax-and-loan-backed war component of European manufactures has also to take account of the misleading impression that can be derived from the arms collections of today. Overwhelmingly, these show not what was used in war but what was produced for parade, joust, hunt or self-defence in peacetime. The more famous armourers carried on a tailor-made and a *prêt-à-porter* business at the same time. In 1464 Duke Philip the Good called Francesco Missaglia of Milan, travelling on business in Burgundy, to take patterns 'from the body' to make up on his return to Italy. In 1514 François de Valois, wanting to cut a stylish figure at the marriage celebrations of Louis XII, summoned Jacques Merveille to Paris from Tours to measure him for a tournament suit and then, again, to fit it on. Shakespeare's Benedick, in *Measure for Measure*, would 'have walked ten miles to see a good armour'. Some commanders, well into the sixteenth century, insisted on obtaining smarter or simply better weapons for their companies than could be obtained locally. Thus Filippo Strozzi, while in French service, regularly ordered Milanese arquebuses for his men in defiance of embargoes on imported arms. For reasons of ceremony – did princely guards take their elaborately chased halberds into action? – or of prestige, as well as the humbler reasons for being armed against adversity, the privately sponsored sector of the arms industry was a thriving one.

After these qualifications, it can be said that early modern warfare, by boosting production, not only affected the places where armaments were made or marketed, but introduced the bureaucraticization of control over the industry, and to some extent altered the composition and status of the workforce involved.

The old specializations, especially for hunting weapons, still persisted. In 1517 Antonio de Beatis toured Malines with the cardinal of Aragon and noted that 'in this town they make all sorts of crossbows extremely well, stocks and bows as well as bindings, sheaths, cranequins and all necessary equipment. The Cardinal had already [when passing through a couple of weeks earlier] ordered a large number which reached him later in Rome.' And because weapons of a sort could be made or repaired anywhere, especially the straightforward, undecorated ones used in war or for self-defence, the earlier pattern whereby most towns had a streetful, or a small cluster of armourers' workshops, was maintained. Thus in 1550 Rouen had two crossbow makers and four swordsmiths (compared with three makers of rcaquets for the *jeu de paume* and twelve playing-card makers). Milan's reputation as a centre for *de luxe* armours, built up from the fourteenth century by successive members of the Missaglia family, was sustained until the end of the sixteenth by the Negroli. The fifteenth-century clockmakers of Nuremberg turned naturally to the manufacture of spring-driven wheel-locks in the sixteenth. But while the late medieval substructure of the industry remained, this was largely determined by civilian demand; of course, its tools and forges could play a small part in military emergencies, but three factors, new in intensity if not in origin, helped to transform the concentration and the siting of the armour and weapons industry: the wish to be nationally self-sufficient, to cut transport costs, and the need for centres which could cope with orders of exceptional magnitude.

One example may suffice to show how large orders could be. Brescia, fed with blades and sheet steel from the forges of Gardone, the chief town in the iron- and fuel-rich Val Trompia, was one of the chief centres in fifteenth-century Italy where simple armours were finished and weapons of all kinds fitted with hafts and stocks. With the increasing importance of firearms, more and more of the Gardone forges specialized in gun barrels and locks, either sent to Brescia for butts and (for sporting weapons) ornamentation to be added, or exported direct to nations who preferred their own native style of finishing. By the 1530s virtually all handgun production in Venice's land empire was concentrated there, and from 1537 export was only permitted under government licence. Even so, production was at such a level that in 1542 permission to export at least 7800 arquebuses and muskets was given. By 1562 Brescia was exporting 25,000 guns (not all mounted) a year, nearly seventy a day over and above national requirements. By 1570 production had – temporarily, it is true, because of the demands of the Turkish war – risen to 300 a day. By 1600 the production of barrels had settled at an annual 77,000, of which perhaps 50,000 were for military use. Between the digging of the ore and carting away of dross from the forges, to the tempering and polishing of the metal parts to the finishers in Brescia, the Val Trompia arms industry provided employment for some 40,000 workers. Brescia, meanwhile, not only completed the fabrication of the firearms and their accoutrements (powder flasks, rammers, bullet moulds) but continued to turn out armour, swords, pikes and halberds. Craft tradition, symbiosis between raw material and city-based manufacturing expertise, governmental protection – often resented because of the restrictions it imposed on the movement of goods and men – and reasonable access to river or mountain-pass means of communication, made the Brescia-Gardone region something of a freak. It is indicative, nonetheless, of the change brought about by the military reformation.

This also involved a shift in the locations where cannon were founded. In the second half of the fifteenth century it was still common for these to be forged in countryside smelteries, as it was cheaper to haul the finished cannon from the source of ore and fuel than to bring these to an urban foundry. With the increasing use of alloys, however, bronze or brass, this motive lost enough of its force to be displaced by governments' desire to supervise quality and impose licensing controls. Thus from 1537, though Brescia-Gardone was permitted to produce cast-iron guns for export, the far greater production of bronze artillery was restricted to the arsenal of Venice itself, as was the ironwork of gun-carriages and balls and the fabrication of gunpowder. This was aided by Venice's position as a port with access to a river system threading through its mainland possessions, but it represents a tendency towards concentration that was happening elsewhere. So was the splitting off of functions; as more and more cannon were needed, founders ceased to make bells, guns and sculptures indiscriminately as had been the rule. Indeed, the casting in Venice in 1556 and 1559 of the great bronze decorative well-heads in the courtyard of the Ducal Palace by the current representatives of the republic's multi-generational gunfounder families Alberghetti and dei Conti was an exceptionally late example of such versatility.

While some armaments centres stably expanded their traditional activity, others developed and declined according to the attention of rulers and the fortunes of war. When the dukes of Burgundy looked on Lille as a capital, its arms trade flourished; when their attention switched to Bruges, it faltered, and Bruges was to be overtaken by Brussels and Antwerp when the Burgundian inheritance passed to Charles V and these cities became the favoured bases of Habsburg industrial-military administration. Liège, under its independent prince-bishops the leading fifteenth-century arms centre in the north, retained its productive stamina in spite of occupation by one side or another, and sold impartially to Spaniards and Dutch throughout the Netherlands wars. In France Charles VII and Louis XI deliberately built up Tours as a more productive arms centre by encouraging foreign armourers and gunfounders, chiefly Italian, to settle there. Under Francis I, whose marketing bureaucracy was more effective and whose military needs were greater, it became simply one of many state-encouraged centres, from Paris itself to Breteuil to the west and St Etienne and Forez in the south east. To the east, the sixteenth-century dukes of Lorraine built up the arsenal of Nancy as a model combination of production and readily available stockpile. Comparable production and warehousing centres developed in Nuremberg, Augsburg and Innsbruck, though without sucking away the production of local specialisms, like the swordblades of Solingen, from towns able to protect profitable crafts of their own.

In Italy, because of Milan's importance as a staging and equipping post for troops raised in Spain, successive governors fostered the city's rivalry with Brescia; Genoa imported iron from Elba for its own lively arms industry; Lucca maintained its traditional role as an exporter of fine swords and daggers. Despite repeated efforts, the Spanish crown never achieved self-sufficiency. Neither the gunfoundries of Malaga nor (after the conquest of Portugal) of Lisbon were able to provide enough artillery even for the navy, and by the end of the century so many had been imported from England that Sir Walter Raleigh was moved to protest: 'I am sure', he told the House of Commons, 'heretofore one ship of Her Majesty's was able to beat ten Spaniards, but now, by reason of our own ordnance we are hardly matched one to one.' The peninsula's one true arms centre, the pike and firearms industry in Guipúzcoa and Vizcaya, was by 1591 capable of producing 20,000 arquebuses and 3000 muskets a year, but Spain still relied on imports from Italy and the Netherlands, as it did for gunpowder and, in spite of busy streets of armourers' workshops like the Calle Sierpes of Seville, for additional helmets and cuirasses. The Dutch, however, faced with being cut off from the arms centres of the south Netherlands and the need to arm a rapidly growing navy, not only imported iron cannon from England and sponsored local foundries in iron-bearing parts of

Westphalia, but built up foundries in Maastricht, Utrecht and The Hague which gave them a large measure of independence in the production of bronze cannon. Made with copper imported from Sweden and even from Japan, alloyed with English and German tin, these weapons are perhaps an extreme example of war's impact on Europe's industrial and commercial economy (we can add the sulphur from Italy and the saltpetre from the East Indies that was used in their charges), and they represent the peak of an international basis of production that would not have been so broad without it.

The Dutch also cast guns in Amsterdam and Rotterdam, but these cities, like Lyon, Mechelen (Malines), Antwerp, Hamburg and Augsburg, were more important as marketing than as arms centres. Much production remained dispersed among forest forges and provincial towns, in spite of rulers' preferences for a few easily controllable centres. Crisis mobilizations could call for extra purchases abroad. Normal imports of raw materials could be blocked. War produced, as no peaceable project could, a need for quickly accessible reserves of warehoused supplies and for contacts with dealers who could tap other sources and arrange – often surreptitiously ('if it be known here, the party is in danger of his life', wrote an English negotiator for gunpowder in Antwerp of his local contact in 1559) – for their delivery. These operations were normally arranged by merchants as part of their handling of a variety of commodities, but from Jean Cambier, whose arms dealership was based on Mons from about 1450, to Albert de Gondi, whose expertise in the arms-supply business from the 1550s brought him a French title of nobility and the office of marshal, and on to such careers as those of the late sixteenth-century armaments barons Jean Curtius and Louis de Geer of Liège, Jacques Le Roy of Antwerp, and Elias Tripp of Dordrecht, the capitalistic skills that had brought fortunes to the Medici and the Fugger were increasingly – though never exclusively, for there were parallel pickings to be made from the feeding and clothing of armies, and never safely, for governments were unreliable clients – concentrated on dealing in military hardware.

Given the constant demand for military goods in peacetime, the stockpile effect this led to, and the longevity and recycling factors we have noticed, it would be unwise to argue that wars stimulated manufactures to a degree that appreciably aided the industrial-bourgeois element in society. While sadly underinformed and impressionistic, figures like 2 per cent of total manufacture for

war-related products in peacetime and 4 per cent in wartime –
including both armies and navies – are probably of the right order
over the period as a whole. Though even more difficult to trace,
the stimulus to commercial and financial dealings probably
played a more pervasive role.

There is no doubt that for men with sticky fingers more war
material was on the move to be caught, profited by, and passed on
as a result of the military reformation. English cannon went to
Denmark and Sweden (until that country became self-sufficient
around 1620) and Moroccan gunpowder joined sugar as part of
north Africa's exchange for European firearms, metals and
sulphur. Of Spain's and Portugal's copious purchase of foreign
arms of every variety, part, especially firearms, was destined for
the Americas and for the west African slave trade. Yew staves
wound their way to the yeomen of England until late in the
sixteenth century less from local country churchyards than from
Venice, the Rhineland and Poland. War itself, however, caused no
fundamental changes in commercial techniques, and the big
dealers trod in the footsteps of the fourteenth-century Bardi and
Datini, using similar partnerships, agent networks and credit
facilities. In any case, far more typical than Cambier and his
successors were the Milanese merchants who hawked their suits of
armour among the tents during the 1488 war in Brittany. Indeed,
much war-related trade remained on a very small, day-to-day scale.
Grocers stocked arms among their cheeses and candles, and
apothecaries speculated in gunpowder as well as ginger and aloes.
If we add the very considerable trade in smuggled war material,
and the continuity of peacetime demand, the arms trade can be
seen as having a variety and resilience of earning power that did
much to compensate for war's interruption of other types of
industrial and commercial activity – activity that, in any case, was
more drastically dislocated by plague and the quarantine regulations that accompanied it than by any war. It is largely because of
its permeation of the economic fabric as a whole that it is
impossible to distinguish the role of the arms trade within the
commercial demands created by other factors, whether the
population rise, a more widespread taste for comfort and luxury,
the needs of colonists, or an increase in the monetary supply. All
the same, it is worth noting the mid-seventeenth-century opinion
of the Dutch chronicler Lieuwe van Aitzema as he reviewed the
pause in hostilities in the Netherlands between 1609 and 1621:
'The ordinary man was weary of the truce. . . . Many recalled that

225

in times of war there had been a good penny to be earned, and they were quite certain that there had been more trafficking during the war than under the truce.' And it is worth contrasting this with Philip II's downcast comment that the same wars have 'consumed the money and substance which has come from the Indies while the collection and raising of revenues in these kingdoms has only been done with great difficulty because of the dearth of specie in them, and because of the damage which this does and causes to the commerce and trade on which the yield of our taxes depends'.

Even more energy could have been fed into the economy by the arms industry had it not been for government intervention. In the interest of national security and, later, to a lesser extent, of profit derived from monopolistic contracts, governments from the late fifteenth century attempted to control labour and sale as well as to peg prices to suit their own pockets and those of their subjects, who were the most valuable military raw material of all.

In 1488 Ferdinand and Isabella forbade the export from Aragon and Castile not only of artillery – which, together with saltpetre, was the earliest arm to attract rulers' vigilance in this respect – but of 'handguns, crossbows and bolts, lances, cuirasses and shields, casques, helmets and beavers, and other forms of weapons and equipment'. At about the same time Charles VIII wrote to Lodovico Sforza, the effective ruler of Milan, asking him to waive the legislation forbidding the export of war material or the emigration of skilled craftsmen. 'We beg you most affectionately that you allow Jacquemin Ayrolde [an armourer from Tours] to bring from Milan up to twelve armourers, with their consent, to our city of Tours and also to carry with them the things necessary for the fabrication of a certain number of suits of armour for us.' Much earlier legislation was summed up in a French ordinance published in 1572: 'because the founding of cannon and ball and the gathering and manufacture of the materials for gunpowder are a sovereign right, belonging to the King alone for the safeguard and defence of the realm', no subject whatsoever was to make or seek to sell such war material without licence from those deputed to act 'in the interest of the prince and of the public good'. And Henry VIII's concern for having troops who could bring their own arms when recruited was expressed in a proclamation of 1542. 'The King's most excellent majesty, being informed that divers covetous persons having harness, artillery [i.e. weapons] and other habiliments of the war to sell, hold them at such unreasonable and excessive prices that his loving and obedient subjects cannot buy nor provide the same at reasonable and convenient prices to serve his majesty and the realm . . . hath . . . set reasonable prices of bows, arrows, bills, harness, and other habilments for the war as hereafter followeth' – and there succeeds a list of prices of weapons and pieces of armour according to manufacture of 'the best sort' or 'the second sort'.

The effectiveness of such controls depended on three things: the number of bureaucrats (using the word loosely to include all those who had a salaried or landed, 'feudal', responsibility to impose the ruler's will) in relation to the volume of the traffic; the marketing sophistication of the economy concerned (the more sophisticated, the shrewder the falsification of invoices, the more numerous the contacts with foreign dealers and smuggler intermediaries); and the degree to which individual producers or their politically weighty supporters had the constitutional right to challenge the extension of regalian rights into the market place.

These issues have not as yet a documentation adequate to permit a chronological or comparative survey. Venetian state control, which began with its permanent acquisition of Brescia in 1440, was perhaps the most consistently effective not only because the republic had been able to negotiate conquerors' rights but because the standard of supervision by the governors sent to reside there was high and continuous, and because, under the Council of Ten (from 1582 the Senate), a permanent central magistracy existed to check the production and sale of firearms, artillery and gunpowder. The very size of France militated against overall control. From the reign of Charles VII it was government orders which built up the heavy armaments industry, but the extraction of saltpetre and the making of gunpowder remained the only area of monopolistic restriction until the reform of the whole system at the conclusion of the civil wars by Sully, after which the production of gunpowder, cannon and non-sporting firearms alike had to be channelled into the Parisian and seventeen provincial arsenals, and sales could only be made from them when state quotas had been filled. In Spain the principle of royal control over arms production had been repeatedly proclaimed since 1488, but though the crown administered a number of arsenals directly, inadequate bureaucratic supervision elsewhere had led to what was the effect overall of a free market. To prevent the drain of pikestaffs, firearms, cannon and saltpetre abroad while the crown was forced to buy foreign arms and ammunition to make good the loss, a sustained but unsuccessful attempt was made in the 1570s to subject almost the whole range of arms production to royal licensees who had to satisfy government needs before indulging in private sales. Its failure by the 1590s, largely because the state could not pay its own bills on time, meant that Spain, of all countries the one with the greatest need of arms, continued to pay for them at the most uneconomical rate.

In England, despite the high cost of purchasing arms abroad for Henry VIII's campaigns, control was desultory. Inadequately patrolled by administrators, price fixing seems to have failed. The claim that all saltpetre deposits belonged to the crown was not in itself challenged, but their exploitation on the basis of a monopolistic licence (granted to the Evelyn family from the 1560s) was; it was a considerable victory for the crown's influence in parliament that this was exempted from mention in the anti-monopolies statute of 1624. And though reliance on cannon imported from the Netherlands, or made in London by German, French and Italian founders was superseded in the mid-sixteenth century by natives working under royal licence to supply the Ordnance Office at the Tower of London, little vigilance was paid to the protection of the licensees. In 1573 Ralph Hogge, petitioning the Privy Council, angrily anticipated Raleigh's argument by pointing to unlicensed manufacturers, thanks to whose private sales of cannon abroad 'your enemy is better furnished with them than our own country's ships are'. On this occasion the reaction was unexpectedly quick. No fewer than fifty-eight errant founders were detected and warned under a bond of £2000 not to export without special licence. All the same, smuggling continued, and when Hogge's successor as licensee, John Browne, found himself forced to sell abroad because of government orders falling short of his productive capacity, he was merely reacting to one of the recurrent problems set by governmental control: the contrast between the rhythms of governmental needs and of peacetime spending capacities, and the steadily rising line on the graph of international demand. It was for this reason that the latecomers to the scene of government-sponsored and -controlled arms production, Holland and Sweden, adopted a mixed-economy policy that ensured a public-sector stockpile while not inhibiting the capital-generating activity of private firms.

The emphasis on cannon and gunpowder in the records of state intervention is striking. But it was easier for officials to spot the somewhat complex plants required by gunfounders than to patrol the multifarious activities of rural bowyers or urban gunsmiths and armourers. Most of the traffic in armour, firearms, swordblades and polearms, all of which cost governments dear when shopped for in a hurry, by escaping control enabled the arms trade as a whole to find pretty well its own level.

The trade encouraged a certain amount of migration among specialist craftsmen, notably the makers of fine armour and gunfounders. The former, chiefly Milanese, settled especially in northern towns like Bruges and Tours, centres which were hard put to it to satisfy fashion-conscious court and noble demand for the novel combination of practicality and decorative effect pioneered in south Germany and northern Italy. Encouraged by tax exemptions and the guarantee of princely protection, such men were rapidly absorbed through market contacts and marriage and, by modifying their names to accord with local usage, become progressively more difficult to trace by the second decade of the sixteenth century. By then, however, such migration had practically ceased with the decline in the use of the finest armour on campaign. Fashion armour retained its popularity, but local armourers learned to make it and, if they could not, purchasers used dealers whose networks dealt adequately with less urgent needs. Some migration on the part of skilled, but less prestigious craftsmen continued, but against a growing current: tightened guild regulations which made entrance to them more difficult, protectionist policies whose success, if slight, is suggested by the exceptional reliance by Spain on its Milanese dependency.

The migration of gunfounders from Germany and Flanders and to a lesser extent from Italy to build up the industry in France, England and Spain was also initially encouraged by tax exemptions and grants of naturalization. Less subject to guild regulations and protected by rulers against the rising tide of resentment against foreign craftsmen, this migration lasted longer. All the same, with the build-up of native industries, by the mid-sixteenth century it had – save to Spain and Portugal – practically ceased. And neither ripple of migration can be compared with the waves that carried, say, silk, ribbon and glass workers away from their countries of origin. Indeed, it is possible that traffic in practitioners of the arts and their talented minions (stucco and intarsia specialists, illustrators, printers and instrumental players) played a greater part than the needs of war in inducing skilled men to change their place of residence.

Did war, then, affect the place that money considerations had in society's consciousness?

Though loans, credit operations and industrial organization involved no techniques that would encourage novel manifestations of the capitalistic spirit as such, and cannot, in any case, be disentangled from the moods and methods of non-war-related economic expansion, military logistics undoubtedly increased the number of transactions that disseminated the imprint of that spirit. It may be true that high rates of war taxation diverted cash that could have been used for profitable investment. The argument has been used to explain the comparative sluggishness of Spain's industrial output. But it cannot be proved, because so many other explanatory factors have to be fed in, from the cost of transport to social and racial temperament and to alternative forms of that adventurousness which, however methodical and 'bourgeois' its surface, lay at capitalism's psychological core. There is no need to review the industrial and commercial terrain we have already crossed; there is little doubt that Amsterdam's new prosperity was linked to its role as an armaments and loan-marketing centre and the welcome its guilds extended to entrepreneur-refugees; English clothiers had never had such opportunities to pass off shoddy as hardwearing military jerkins and hose; no Milanese entrepreneur had received so demanding a contract as did Carlo Pedrone in 1605 when he was charged to provide quarters, utensils, fuel, fodder, firewood and transport for 5000 troops. It is enough to remember that each military business situation or deal involved not only the principals but their agents and their agents' employees in the tempting game that could be played with figures; due to war, more men learned the ways in which coins as well as animals could be coaxed to breed. And the same phenomenon appears on turning from logistical support to armies themselves: more colonel or captain entrepreneurs, more soldiers aware as never before of the ability of hard cash to purchase or, by its lack, punish; men isolated from the local support systems of family, relations, neighbours, local vendors and their bridging loans, and of landlords who, under the share-cropping tenancies of France and Italy, supplied seed and equipment in return for produce. If we include the extension of the scope of indirect and of the scale of direct taxation (with its associated valuations of property and possessions) and add the probability that the wider circulation of debased, non-bullion-equivalent coins fostered an acuter awareness of the artifice within the working relationship of money to goods and services, war can be seen not only as extending the scope of capitalistic enterprise but of inducing reverberations of its spirit, however faint, in society at large.

That scope included opportunities for all the familiar mani-festations of profit-making moods. For those who relished high-risk, high-profit enterprises there was the smuggling of war supplies and a greatly extended opportunity to invest in priva-teering. For those who saw capital accumulation as a way of buying social prestige either through the purchase of administrative offices which cash-hungry rulers were forced to offer for sale, or through becoming the trusted financial agents of a court, the opportunities multiplied as never before. And for those who liked to play safe there were war-loan bonds offered on an unprecedented scale. These bonds, secured by governments on anticipated revenues, provided a modest yield: 6 per cent was typical. And though the rate was at times cut or interest payments deferred, they were considered safe. War bonds were not an innovation. It was through investment in state debts that Florence and Venice had been able to persist in their frontier-defining wars in the first half of the fifteenth century for year after year with the committed support of the bondholders. It was a Venetian ambassador who noted in 1620 that bonds were looked on as a sound investment in the United Provinces although 'the province of Holland alone has a debt of forty million florins, for which it pays six and a quarter per cent interest. It could easily get rid of its debts by raising taxes, but the creditors of the state will not have it so.' And if investment in bonds, like the parallel low-yield investment in land for reasons of business caution or the acquisition of social repute, limited the productive power of war-related profits and, as in France, was recognized as a check on a turnover that might have contributed more to revenue by other means, it was nevertheless a political advantage to governments to have subjects linked in this way to an increased dependence on their exercise of power.

making profits.

9

The indirect impact: war, taxation and government

The Florentine secretary who kept the minutes of a discussion about proposed new taxes in 1495 headed his account with what had long been a cliché: 'Bellorum nervi sunt pecuniae' (sums of money are the sinews of war). Urging Louis XII to invade Milan in 1499, the Milanese exile Gian Giacomo Trivulzio reminded him that 'three things are necessary: money; more money; and still more money'. Though occasionally challenged by military reformers who pointed out that the quality of soldiers was as important, if not more so, as the cash raised for war, there was no dissent from Thomas Wilson's pronouncement of 1600 that of all state expenditure, war constituted 'the greatest and arch-point of expense'.

As a proportion of gross national product the expenses of wars were, by modern standards, not immoderate: some 5+ per cent in the fifteenth century, in the late sixteenth century perhaps 3–4 per cent for England, 8–9 per cent for Spain and possibly 16 per cent for the United Provinces – a great burden for a small, if rich, economy. But the means of tapping GNP into revenue were then primitive; war expenses were related not to what was there, but to what could be got.

War was so outrageously the most weighty cause of public expenditure that the only figures usefully to be compared with its costs are those of states' total normal, or 'ordinary' revenues: income, that is, arising from rents, fees, fines and traditionally accepted customs dues and forms of direct taxation on assets.

Given the imprecision that dogs the records of both military costs actually disbursed and of revenue actually received, these figures are to be treated with caution; the proportions, however, are probably not far out. In general it can be hazarded that the direct costs of war were seldom less than half the amount of peacetime revenues, and that apart from the examples of 1537–40, 1544, 1550 and 1570–3 given opposite, other cases when costs exceeded revenue (the Papacy in 1529–31 and Holland in 1599 would be further examples) were not rare. The drama inherent in these figures, moreover, can only be appreciated if two other factors are borne in mind.

The cost of war

	Theatre	Cost p.a.	Revenue p.a.	Currency
1482–92	Spain v. Granada	80,000,000	150,000,000	Maravedis
1515	France v. Milan	1,800,000	4,900,000	Livres tournois
1523	France (mobilization for Italy and expedition to Scotland)	2,600,000	5,150,000	Livres tournois
1526	Florence v. France (subsidy to Holy League)	261,000	268,000	Florins
1537–40	Venice v. Turks	1,500,000	1,340,000	Ducats
1544	France v. England and Charles V	6,000,000	9,000,000	Livres tournois
1544	England v. France	650,000	250,000	Pounds
1550	Nuremberg v. Brandenburg	1,500,000	170,000	Gulden
1554	France v. Charles V	13,275,000	11,000,000(?)	Livres tournois
1570–73	Venice v. Turks	2,500,000	2,000,000	Ducats
1585	England in Netherlands	126,000	250,000	Pounds
1590s	Spain in Netherlands	9,000,000	22,200,000	Florins
1600	England in Ireland	320,000	374,000	Pounds
1615–17	Venice v. Austria	1,580,000	3,000,000	Ducats

First, as a rule, peacetime revenues were fully committed to housekeeping expenses: court salaries, entertainment and buildings; administrative costs (judicial, financial, diplomatic); and defence (garrisons, fortifications, navies). Significantly, when there were, exceptionally, surpluses, these were placed, in the form of coin or jewels, in 'war chests': stout coffers, provided with several locks so that they could be opened only by mutual agreement among the official keyholders, and placed in jealously guarded strongrooms. Henry VII saved such a treasure, which Henry VIII spent, and Lord Burghley had built one for Elizabeth to the sum of over a quarter of a million pounds before it had to be raided to nothing by the expenses of the Netherlands and Irish wars. Julius II was the first pope to establish a war chest, in an innermost room of Castel S. Angelo; it was quickly emptied by his successors. Francis I in 1535 aimed to build up a war reserve of three million livres from revenue surpluses and windfalls such as fines levied on peccant officials and the dowry he forced Catherine

233

de Medici to bring on her marriage to his son Henry. The experiment failed after two years of renewed war expenditure. When the massive debts incurred during the war of 1570–3 had been paid off, Venice set one up in 1584 with the warning to senators that it 'cannot be invaded for any reason whatsoever save that of open war, with a penalty of 1000 ducats to whosoever should propose otherwise'. It was the most successful chest of the period, and enabled the republic to go to war with Austria in 1615 with a fairly light financial heart.

In the second place, normal revenue had, at least by the 1530s, exploited to the limits of fiscal practicality and political goodwill the revenues earmarked for defence. Larger permanent forces, government contributions to modernized urban and coastal fortifications, the stocking of precautionary 'parks' of artillery: these aspects of the military reformation meant that although revenue rose along with the population that paid head or hearth tax, and with the increased volume of commercial transactions that involved tolls or purchase taxes, war-related expenditure in peacetime, however effectively it was diverted on to local communities in accordance with the principle of self-help, pressed alarmingly on governments' ability to balance their books. One half of Louis XI's revenue was absorbed by the permanent military establishment and subsidies to Swiss troops on stand-by contracts; between 1539 and his death in January 1547 Henry VIII spent an average 29 per cent of normal income on fortifications alone. Spain was spending over five times as much on fortifications in 1611 as in 1577. In 1600 defence accounted for 6.5 million livres out of 20.5 in France; in 1615 10 million out of 24.4. Apart from the exceptional war-chest episodes, defence spending, like a malign growth spreading within the bottle shaped by medieval conventions limiting 'ordinary' revenues, ensured that all the expenses of actual war had to be paid for in 'extraordinary' ways. And the fact that local communities (many of them, as ports or commercial centres on strategically important routes, the most prosperous ones) had to contribute heavily to their own defences, made them the more reluctant to contribute to national defence as a whole. In the second half of the fifteenth century Rennes was spending an average of 42 per cent of the municipal budget on its walls; in the second half of the sixteenth, many towns – Como and Bergamo, for instance – had to earmark over 50 per cent for military expenditure. The budget of the kingdom of Naples – theoretically a source of national income for Spain – reflected a similar proportion: 55 per cent for defence. And, as with national budgets, these figures relate to normal revenue. For sudden bursts of modernizing defences 'extraordinary' revenue had to be generated locally: in Plymouth a tax on pilchards as well as loans from residents, for Antwerp, the sale of civic property, increased citizenship fees, heavier sales and import duties on beer and meat, in addition to loans. At times of mobilization, when governments needed exceptional fiscal cooperation, communities could be spending on raising combat troops, readying defensive forces and contributing to navies, as much as, or even double what government was extracting from national assemblies.

Preparing for war and waging it had always forced rulers themselves, and their councillors and officials, to think with unaccustomed zeal about money. But there had been no medieval precedent for the intensity of the concern that had to be devoted to the topic as one aspect after another of the military reformation presented its bill. 'Those who try to be tightfisted while waging war always end by spending more. For nothing requires a more boundless effusion of money. The greater the provisions, the quicker the undertaking will be ended. Failure to make provisions, just to save money, will make the enterprise last longer and, what is more, will result in incomparably greater cost.' It is not that any government was unaware of the truth of Guicciardini's observation. The problem was how to raise the money.

Though normal tax revenues increased to offset the effects of inflating prices on peacetime government, expenditure on enlarged legal and fiscal bureaucracies, wider diplomatic networks and more splendid courts and building programmes, as well as on defence preparations, was in any case causing increased recourse to taxation that was 'extraordinary' either in the sense of increases in the revenue derived from traditional sources such as customs dues or the sales tax on salt, or of demands so unusual that their imposition required a form of assent, varying with the constitutional practice of different countries. The explanations given for raising extraordinary revenue through the Tudor parliament show how far normal expenditure was outrunning normal revenue (crown lands, customs, fees for instituting proceedings in royal courts, feudal windfalls like the falling-in of heirless estates or the exercise of wardship over estates whose inheritors were minors). Up to the 1540s such demands had always centred on open warfare – foreign or against rebels – or its threat as their justification. Thereafter, though this excuse was added whenever it was colourable, it became usual to plead the cost of the national administration in general. And this in a country with no permanent army apart from very small garrison forces, and with a fortification programme that after the mid-century was small compared with those of other countries.

This enhanced pressure on normal revenues made the retention of credit balances only rarely possible. And it made the extraction of additional money from populations whose taking war for granted bore little relationship to their willingness to pay for it all the trickier. The extortionate demands made by campaigns on revenues would have been easier to anticipate – and justify – if they had arisen solely from the direct logistic consequences of the military reformation. But they did not. With the military wage declining against the cost of living, troops relied more and more on government purchases of food and clothing which reflected the endemic inflation. It was not wages but supply and the losses to the fisc (not the economy) from peculation, growing with growing numbers, that caused a Spanish secretary of war to complain in 1596 that 'if comparison were made between the present cost to His Majesty of the troops who serve in his armies and navies and the cost of those of the Emperor Charles V, it will be found that, for an equal number of men, three times as much money is necessary today as used to be spent then'. Outside strictly 'reformation' costs was, again, the charge of servicing not only national war debts but those incurred by the failure of allies to repay subsidies on time: in 1598 England was paying interest on debts of some £1,560,000 incurred by her French and Dutch allies. Hard-pressed to get an expedition going, no government dared add the figure (which could have been at least roughly worked out from past experience or present consultation with serving officers) relating to the costs of replacing men who fell sick or deserted; yet the expense of sending round more recruiting bands, giving the replacement men equipment and subsistence pay, and escorting and transporting them to the front was a formidable item in war expenditure, even if much of it was passed on by central to local government.

'One readily understands the close connection between war with its prodigious expense and the revenues of a ruler.' Fernand Braudel's remark is as justified as is his corollary: 'Through these revenues, war ultimately touched every human activity.' But it is important, too, to bear in mind not only the incidence of extraordinary revenue but the cumulative effect of its timing; not just the launch fee, as it were, which could be called for with a brave declaration of need, and the supplementary and more or less self-explanatory charges caused by the fortunes of war (defeats in battle, stalemates in sieges), but those additional demands, caused by administrative blunders, that imposed further tests of the cooperation between those who started and waged aggressive wars and those who found themselves paying for them. No war, even if fought in the guise of crusade – external or internal – could count on continued willing and direct support from subjects whose loyalty and chauvinism, however vocal, did not go pocket-deep. Hence the state bankruptcies, from those of the Papacy in 1521, of France in 1557, to those of Spain not only in 1557 but in 1575, 1596 and 1607. Hence the ad hoc flurry of expedients and experiments that, alongside a new rigour applied to old methods, characterized the financing of wars. To give but one anticipatory example: in the early months of 1527, Florence, pledged to engage troops for Clement VII's campaigns both at home against the rebel Colonna clan and abroad against the Spanish kingdom of Naples, increased the incidence of direct taxation on person and property, imposed loans on wealthy individuals and guilds (repayable at 6 per cent), offered shares in government stock for a smaller capital investment than hitherto, commuted death or mutilation sentences in return for fines (save for premeditated murder or assault which the victim's family would not accept as adequately revenged in this way), allowed, for a fee, the rights of full citizenship to those families whose heads had not yet completed the normal require-ment of thirty years' taxpaying residence, and confiscated silver plate from churches and guilds for melting into coin.

Recourse to expedients of this sort reflects not the theoretical inadequacy of the traditional tax structure but the difficulty of making it work. Taxes related to individual male adults, to 'hearths' or families, to movable assets including cash balances, and to property, could all be suspended or doubled or trebled according to a government's need and the obtaining of the necessary form of assent. In the same way, indirect taxes on the sale of such things as salt, grain, meat, wood, wax or playing cards, and value-added taxes on the milling of wheat or the casking of wine or simply on the access to town markets of country produce, could be varied in their incidence. While the objects taxed differed from country to country, as did the tax point in the process of manufac-ture or distribution, an administrative turn of a tap should everywhere have produced calculable changes of flow.

But while all wars involved the use of this mechanism, none

depended on it. 'Assent' was not simply a matter of constitutional form; taxes were as difficult to collect after they had been granted by the English parliament as when they were imposed by central fiat in France; standing armies were not used – were too small to have been used – to enforce tax legislation. Whatever pressure administrative systems were able to exert, they could not bring it fully to bear on the passive resistance of the tax-liable population, as individuals or as corporations. The traditional tax system was based on precedent. And every precedent, in an eagerly litigious age ('a peasant has spent twelve ducats on legal fees to contest a bill of six soldi' noted a maddened Venetian administrator in 1578), had come to be dogged by an attendant horde of claims for exemptions, mitigations and postponements. No body of evidence relating to this period reveals the weakness of central government so clearly as does that of tax protest. And when protest on the grounds of privilege failed, there was always the possibility of charging that the records on which direct taxation was based were out of date and therefore open to challenge. When to this thicket of obstruction to the advance of the always-too-few tax gatherers is added the proclivity of representative institutions, whether parliament, estate, municipality or the clergy, to agree to tax demands only if they were spread over a number of years, it is not only clear why governments farmed out the collection of taxes to individuals, thus accepting a net loss of revenue, but why in the short term taxation was chiefly looked upon as a background – if an essential one – to expedience financing. Fiscally speaking no war, even if defensive, was 'popular' in the sense that it was waged with the immediate response of taxpayers.

The most obvious expedient was, of course, for conquering armies to live off contributions gouged from the vanquished or their neutral neighbours. But these demands, though peremptory, still had to be filtered through local resistance, and muted lest they caused revolt; however triumphant, armies abroad never ceased to need supplies pumped through from their national base. This remained true from the periods of French occupation of Italian territory in the early sixteenth century to the prolonged Spanish presence in the late sixteenth-century Netherlands.

At home, forced loans from wealthy individuals or communities had the advantage that rulers could go straight for easily identifiable nuggets rather than wait for the gold dust to be sifted from the taxable seam as a whole. The loans were repayable. Rulers had reprisals (imprisonment, confiscation of property) at their command, or favours – titles, monopolies, offices – that prompted agreement. Comparably speedy was the selling of public offices, from collectorships of tolls and customs to legal and fiscal positions within central and provincial administrations. During the dark days that followed Venice's defeat at Agnadello even a few positions in the Senate were offered for cash. There were medieval precedents for the sale of office. But the late fifteenth and sixteenth centuries saw not only a great surge in the numbers of these transactions, especially in France and Spain, but an extension of the principle that for still more cash such offices could become as heritable as property; there was also introduced the practice of creating unnecessary but prestigious offices solely for the purpose of selling them. Francis I added twenty councillors to the already adequate legal staff of the *parlement* of Paris at 6000 livres a time. Leo X, as well as putting a price-tag on cardinals' hats and key bureaucratic posts (Francesco Ermellino paid 50,000 ducats for the chamberlainship), stuffed the papal civil service with extra posts which gave their holders either a satisfying title or the right to intercept a proportion of the church's revenue before it fell into the treasury. Not all those who bought posts were unworthy of them. On the whole, however, the sale of offices raised short-term income for war purposes at a cost of self-remuneration from fees, taxes or tolls that added to the burden governments had to lay on their people whether in war or peace. An indication of the scale on which this form of expendient war financing was carried on – admittedly an extreme one – is that while towards the end of Francis I's reign direct taxation was bringing in some 5 million livres a year, his income from the sale of offices was estimated at a weighty 900,000.

The chief example of another common way of raising money, the sale of lands belonging to or confiscated by the crown, is provided by England. The dissolution of the monasteries was largely motivated by the need for campaigning money by Henry VIII; disposing of their lands paid for 32 per cent of his French wars, and after further sales for military purposes under Elizabeth some 25 per cent of the country's soil had changed ownership.

Compared with these sales of offices and land, none of the other expedients adopted to bridge the waiting period between the passing of a tax law and the garnering of its yields – the pawning of plate and jewels; the employment of commanding officers rich enough to pay the troops in the early months of a campaign out of their own pockets or credit (the duke of Medina Sidonia in 1588, the earl of Essex in 1591); the state lotteries authorized by Francis I and that were another post-Agnadello Venetian device; moratoria on official salaries – none, even the occasional revaluation or debasement of the coinage, had any important long-term economic or social effect.

Even with the sales of offices and lands, however, there could be delays until purchasers offered themselves. So more than on these and other expedients, governments relied on the up-front money of loans. There was, again, nothing new about waging war on credit. But never before this period had loans attained so high an overall volume, involved so many simultaneous transactions or shaped the course of so many financial careers. And though credit remained the familiar means of achieving non-military aims (the most striking example being Charles V's borrowing in Germany and Italy of 851,000 florins for the diplomacy and bribes that secured his Imperial title from the electors in 1519), it was war that challenged this aspect of the techniques and temperament of capitalism most pervasively. This was true not only of banker merchants who became almost legendary in their own lifetimes like Jakob Fugger (d. 1525) of whom the chronicler of his home city, Augsburg, wrote that his name was 'known in every kingdom and every region, even among the heathens. Emperors, kings, princes and lords sent emissaries to him; the Pope hailed him and embraced him as his own dear son; the cardinals stood up when he appeared.' It was also true of the host of lesser men among whom the big lenders spread their risks and whose contributions helped them preserve enough capital to keep on trading in the metals, grain and foreign exchange markets; for the uncertainty of the timing and, in the case of state 'bankruptcies' (i.e. suspensions of interest pending renegotiation of the terms), of the rate of repayment, meant that the disasters of war were not limited to its combatants.

The sums borrowed were enormous. In one three-year period Henry VIII – despite the ex-monastic lands – became indebted to foreign bankers, including the Fuggers, to the tune of 3 million pounds. Spain borrowed over 39 million ducats between 1519 and 1556; normal tax revenues over the period, fully committed to peacetime expenditure, amounted to roughly 55.5 million. The Italian states had been fighting for their lives and frontiers with borrowed money during the small wars that preceded the major engagements that began in 1494. France, with the highest peacetime tax base in Europe, managed, with a modest tuning up of this and an exploitation of every form of expedience financing mentioned above, to postpone recourse to money-lenders on a large scale till both sides turned to them in the civil wars. But when the Netherlands conflict forced the northern provinces into seeking quick infusions of ready money there was scarcely a vein of surplus capital in Europe left untapped, or at least unbesieged, by government agents acting openly in peaceful countries, and clandestinely in those monetary centres – Lyon, Rouen, Besançon, Antwerp, Genoa, Augsburg, Cologne – whose bankers had to act covertly if considering loans to actively hostile powers or to those outside their traditional financial alignment: Genoa to Spain, for instance. Nor did the complexities induced by war into the financial scene end here, for loan-dealing was seldom straightforward but could involve the acceptance as well of commodities – alum, lead, grain, currency – on unnaturally favourable terms to the lender, or on mortgaging receiverships of customs or tolls as additional security, or on persuading native merchants to offer bonds guaranteeing the crown's repayments to foreign bankers.

These negotiations were further complicated by the news networks stretched among the financial centres which appraised the short- and long-term chances of political clients' creditworthiness; also, inevitably, by the conflict between military and ordinary commercial demands on capital: very few bankers of any weight were not also traders, and if a local dearth meant that large profits could be made from importing grain on a larger scale, that opportunity was likely to be given precedence. Though governments could threaten to imprison their own subjects for putting private before national interest (and occasionally did) and to deprive foreign merchants of their residence rights, the need for golden eggs kept coercion at a minimum. Thus alongside armsdealer financiers of the newly specialized stamp, like Albert de Gondi, there was forced into existence a new race of government financial agents, some of them merchants themselves, who were charged to scour foreign money markets in search of loans and to chaffer with principals and their agents as equals in wile and knowledge. For England the new model was established by Stephen Vaughan, who served from 1538 to 1546 as Henry VIII's financial – and sometimes diplomatic – agent from his base in Antwerp. His successor, Thomas Gresham, who served Mary and Elizabeth in the same capacity, and added covert deals in arms to his other activities, boasted with reason that in Antwerp 'no [meeting of the] bourse passes wherein I am not furnished with a statement of all monies borrowed on that day'. On his death in 1579 his successor, the Genoese Horatio Pallavicino, began a career (he was granted naturalization papers in 1585) that was even more remarkable for his ability to raise and transfer funds between England and its continental allies, hire troops and conduct straightforward diplomacy while at the same time building up a formidable fortune by trading on his own account.

The activities of such men conceal those of a host of others. It is not underestimating the business commonsense of medieval officials and statesmen to suggest that the bureaucracies and councils that had to digest and approve the negotiations of financial agents were forced now to become numerate to an extent different in degree if not in kind. Within these circles veritable financial wizards were rare. Jacques de Beaune, son of a cloth-trading family in Tours, became a civil servant of the duchy of Brittany as a young man, and when the duchess married Louis XII he passed into the financial service of France. The tact and business expertise that enabled him to woo loans from native and foreign merchants – nearly 2 million livres in 1521–2 alone – led to ennoblement as the sieur de Semblançay and to his recognized primacy within the national fiscal system. So conspicuous a position was, of course, dangerous, as was his amassment – in complete accord with the mores of his colleagues – of a socially advantageously noble marriage and a considerable private fortune. A perfect example of both the importance of war financing and the hazards it could lead to occurred in 1522. On 26 April of that year, the Swiss, cream of the French army defending Milan against growing Imperialist pressure, announced that they would decamp in protest against arrears of pay unless they were allowed on the very next day to try their fortunes against the fortified position in which the enemy had entrenched themselves at Bicocca. It was a position against which morale, however defiant, simply could not win, and the French commander, Odet de Foix, knew it. Rather than be rendered helpless by the desertion of his key infantry, however, he consented. His excuse for the debacle that followed was that Semblançay had deliberately held back the pay he was meant to send to the Swiss. It was, in fact, on its way; a few more days and the Franco-Swiss force would have been able to choose a more favourable opportunity for battle. Francis I himself was too shrewdly aware of the financial component as one among the many incalculable imperatives that shaped campaigns, to yield at once to the cry that the flower of aristocratic militancy had been betrayed by a parvenu. But Bicocca was the reddest skein in the rope of accusations that finally tightened round Semblançay's neck in 1527. The records do not sustain the charges against him. There was nothing new about an administrator being made a scapegoat for the failures of men of birth and action (Wolsey's disgrace and death came three years later). And, in any case, rulers could not afford not to entrust professional businessmen with fund-raising and accounting tasks beyond normal bureaucratic competence. Francis's successor, Henry II, employed Albizzo del Bene, the leading member of an exiled Florentine banking family living in Lyons, to put up the money for his Italian campaigns and recover it as he could from the treasurer of 'extraordinary' war costs. Albizzo was amply justified in claiming that 'without me and my associates all the affairs of Italy would have foundered a hundred times for lack of ready money'. But it was Spain's turning to the private sector that became the outstanding example of the inadequacy of central government to pay, equip and feed the armed forces, and the engagement of entrepreneurs reached a climax in the career of the Madrid financier Juan Pascual, and his appointment, as the Council of War suggested in 1597, 'to all the paymasterships of Spain'.

War, then, was not waged with additional taxation raised all at once. If it had had to be, there would have been fewer campaigns. Its costs were spread. There might be protest and complaint; some campaigns had to be cut short for governments' lack of confidence in their ability to raise yet more money. Yet thanks to the expedients described above, wars were embarked on with little fear of provoking into revolt those who in the end paid for them. Francis I spent lavishly, over and over again, on war. Yet the tax rate in his reign rose annually only by rather less than 2.2 per cent. A further dilution of the sudden, direct crown-subject confrontation, was the use rulers made of civic finance to help cover their major borrowings. In this way war costs were diffused amongst familiar financial expedients – often involving the issuing of annuities on the lines of state-organized war bonds – that had been adopted by a number of widely separated municipalities.

Eventually war was paid for by taxes, and every expedient to spread their incidence increased the final bill. Sales of crown land meant that extraordinary revenue had to be increased to compensate for the loss in normal royal income. The farming out of taxes (accepting a fixed sum in exchange for a licence to collect them) lessened the yield to the treasury: otherwise no one would have applied for the farm. Interest on loans, and on loans to pay for loans, rarely went above 16 per cent but was seldom less than 10. These were all part of the cost of making the financing of war politically safe, and they caused post-war taxation levels to reflect not only administrative, defence and other costs that were rising anyway, but prolongations of part of the expenditure caused by war itself. Here again, by being concealed among the housekeeping accounts of peace, war's costs appeared less provocatively shocking.

It is difficult, therefore, to isolate the reaction to, and the effect of, war taxation. While tax money raised for defence purposes – in Venice for the maintenance of men-at-arms and fortification programmes, in France for Charles VII's *ordonnance* and, in 1543, for Francis I's infantry reserve, in Spain the *cruzada* for frontier garrisons – was named and earmarked for these purposes, wartime increases, however justified by pleas of emergency, were folded into tax demands as a whole. All additional taxation was, of course, resented. And the military component within the tax burden did lead both to more frequent pressures by central on local administrations and to a weakening of the sense of provincial identity. But the expression of resentment had so many other targets – infringement of privileges, relevance to the local economic position of the moment, the basis of assessment – that protest can very rarely be identified as anti-war as such. Nor, given the immersion of war finances in the overall subject-government cash nexus, can war's role in determining this relationship be clearly defined. Certain generalizations can be made. War, by leading to a proliferation of bondholders (Italian *monte* shares, French *rentes*, Spanish *juros*) may, as we have seen, have encouraged a passive, rentier frame of mind among those with otherwise productive capital to invest; the sales of offices, noble titles and crown lands probably hardened – in Spain and to a lesser extent in France it certainly did – the frontiers between class and class; most surely of all, the recourse to indirect taxation, much of which, introduced in war, was retained thereafter, inequably penalized the semi- and the absolutely poor. It was upon their chronic indebtedness (6 per cent of the population of Rome was in gaol for debt at any single moment of the peaceful year 1582) that the long process of paying for war weighed most grievously.

Worth noting, at least, was the divergence between the standards applied by governments to financial affairs and by individuals who were adding to the tax base by manifesting the 'capitalistic' attitudes of deliberate accumulation, effective control and calculated disbursement. As war financing was emergency financing, it was raised at a cost in investment rates or loss of assets no businessmen would have found acceptable. Worse, no government had a financially trained administration large enough, or accounting procedures adequately refined, to keep track of all the routes through which credit or cash reached the treasury, let alone to check them as they were disbursed. And commanders-in-chief were not qualified to monitor expenditure. When enquiries were made from Spain about the accounts of Francisco de Lixalde, Alba's paymaster in the Netherlands, the duke confessed that after seven years as governor he still did not understand the system; all he had wanted was money to pay his troops. Lixalde died in 1577, but the file on him was not closed until 1612. It was not so much that forecasts of costs were wrong (Henry VIII's 1544 invasion of France was estimated at £250,000 and turned out to be nearer £650,000), or that at a campaign's end expenditure was not clearly related to costs for future reference – for budgeting in peacetime was sporadic and precariously trustworthy: what may have rankled with those in a position to know was the accuracy demanded by governments when assessing individuals for tax purposes in contrast to the waste that so conspicuously attended the same governments' conduct of wars.

It is, however, when asking this very question – how far the exercise of centralized power and the relationship between ruler and ruled were shaped by and for war – that the theme of this book acquires a perspective which necessarily conceals the answer within the contours of far wider prospects. Every country was undergoing a development that in its continuity and scope was largely independent of war, even if internal violence and campaigns abroad were often part of it. In England there was the re-establishment of administrative contact within the country as a whole after the Wars of the Roses, and the subsequent 'Tudorization' of every aspect of life that was susceptible to the influence of government and its agents. The internal history of France, from its territorial redefinition after the Hundred Years War to its recovery from its civil conflicts in the late sixteenth century, can be told, indeed, usually is, without emphasis on the formal wars waged by or against its monarchs. Even that of Spain, with its practically non-stop record of wars from Granada through Naples, Algiers, Lepanto and the Armada to the fighting that petered out in the Netherlands in 1609, cannot afford not to place a far greater emphasis on the efforts towards, and the rebuffs to, national consolidation within a traditionally divided peninsula, the initial adventure and then the continuing business of transatlantic empire, the strain of religious-racial conflicts, and the social symptoms induced by the forced run of specie through its economic digestive system.

So the compass can be boxed. Through the accommodation to yet another form of conquest in Sicily and Naples, the consequences of the substitution of ducal for republican rule in Tuscany, the judders induced from top to bottom of German society by the intensity of Reformation and (to a lesser extent) anti-Reformation fervours, to the institutional realization in the Netherlands that, while plagued by both old and new political dissensions, it had become the chief beneficiary of the swing in commercial activity from the Mediterranean to the Atlantic seaboard; the national portraits, however different in style, have a characteristic in common. They reflect the fact that while taking defence measures, and dealing with war when it came, governmental procedures and institutions were primarily affected by the problems generated in time of peace. However continuous war might be, its imperatives never overrode the familiar governmental activities of guaranteeing legal processes, ensuring, as far as possible, law and order, garnering and accounting for 'ordinary' revenues, responding to petitions from individuals and communities, conducting diplomacy.

The growth of this last activity, which led to the establishment of permanent embassies in foreign capitals, was certainly encouraged by war. There was the need to seek and maintain alliances, to recruit and to raise money abroad, and to have an early warning system which could report military preparations or hostile negotiations. But it was also fostered by mutual suspicion caused by Reformation animosities and nervousness about the behaviour of exiles, and by governments' increasingly direct concern with international commerce. Apart from an extended diplomatic network, it was probably defence rather than war that led to the creation of new offices: to supervise standing armies, artillery services, militias, fortification programmes and, above all, enlarged navies. The financial and recruiting burdens of actual war administration were, as we know, in the main borne as additional duties by existing civil servants or by local authorities, or by territorial magnates who, together with their own men of business, acted as temporary ones. It was when England's commitment to war in the Netherlands, France and Ireland was at its height that Elizabeth's justices of the peace and county lieutenants grumbled at the 'stacks of statutes' that were unloaded on them concerned with raising, equipping and transporting soldiers and dealing with their poverty and ruffianism when they returned. In Spain, it is true, a Council of War was created with a permanent secretariat (two from the 1580s) dealing with military and naval matters in peace – as well as in wartime. But Spain's commitments in Italy, the Americas, the Netherlands and Portugal led for other reasons to a proliferation of bureaucratic offices; it was, in any case, only from the mid-sixteenth century that direct central control over military matters gained at the expense of powers previously delegated to loyal major landowners or merchant contractors, and two generations later the system was already going into reverse, crippled by the lack of adequate central funding and of civil servants who could put devoted service to the state above the use of an office as a means of enhancing personal gain and social standing. Similarly, the 1594 measure whereby the French secretary of war ceased to be also in charge of the *Maison du Roi* (reflecting the personal nature of war) and became instead the official responsible for foreign affairs, did possibly reflect a more national approach to conflict, but it had no significant bureaucratic consequences. The most efficient central bureaucracy came to be that of Savoy–Piedmont under Emanuel Philibert (1553–80) and his successor Carlo Emanuel. This was, to an important degree, a response to war. But the duchy was small and, in comparison with other countries, socially and economically unresistant to direct control.

If war played as yet only a minor part in fostering the development of modern-looking bureaucracies, what of its contribution to the growth in other ways of central authority?

The military reformation involved innovations any or all of which might seem to have been moulded to authority's hand: decreasing dependence on magnate retinues, permanent forces, an extension of the use of mercenaries, artillery, centrally organized militias and other armed self-defence citizen forces, theoretically impregnable citadels suited to the overawing of cities of doubtful loyalty.

The reliance on native troops directly engaged by government did not mean that magnate cooperation could be brushed aside. The magnate turned military governor, or lord lieutenant, was no less necessary to the raising of soldiers. He, and, indeed, other authorities in town and country could make capital out of governments' need to rely on their partnership in an emergency administrative effort. But the defeudalization of recruiting methods led to the substitution for it of a wary managerial stance that had little to do with the streamlining of ruler-subject contacts. Permanent forces? They were not, could not have been, used for the purpose of coercion. Indeed, we know that a major problem was to keep them from civilianizing themselves. Mercenaries, though imported German infantry were largely responsible for the suppression in 1549 of anti-government revolts in south-western England and in Norfolk (Kett's rebellion), played no part of any significance in the internal development of state-subject relations. The stage when a mercenary army could displace its employer had closed with the takeover by the Romagnol *condottiere* Francesco Sforza of his sickly employer, the temporary republican government of Milan in 1450. Thereafter, though mercenaries were used in campaigns abroad – where their occasional mutinies were for pay, not control – the few who were admitted into permanent domestic forces or used to supplement local police functions, were of no political significance.

The case for the suggestion that artillery was an instrument centralizing power is similarly feeble. Governments, as a result of regalian rights over metals and their heavy investment in having guns made, insisted on making the manufacture of artillery a monopoly. But though an occasional rebellious magnate may have been brought to heel by royal cannon (but never just because of cannon) the complex shifts towards more effectively centralized forms of government began before cannon were effective or readily transportable and can be explained without reference to gunpowder weapons. In any case, cannon did leak into private hands through the black market. Some openly displayed their owners' coats of arms. Kett's rebels bullied their artillery out of local landowners. A number of the showier fortified mansions of Elizabethan England were stocked with at least a few of these unlicensed but essential articles of aristocratic furniture. It was after two quite exceptional generations of provincial self-sufficiency that Henry IV started calling in unauthorized cannon from private properties; even so, his own master of the royal artillery, Sully, equipped his château on the Loire with guns. As for walled towns, equally liable to be foci of discontent because of the demands for extra taxation channelled through them, none was without its carefully inventoried artillery, ball and powder: covered, it may be, by general royal licence in the interest of the defence of the realm and including loans from rulers, but seldom investigated, and never challenged save on the grounds of its inadequacy.

With regard to portable firearms, arquebuses, calivers and pistols (no individual wanted the unwieldy musket), every indication from licences to carry, or prohibitions against bearing them, is that what governments feared was their use in crime, not rebellion, or the consumption by individuals of the always scarce supplies of gunpowder that governments themselves might need: hence militia training that placed more emphasis on the flash in the pan (of priming powder only) than on the use of the full charge necessary to project a bullet.

The establishment of militia forces had nowhere met with the objection that they might be used to force governments' will against the grain of their subjects' feelings. Indeed, apart from local mutterings that giving modern arms to peasants would encourage them to rise against their betters, considered criticism pointed to them as likely to impede rather than further the growth of central authority. When called out, as they occasionally were at times of riot or revolt by local authorities to aid the forces raised by landowners and townsmen from their own tenants and other dependants (reinforced if it were logistically possible by companies of garrison troops), their support was recognized as being conditioned by the extent to which they shared or feared the rebels' programme. Scattered across rural farms and hamlets as they were, and only infrequently drilled together in large numbers, theirs was but a token allegiance to causes less burning than those shared with their neighbours. And the same can be said of gate guards and self-defence municipal militia forces; the French civil wars clearly revealed that their military effectiveness was almost solely conditioned by narrowly construed 'class' solidarity and economic self-interest. Some mobs they would break up. Others they would not. In the town as in the country, authority could encourage but not enforce. And encouragement was most effective when the threat of foreign invasion produced a tentative solidarity between ruler, rich and poor. In this case the promise of a full military wage and the threat of loss of privileges brought militiamen on to ramparts and, less willingly and in smaller numbers, into the field. By the end of the sixteenth century political theorists were reproaching rulers for not making enough use of their own subjects-in-arms. Only tyrants, chided Justus Lipsius, had anything to fear from them. The Savoyard Giovanni Botero, one of the

249

best informed students of contemporary forms of government, asked, 'What of the rulers of Venice, his Most Serene Majesty of Savoy and the Grand Duke of Tuscany? Have they not each of them an excellent militia? . . . These have never been known to rebel or riot, to loot the countryside, attack towns, fight in the streets, disturb the public peace or do any other harm. . . . We conclude, then, that a ruler should train his subjects in the use of arms.' Discussion of this topic never raised the suggestion that governments might use militias to coerce the wider body of subjects from whom they were selected.

The most obvious symbol of coercion was the citadel. After his reconquest of rebellious Liège in 1468 Charles the Bold built one to ensure its continuing obedience to Burgundy. Julius II ordered one for Bologna in 1511 after his army's expulsion of its disobedient signori the Bentivoglio, which the citizens promptly tore down as a badge of tyranny. The construction of the vast Fortezza da Basso by Alessandro de' Medici from 1534 to keep the Florentines henceforward in awe of the new ducal regime was criticized as 'a thing totally inappropriate to a free city'. From time to time Venice's military experts proposed the construction of citadels in its subject cities. In 1546 the garrison commander of Verona urged the government 'to transform the castle of S. Felice into a fortress against both internal and external threats. . . . I do not say this because I am unaware that the justice and charity of this most excellent government towards its subjects is such that they should in all reason remain faithful . . . but because of the ill-will that many men nourish, although they should not.' But the republic did not follow up any of these proposals. Citadels were, indeed, justifiable simply as strong-points athwart city walls, but their anti-popular associations were widespread enough for Henry VIII later to explain his ordering one for Carlisle as being intended purely as a rallying point in case the Scots broke in. Some citadels were built specifically as threats. After the Dutch revolt of 1567, Spanish garrisons and citadels were decreed for 'towns which have sinned', as Alba put it, and he personally urged on the building of the citadel of Antwerp. On the other side, the States General had one constructed in the 1590s in Groningen to punish the city for refusing contributions for the war. But by the second half of the century citadels had become so standard a technical feature of bastioned fortification theory that, save in such examples, their connection with tyranny was dimmed. In any case, situated, in the great majority, in frontier regions or on strategic routes where towns had commonly been provided, or had provided themselves, with rallying strong-points, Renaissance citadels projected little more than an extra whiff of naked force over the vast landscapes covered by authority in general. Florence remained the only capital city with a knife, as it were, constantly held at its throat, and became even more of an exception when Ferdinand I built the Belvedere fortress with its tiers of artillery glowering against the city from the heights of the Boboli Gardens.

As with the effect of war on bureaucracies, changes in military organization and practice offer, then, little to an understanding of what was on the whole a distinctive, if not everywhere impressive feature of the period: the continuing growth of effective, centralizing authority. War cannot be thought out of history and then be put back in order to measure the difference it made to what else was influencing the course of administrative and constitutional affairs. For these were many, and inseparable themselves one from another: from price and population movements to personalities with the exceptional efficacy of a Thomas Cromwell or a Cosimo I or a Henry IV, and to the effect of post-Reformation religious ardours and accommodations on the sense of national self-identity. Given its grandiose proportions, cash for war, as it was squeezed and cajoled out of the economy, left a mark on all those traditional points of contact which had become organized in the form of parliaments, provincial estates and corporations. But because the response to these demands was spread in a way that allowed non-military needs to be folded into them en route to the quenching of war debts, it is rarely possible to isolate the very stimulus we are looking for.

There were, nonetheless, surges in tax demands clearly attributable to war that did have an identifiable and lasting effect on constitutional procedures. Thus the highly vocal French States General were not summoned after 1484, monarchs choosing instead to apply pressure to smaller targets: ad hoc assemblies of notables or provincial estates. In Castile, to retain the support of the nobility, Charles V abandoned in 1538 an attempt to subject it to tax burdens which henceforward fell increasingly on the towns; under Philip II the Cortes of Aragon, Valencia and Catalonia were, save on rare occasions, summoned separately instead of in their more resistant joint form. Without the continuous need for extra taxation for Elizabeth's wars, parliament would probably not have met frequently and confidently enough to have challenged not only the military plans but the peacetime, personal spending of James I and Charles I. However, war cannot be invoked to explain the overall development of parliament's role in the government of England, nor the relationship between crown and representative institutions in those large land masses, France and Spain, where central government had to come to terms with previously independent regions possessing deeply entrenched law-making and administrative systems of their own. War conditioned but did not create those changes that occurred between 1450 and 1620: this much can be said between the extreme cases of Spain's drive towards, and then withdrawal from, a centralizing policy, and Venice's weathering of one expensive war or crisis after another without any significant change in the nature of its methods of government at all. And however different formal constitutional analysis can show one country to have been from another, in all of them support for war was the result of bargains and dialogues with subjects. It is by looking at government in this wider context of consent that historians have reduced the difference between its 'absolutist' and 'constitutional' forms.

This playing down of war's impact on political life – save, obviously, in the case of civil war – can be supported by two other considerations.

Except in Spain, where by 1600 there was considerable feeling that the peninsula was being robbed to make the Netherlands rebels rich, consent was not grudged on the score of the rights or wrongs of a war as such, but of wasteful administration and government's reluctance to listen to grievances of a quite other sort. And in the second place, revolt: whether on the scale of that of the Comuneros of 1520–1 and the German Peasant War of 1525, or of the English Pilgrimage of Grace of 1536 and the Rebellion of the Northern Earls in 1569, or of the numerous outbreaks of antagonism that can be knotted together to form a skein of violent protest reaching from Venetian Crete to Devon and Cornwall, uprisings against government were the result of local issues. That rulers had the right to initiate or respond to wars was only weakly challenged. In spite of its expense, its horror, the contrast between the precision of its aims and the almost limitless permeation of its consequences, war in this period, perhaps for the last time, was largely a non-constitutional, only marginally a political issue. And this is among the justifications for having treated it at such length as a social one.

Notes

Select bibliography

Index

Notes

(Authors of books listed in the Bibliography are in small capitals)

Chapter 1

Page
20   Montaigne   Tr. John Florio (Everyman ed., London, 1915) ii, 345–6.
21   Barrillon   Quoted in KNECHT (1982) 69.
21   English captain   Quoted in CONTAMINE, 'The war literature . . .', 118.
22   Valla   *The treatise of Lorenzo Valla on the Donation of Constantine,* tr. C. B. Coleman (Yale University Press, 1922) 167.
23   Duaren   Quoted in William Fulbecke, *The pandectes of the law of nations* (London, 1602) 41v.
23   Montchretien   Quoted in SILBERNER, 26.
24   Ivan IV   Quoted in KOENIGSBERGER AND MOSSE, 198.
24   Winwood   Quoted in BUISSERET (1984) 85.
28   Elizabeth   Quoted in LLOYD, 21–2.
29   Galileo   Quoted in G. Diaz de Santillana, *The crime of Galileo* (London, 1958) 3.
29   More   *Utopia,* ed. Edward Surtz and J. H. Hexter (Yale University Press, 1965) 205.
29   Machiavelli   'Memoriale a Raffaello Girolami', *Opere,* ed. A. Panella, vol. 2 (Milan, 1939) 726.
29   Cavalli   Quoted in KNECHT (1984) 95–6.
30   Alba   Quoted in MALTBY, 82.
30   Duodo   Quoted in J. C. DAVIS, 268–70.
31   Seyssel   Ed. Jacques Poujol (Paris, 1961) 195.
31   Vettori   *Sommario della istoria d'Italia. Scritti storici e politici,* ed. E. Niccolini (Bari, 1972) 202.
32   Ferdinand I   Quoted in FICHTNER, 4.
32   Philip's ministers   Cardinal Quiroga and the duke of Alba, quoted in PARKER (1972) 133.
32   Spanish adviser   Juan de Idiáquez, quoted in ELLIOTT (1968) 317.
33   Dutch ambassador   Francis Aersen, quoted in BUISSERET (1984) 173.
33   Guicciardini   *Maxims and reflections of a Renaissance statesman,* tr. Mario Domandi (New York, 1965) 73.
33   Cromwell   Quoted in ADAMS, 213.
33   Burghley   *State papers relating to the defeat of the Spanish Armada,* ed. J. K. Laughton, Navy Records Society (1895) i, 109.
35   Christ   Matthew, xxii, 21.
35   Luther   Quoted in H. Bender, 'The pacifism of the sixteenth-century Anabaptists', *Mennonite Quarterly Review* (1959) 7–8.

35 Devout author   Lodowick Lloyd, opening paragraph of *The stratagems of Jerusalem* (London, 1602).

36 Erasmus   *The education of a Christian prince*. tr. L. K. Born (Columbia University Press, 1936) 251.

36 English divine   Matthew Sutcliffe, *The practice, proceedings, and lawes of armes* (London, 1593) 2.

36 Francis I   Quoted in GARDOT, 429.

36 Duty   Sutcliffe, op. cit., 12.

37 National chivalries   VALE, 168.

39 Raleigh   Opening words of *A discourse of the . . . cause of . . . war*.

39 Da Porto   *Lettere storiche*, ed. B. Bressan (Florence, 1857) 26, 46.

40 Pastimes   Innocentio Ringhieri, *Cento giuochi liberali et d'ingegno* (Bologna, 1551) book 5, chap. 44.

40 Digges   Thomas and Dudley Digges, *Four paradoxes . . .* (London, 1604) 109.

42 Commines   *Memoirs*, ed. A. R. Scobie, 2 vols. (London, 1855) i, 379 seq.

42 Erasmus   *Education . . .* , cit., 255.

43 Budé   *De asse et partibus* (1514).

44 Lambarde   READ, 129–30

45 More   Op. cit., 203–5.

45 Du Bellay   *Mémoires*, ed. J. A. C. Buchon (Paris, 1936) 582.

Chapter 2

47 Council of Ten   Quoted in MALLETT AND HALE, 395.

48 Charles VIII   *Campagne et bulletins de la grande armée d'Italie commandée par Charles VIII*, ed. J. de la Pilorgerie (Paris, 1866) 176–7.

51 Privy Council   Quoted in J. S. D. Scott, *The British Army*, 2 vols. (London, 1868) ii, 96.

56 Costanzo   Quoted in MALLETT AND HALE, 369.

56 Report   Ib., 372.

57 Granvelle   Quoted in J. A. Froude, *History of England*, 12 vols. (London, 1970) vi, 286.

57 Williams   *A briefe discourse of warre*, ed. John X. Evans in *The works of Sir Roger Williams* (Oxford, 1972) 27.

57 Jonson   III, ii.

58 English writer   Robert Barrett, *The theoricke and practicke of moderne warres* (London, 1598) 75.

60 Machiavelli   *The art of war*, tr. E. Farnsworth, *Works*, 4 vols. (London, 1775) iv, 87.

61 Monluc   Quoted in C. S. L. DAVIES in LOACH AND TITTLER, 178.

61 De Bueil   Quoted in VALE, 148–9.

64 Essex   Quoted in L. W. Henry, 'The Earl of Essex as strategist and military organizer, 1596–7', *English Historical Review* (1953) 370.

67 La Noue   *The politicke and militarie discourses* (London, 1587) 170–1.

68 Williams   Ed. cit., 11.

68 *Discourse*   Ed. E. Lamond (Cambridge University Press, 1893) 94–5.

68 States General   KOENIGSBERGER (1971) 20.

70 Sanuto   MALLETT AND HALE, 217.

70 Welsh professional   Elis Gruffydd quoted in G. S. Millar, *Tudor mercenaries and auxiliaries 1485–1547* (University of Virginia Press, 1970) 48.

70   Sully   *Memoirs*, 5 vols. (London, 1812) i, 195, 198.
71   La Noue   *Discours politiques et militaires*, ed. F. E. Sutcliffe (Geneva, 1967) 257.
71   Crete   Quoted in MALLETT AND HALE, 235.
72   More   Quoted in ADAMS, 267.
73   Bacon   'On the true greatness of kingdoms and estates', *Essays* (London, 1902) 76–7.
74   1495 decree   Quoted in QUATREFAGES (1984).

Chapter 3

78   Falstaff   Shakespeare, *Henry IV, part I*, IV, i.
79   Gates   *The defence of the militarie profession* . . . (London, 1579) 45.
79   Olivares   *Memoriales y cartas*, ed. John H. Elliott and José F. de la Peña, vol. 1 (Madrid, 1978) 193. I owe this reference to Professor Elliott.
83   Landucci   *A Florentine diary from 1450 to 1516*, ed. A. de Rosen Jervis (London, 1921) 176.
84   Paré   *The works* . . . , tr. Th. Johnson (London, 1678) 44.
85   Proclamation   P. H. Hughes and J. F. Larkin, *Tudor royal proclamations*, vol. 2 (Yale University Press, 1969) 116.
86   Spokesman   Quoted in GOODMAN, 198.
86   Poetaster   Quoted in L. C. Knights, *Drama and society in the age of Jonson* (London, 1937) 332.
86   Lambarde   Quoted in READ, 61.
87   Haton   Quoted in PABLO, 199.
87   Copland   'High-way to the spital-house', in A. V. Judges, ed., *The Elizabethan underworld* (London, 1965) 7.
87   Merchant   *Letters and papers of Henry VIII*, ed. J. S. Brewer and J. Gairdner (1862–1920) vol. 18, part ii, no. 460.
88   Common Council   Modernized from a transcription generously sent me by Dr Susan Brigden.
91   States General   In MANDROU, 90.
91   Bernáldez   Quoted in VIGON, 112.
91   Hôpital   Quoted in BARRE-DUPARCQ, 290.
91   Wilson   Quoted in J. M. Hexter, *Reappraisals in history* (New York, 1963) 90, f.n.
92   Chabannes   Quoted in CONTAMINE (1972) 445–6.
95   Ramirez   Quoted in MARIÉJOL, 203.
95   Lisle   Quoted in GOODMAN, 173.
96   Gonzaga   Quoted in MICHAUD (1977) 35, f.n.
97   Clerics   Quoted in KIPLING, 170.
98   Montaigne   Quoted in BITTON, 27.
98   Segar   *The booke of honor and armes* (London, 1590) 72.
98   Alba   Quoted in PARKER (1972) 41.
99   Burghley   Quoted in Joel Hurstfield, *The queen's wards: wardship and marriage under Elizabeth I* (London, 1958) 257.

Chapter 4

102   Nardi   *Istorie della città di Firenze*, 2 vols. (Florence, 1858) ii, 166, 207.

106 Parisian Pierre de l'Estoiel. Quoted in *The Paris of Henry of Navarre*, ed. Nancy L. Roelker (Harvard University Press, 1958) 122.

106 Bodin Quoted in KAMEN, 59.

107 Utopians *Utopia*, ed. cit., 211.

109 Savorgnan Quoted in MALLETT AND HALE, 324.

109 La Noue Ed. cit. (Sutcliffe) 209–10.

109 Beolco *Parlamento de Ruzante che iera vegnú de campo. Due dialoghi*, ed. L. Zorzi (Turin, 1968) 24.

112 Savorgnan Quoted in MALLETT AND HALE, 386–7.

113 Edward VI *Tudor royal proclamations*, ed. P. L. Hughes and J. F. Larkin (New Haven, 1964) i, 446.

114 North Quoted in H. H. Davis, 'The military career of Thomas North', *Huntington Library Quarterly* (1949) 320.

115 *Pericles* Boult in IV, v.

116 Leicester *Correspondence of Robert Dudley, Earl of Leycester* (Camden Society, 1844) 181, 338.

116 Gascoigne *The complete poems*, ed. W. C. Hazlitt, 2 vols. (Roxburgh Library, 1869) i, 167.

116 Swiss order Quoted in C. Kohler, *Les Suisses dans les guerres d'Italie de 1506 à 1512* (Geneva, 1896) 25.

117 Luther Quoted in REDLICH (1956) 25.

118 Postan *Essays in medieval agriculture and general problems of the medieval economy* (Cambridge University Press, 1972) 73. My italics.

119 Crucé Quoted in PARKER (1972) 120.

120 La Noue Ed. cit. (Sutcliffe) 222.

120 Paré *The apology and treatise*, ed. Geoffrey Keynes (London, 1951) 49.

121 Requesens Quoted in PARKER (1972) 168.

121 Cervantes *Don Quixote*, prologue to the second part.

121 Palmanova Quoted in MALLETT AND HALE, 364.

121 Botero *The reason of state*, tr. P. J. and D. P. Waley (London, 1956) 192–3.

122 Turks Quoted in Sir Godfrey Fisher, *Barbary legend . . .* (Oxford, 1957) 91.

123 Becon *The policy of war*, in *Early works*, ed. J. Ayre (London, 1843) 251.

124 French author Michel d'Amboise, *Le guidon des gens de guerre* (repr. Sceaux, 1880) 8.

124 Peasant lads Quoted in ROBERTS (vol. 2, 1958) 209.

125 Alba Quoted in FALLS, 44.

125 Monluc Quoted in BITTON, 32.

125 Gustavus ROBERTS (vol. 2, 1958) 237.

125 Heywood Quoted in JORGENSEN, 157.

125 Rich Ib., 142.

125 Wilson *The state of England in Anno Dom. 1600*, ed. F. J. Fisher (Camden Miscellany XVI, part i, 1936) 19–20.

125 Naval recruits Quoted in J. S. McGurk, 'A levy of seamen in the Cinque Ports, 1602', *Mariner's Mirror* (1980) 139.

126 Bacon Op. and ed. cit., 78–9.

Chapter 5

127 Erasmus 'The soldier and the Carthusian'. *Colloquies*, tr. N. Bailey (Glasgow, 1877) 139.

128 Machiavelli *Arte della guerra*, ed. S. Bertelli (Milan, 1961) 325.

128 Manuel Quoted in ANDERSSON, 30.

129 Seyssel Ed. cit., 184.

130 Vettori *Sommario*, cit., 184.

130 Urrea Quoted in PUDDU, 198.

133 Da Porto Op. cit., 176.

134 Christmas *Letters and papers of Henry VIII*, cit., vol. xviii, no. 343.

134 Drake Quoted in THOMPSON (1976) 35.

136 Filles de joie Quoted in HARDING, 75–6.

138 Cervantes *Exemplary novels*, tr. W. K. Kelly (New York, 1960) 62.

138 Smythe *Certain discourses military*, ed. J. R. Hale (Cornell University Press, 1964) xv.

139 La Noue Ed. cit. (Sutcliffe) 210–12.

140 Churchyard Quoted in G. Geoffrey Langsam, *Martial books and Tudor verse* (New York, 1951) 153.

141 Louis XI Quoted in CONTAMINE in ALLMAND, 108.

142 Carew Quoted in CORNWALL, 71.

143 Brantôme Quoted in F. Reboul, *Histoire militaire et navale*, vol. VII, part i of *Histoire de la nation française*, ed. G. Hanotaux (Paris, 1925) 270.

144 Rovigo Quoted in HALE (1983) 288.

144 Geometry J. Errard, *La géométrie et pratique générale d'icelle* (2nd ed., Paris, 1602) Dedication.

144 Tavannes Ed. M. Petitot (Paris, 1823) 160.

145 Jonson III, ii.

145 Iago *Othello*, I, i.

145 Barrett Op. cit., 6.

145 Octeranus Quoted in M. Jähns, *Geschichte der Kriegswissenschaften*, vol. 2 (Munich, 1889) 1027.

146 Cleland *The institution of a young noble man* (Oxford, 1607) 267–8.

Chapter 6

154 Ubaldini Quoted in Marcus Merriman, 'Italian military engineers in Britain in the 1540s', *English map-making, 1500–1650*, ed. Sarah Tyacke (British Library, 1983) 57.

157 Guicciardini *Maxims*, cit., 58.

158 Seyssel Ed. cit., 185–6.

160 *Utopia* Ed. cit., 209–11.

161 Londoño Quoted in QUATREFAGES (1979) 272.

161 D'Amboise *Le guidon*, cit., 70.

161 Broadsheet *Tudor royal proclamations*, cit., 113.

161 Council *Letters and papers of Henry VIII*, cit., vol. xix, part 2, no. 187.

162 La Noue Quoted in OMAN, 400.

162 Dutch Articles Quoted in NICKLE, 318.

163 Gruffydd Quoted in M. Bryn-Davies, 'Surrey at Boulogne', *Huntington Library Quarterly* (1959–60) 343.

163 Charles the Bold Quoted in VALE, 148.

164 Henry VIII *Letters and papers*, cit., vol. xix, part 1, no. 448.

164 *Camisades* Ib., vol. xx, part 1, no. 1200.

164 Audley Quoted in HALE (1983) 249.

165 Leicester Quoted in NICKLE, 236, note 50.

165 Maurice   Ib., 155.

165 Palladio   Quoted in HALE (1983) 475.

165 Chieregato   Quoted in MALLETT AND HALE, 362.

166 Observer   *Letters and papers of Henry VIII*, cit., vol. xx, part 2, no. 533.

166 Londoño   *El discurso sobre la forma de reduzir la disciplina militar* (Brussels, 1589). Written in 1568. I use French ed. (also Brussels, 1589) 24v–25r.

166 Della Valle   Ed. of Venice, 1524, 46r.

167 Brantôme   *Discours sur les colonels de l'infanterie de France*, ed. E. Vaucheret (Paris, 1973) 98.

169 Dutch code   quoted in NICKLE, 337.

170 Article 65   Ib., 333.

170 Leicester   *Correspondence*, cit., 167.

171 Tournai garrison   Quoted in CRUICKSHANK (1971) 73.

172 Gonzalo   Quoted in MARIÉJOL, 208.

173 Monluc   *Commentaries*, ed. A. W. Evans (London, n.d.) 187.

173 Machiavelli   Op. cit., tr. Farnsworth, 145–6.

173 Cicero   *Philippics*, tr. W. C. A. Ker, Loeb Classical Library (London, 1926) 245–7.

174 Caesar   *The Gallic war*, tr. M. J. Edwards, Loeb Classical Library (London, 1937) 115–17.

174 Le Roy   *Enseignements d'Isocrates et Xenophon* . . . (Paris, 1568) 70.

175 Alviano   Paraphrased in Marino Sanuto, *Diarii*, ed. R. Fulin et al., 58 vols. (Venice, 1879–1903) xxvii, columns 126–7.

175 Gruffydd   Quoted in M. Bryn-Davies, cit., 344.

175 Guise   Quoted in R. C. Radouant, ed., *Guillaume du Vair, de l'éloquence françoise* (Paris, n.d.) 510–11.

176 Da Porto   Op. cit., 289–90.

177 De Bueil   VALE, 30.

177 Coningsby   *Journal of the Siege of Rouen*, ed. J. G. Nichols (Camden Miscellany, i, 1847) 26, 33, 35–6.

178 Drake   *State papers* . . . ed. J. K. Laughton, cit., vol. ii, 148.

178 Montaigne   Ed. cit., ii, 351.

Chapter 7

179 Guicciardini   *Storia d'Italia*, ed. C. Panigada (Bari, 1929) ii, 245.

179 Dutch ballad   Quoted in FISHMAN, 12.

180 Pavia   English ambassadors to Charles V, from Bologna. Quoted in CIPOLLA (1976) 237.

180 Poor peasant   Quoted in KAMEN, 40.

182 Henry VII   Quoted in GOODMAN, 155.

183 Woman   Quoted in DAVIES (1964) 244.

184 Frenchmen   *The Lisle letters*, ed. Muriel St Clare Byrne, vol. 6 (London, 1981) 22.

184 Surrey   Quoted in DAVIES in DUKE AND TAMSE, 5.

184 Chichester   Quoted in FALLS, 277.

185 Alba   Quoted in MALTBY, 244.

185 Antwerp merchant   Quoted in QUATREFAGES (1979) 269.

185 Dutch Articles   Tr. in NICKLE, 321.

186 Handbook, 1562   Printed in HALE (1983) 283.

186   Centorio   *Discorsi di guerra* (Venice, 1567) 78.
186   Vitoria   Quoted in Bernice Hamilton, *Political thought in sixteenth century Spain* (Oxford, 1963) 152–3.
186   Molina   Ib., 153.
187   Erasmus   'The soldier's confession', *Colloquies*, cit., 39.
188   German officer   Quoted in VAN DEURSEN in DUKE AND TAMSE, 33.
188   Utrecht chronicler   Ib., 24.
188   Landucci   Op. cit., 71–3, 181.
189   Henry VII   Quoted in GOODMAN, 221.
189   Guicciardini   *Storia d'Italia*, ed. cit., vol. 2, 138.
189   Carcès   Quoted in WOLFE, 197.
189   Brantôme   *Discours*, cit., 103.
190   Quartermaster   Quoted in HALICZER, 196.
190   Petition   Ib., 111–12.
191   Brantôme   *Discours*, cit., 137.
192   Bread or peace   Quoted in LLOYD, 146.
192   Novara   Alessandro Benedetti, *Diario de bello Carolino*, ed. and tr. Dorothy M. Schullian (New York, 1967) 159.
192   Monluc   *Commentaries*, ed. cit., 308 seq.
193   Essex   Quoted in BENEDICT, 218.
195   Raleigh   Quoted in JORGENSEN, 152–3.
195   Molina   Quoted in Hamilton, op. cit., 154.
195   Pavia   Nardi, op. cit., ii, 129–30.
195   Antwerp   Quoted in Abraham B. Feldman, 'Playwrights and pike-trailers in the Low Countries', *Notes and Queries* (1953) 185.
197   Frenchman   Quoted in SOLON, 88.
203   Venetian administrator   Quoted in MALLETT AND HALE, 364.
203   Discreet persons   Quoted in CRUICKSHANK (1966) 133.
205   Levelling   Quoted in G. Goold Walker, *The Honourable Artillery Company 1537–1926* (London, 1926) 15.
207   Montaigne   Ed. cit., ii, 339.
208   Palma   Quoted in MALLETT AND HALE, 419.

Chapter 8

211   Hooft   Quoted in PARKER in WINTER, 60.
214   Howes   Quoted in CIPOLLA (1976) 265–6.
215   Cecil   Quoted in DONALD, 363. My italics.
218   1628 Saltpetremen   Quoted in RUSSELL, 210.
220   From the body   Quoted in GAIER (1973) 274.
220   De Beatis   *The travel journal* . . . , ed. J. R. Hale (The Hakluyt Society, 1979) 93.
223   Raleigh   Quoted in H. Hamilton, *The English brass and copper industries to 1880* (London, repr. 1967) 6.
224   English negotiator   Quoted in FFOULKES, 111.
225   Van Aitzema   Quoted in VAN DEURSEN in DUKE AND TAMSE, 35.
226   Philip II   Quoted in PARKER in WINTER, 55.
226   Charles VIII   Ambrosiana Library, Milan, Ms. Z 226 Sup., Folder 2.
226   1572   Quoted in P. Boissonade, *Socialisme d'état: l'industrie et les classes industrielles en France* . . . *1453–1661* (Paris, 1927) 53.
226   1542   *Tudor royal proclamations*, cit., 313–14.

228 Hogge   Quoted in FFOULKES, 74.
231 Venetian ambassador   Quoted in KAMEN, 107.

Chapter 9

232 Florentine secretary   Quoted in Felix Gilbert, 'Florentine political assumptions in the period of Savonarola and Soderini', *Journal of the Warburg and Courtauld Institutes* (1957) 203.
232 Trivulzio   Quoted in GAIER (1984).
232 Wilson   Op. cit., 32.
234 Senators   Quoted in MALLETT AND HALE, 467.
235 Guicciardini   *Maxims*, cit., 79.
236 Spanish secretary   Quoted in PARKER (1979) 100.
236 Braudel   BRAUDEL, vol. 2, 842.
238 Venetian administrator   *Relazioni dei rettori veneti in terra ferma*, vol. 2, *Belluno, Feltre* (Milan, 1974) 259.
240 Fugger   Quoted in JEANNIN, 5.
241 Gresham   Quoted in EHRENBERG, 254.
243 Del Bene   Quoted in FRANÇOIS, 360.
243 Council of War   Quoted in THOMPSON (1976) 87.
250 Botero   Op. cit., 172.
250 Free city.   Quoted in HALE (1983) 33.
250 Garrison commander   Quoted in J. R. Hale, 'Terra ferma fortifications in the Cinquecento', *Florence and Venice: comparisons and relations*, ed. S. Bertelli (Florence, 1979) 180.
250 Alba   Quoted in MALTBY, 151.

Select bibliography

Adams, Robert P., *The better part of valor: More, Erasmus, Colet and Vives, on humanism, war and peace 1496–1535* (Seattle, 1962)

Allmand, C. T., ed., *War, literature and politics in the late middle ages* (Liverpool University Press, 1976)

Andersson, Christiane, *Dirnen, Krieger, Narren; ausgewählte Zeichnungen von Urs Graf* (Basel, 1978)

Armi e cultura nel Bresciano 1420–1870 (Ateneo di Brescia, 1981)

Aymard, Maurice, 'Le coût de la guerre', paper forthcoming in proceedings of Sedicesima Settimana di Studio, Istituto Datini, Prato, 4 May 1984

Barbour, V., *Capitalism in Amsterdam in the 17th century* (University of Michigan, 1963)

Barre-Duparcq, E. de la, 'L'art militaire pendant les guerres de religion, 1562–1598', *Séances et travaux de l'académie des sciences morales et politiques* (1863, pt. ii) 275–315, (1864, pt. i) 247–70, (pt. ii) 89–110, 263–83

Bayley, C. C., *War and society in Renaissance Florence* (University of Toronto, 1961)

Benedict, P., *Rouen during the wars of religion* (Cambridge University Press, 1980)

Bennassar, B., *The Spanish character: attitudes and mentalities from the sixteenth to the nineteenth centuries*, tr. B. Keen (London, 1979)

Bitton, A., *The French nobility in crisis 1560–1640* (Stanford University Press, 1969)

Blickle, Peter, tr. and intro. T. A. Brady and H. C. E. Midelfort, *The revolution of 1525. The German Peasants' War from a new perspective* (Johns Hopkins University Press, 1981)

Boas, Frederick S., 'The soldier in Elizabethan and later English drama', in ib., *Queen Elizabeth in drama and related subjects* (London, 1950)

Bonney, Richard, *The King's debts: finance and politics in France 1589–1661* (Oxford, 1981)

Boutaric, Edgard, *Institutions militaires de la France avant les armées permanentes* (Paris, 1863)

Boynton, Lindsay, *The Elizabethan militia* (London, 1967)

Brantôme (Pierre de Bourdeille), ed. Etienne Vaucheret, *Discours sur les colonels de l'infanterie de France* (Paris, 1973)

Braudel, Fernand, *The Mediterranean and the Mediterranean world in the age of Philip II*, tr. Sian Reynolds, 2 vols. (London, 1972–3)

Brusten, Ch., *L'armée bourguignonne de 1465 à 1468* (Brussels, 1953)

Buisseret, David, *Sully and the growth of centralized government in France 1598–1610* (London, 1968)

Buisseret, David, *Henry IV* (London, 1984)

Burke, P., ed., *Economy and society in early modern Europe* (London, 1972)

Canestrini, G., *Documenti per servire alla storia della milizia italiana dal XIII sec. al XVI sec., Archivio Storico Italiano*, vol. 15 (1851)

Chaunu, Pierre, *L'Espagne de Charles V*, 2 vols. (Paris, 1973)

Chevalier, B., *Tours, ville royale (1356–1520). Origine et développement d'une capitale à la fin du moyen âge* (Louvain-Paris, 1975)

Chevalier, B., *Les bonnes villes de France du XIVe au XVIe siècle* (Paris, 1982)

Cipolla, Carlo, ed., *The Fontana economic history of Europe: the sixteenth and seventeenth centuries* (London, 1974)

Cipolla, Carlo, *Before the industrial revolution* (London, 1976)

Clark, Sir George, *War and society in the seventeenth century* (Cambridge University Press, 1958)

Clark, Peter, *English provincial society from the Reformation to the Revolution: religion, politics and society in Kent 1500–1640* (Hassocks, 1977)

Cockburn, J. S., ed., *Crime in England* (Princeton University Press, 1978)

Cockle, Maurice J. D., *Bibliography of military books up to 1642* (London, 1900)

Cohn, Henry J., *The government of the Rhine Palatinate in the fifteenth century* (Oxford, 1965)

Contamine, Philippe, *Guerre, état et société à la fin du moyen âge. Études sur les armées des rois de France 1337–1494* (Paris, 1972)

Contamine, Philippe, 'The war literature of the late middle ages: the treatises of Robert de Balsac and Beraud Stuart, Lord of Aubigny, (in Allmand)

Contamine, Philippe, 'L'idée de guerre à la fin du moyen âge: aspects juridiques et éthiques', *Académie des inscriptions et belles-lettres: comptes rendus* (January–March, 1979)

Contamine, Philippe, *La guerre au moyen âge* (Nouvelle Clio, Paris, 1980)

Contamine, Philippe, 'Les industries de la guerre dans la France de la Renaissance', paper forthcoming in proceedings of Sedicesima Settimana di Studio, Istituto Datini, Prato, 7 May 1984

Cornwall, Julian, *Revolt of the peasantry 1549* (London, 1977)

Corvisier, André, 'Le mort de soldat, depuis la fin du moyen âge', *Revue Historique* (1975) 3–30

Corvisier, André, *Armies and societies in Europe, 1494–1789*, tr. A. T. Siddall (Indiana University Press, 1979)

Cruickshank, C. G., *Elizabeth's army* (Oxford, 2nd ed., 1966)

Cruickshank, C. G., *Army royal: Henry VIII's invasion of France 1513* (Oxford, 1969)

Cruickshank, C. G., *The English occupation of Tournai 1513–1519* (Oxford, 1971)

Davies, C. S. L., 'Provisions for armies, 1509–1550: a study in the effectiveness of early Tudor government', *Economic History Review* (1964) 234–48

Davies, C. S. L., 'The English people and war in the early sixteenth century' (in Duke and Tamse)

Davies, C. S. L., 'England and the French war, 1557–9', in Loach, Jennifer and Tittler, Robert, *The mid-Tudor polity c.1540–1560* (London, 1980)

Davis, James C., ed., *Pursuit of power. Venetian ambassadors' reports on Spain, Turkey, and France in the age of Philip II, 1560–1600* (New York, 1970)

Davis, Natalie Zemon, *Society and culture in early modern France* (Stanford University Press, 1975)

Davis, Natalie Zemon, *The return of Martin Guerre: imposture and infidelity in a sixteenth century village* (Harvard University Press, 1983)

Davis, Ralph, *Rise of the Atlantic economies* (London, 1973)

Delbrück, H., *Geschichte der Kriegskunst im Rahmen der politischen Geschichte*, vol. iv (Berlin, 1920)

Delumeau, J., *La peur en occident, XIVe–XVIIIe siècle. Une cité assiégée* (Paris, 1978)

Dickinson, G., 'Some notes on the Scottish army in the first half of the sixteenth century', *Scottish Historical Review* (1949) 133–45

Dietz, F. L., *English public finance 1558–1641* (New York, 1932)

Dionisotti, C., 'Lepanto nella cultura italiana del tempo', *Lettere Italiane* (1971) 473–92

Domínguez Ortiz, A., *The golden age of Spain* (London, 1971)

Donald, M. B., *Elizabethan copper. The history of the Company of Mines Royal, 1568–1605* (Oxford, 1955)

Donald, M. B., *Elizabethan monopolies. The history of the Company of Mineral and Battery Works, 1568–1604* (London, 1961)

Doucet, R., 'L'état des finances de 1523', *Bulletin Philologique et Historique du Comité des Travaux Historiques et Scientifiques* (1920) 5–143

Doucet, R., *Les institutions de la France au XVIe siècle*, 2 vols. (Paris, 1948)

Duke, A. C. and Tamse, C. A., *Britain and the Netherlands*, vol. 6, *War and society: papers delivered for the sixth Anglo-Dutch Historical Conference* (The Hague, 1977)

Earle, P., ed., *Essays in European economic history 1500–1800* (Oxford, 1984)

Egg, Erich, *Der Tiroler Geschützguss 1400–1800* (Innsbruck, 1961)

Ehrenberg, Richard, *Capital and finance in the age of the Renaissance* (London, 1928)

Elliott, J. H., *Imperial Spain 1469–1716* (London, 1963)

Elliott, J. H., *Europe divided 1559–1598* (London, 1968)

Elliott, J. H., 'A question of reputation? Spanish foreign policy in the seventeenth century', *Journal of Modern History* (1983) 474–83

Elton, G. R., *Reformation Europe 1517–1559* (London, 1963)

Elton, G. R., *Studies in Tudor and Stuart politics and government*, 2 vols. (Cambridge University Press, 1974)

Elton, G. R., 'Taxation for war and peace in early-Tudor England' (in Winter)

Esler, Anthony, *The aspiring mind of the Elizabethan younger generation* (Duke University Press, 1966)

Essen, Léon van der, *Alexandre Farnese*, 5 vols. (Brussels, 1937)

Falls, Cyril, *Elizabeth's Irish wars* (repr. London, 1970)

Fernandez-Santamaria, J. A., *The state, war and peace: Spanish political thought in the Renaissance, 1516–1559* (Cambridge University Press, 1977)

Ffoulkes, Charles, *The gun-founders of England* (London, 2nd ed., 1969)

Fichtner, Paula Sutter, *Ferdinand I of Austria, 1503–1564: the politics of dynasticism in the age of the Reformation* (Boulder, 1982)

Finer, E. I., 'State and nation-building in Europe: the role of the military', in C. Tilly, ed., *The formation of national states in Europe* (Princeton University Press, 1975)

Fishman, Jane Susannah, *Boerenverdriet: violence between peasants and soldiers in early modern Netherlandish art* (Ann Arbor, 1982)

Flinn, Michael W., *The European demographic system, 1500–1820* (Harvester, 1981)

François, Michel, 'Albisse del Bene, surintendant général des finances françaises en Italie, 1551–1556', *Bibliothèque de l'École des Chartes* (1933) 337–60

Frauenholz, Eugen von, *Entwicklungsgeschichte des deutschen Heerwesens*, vol. 2 parts i and ii (Munich, 1936–7)

Frauenholz, Eugen von, *Lazarus von Schwendi, der erste deutsche Verkünder der allgemein Wehrpflicht* (Hamburg, 1939)

Friedrichs, C. R., *Urban society in an age of war: Nordlingen, 1580–1720* (Princeton University Press, 1979)

Gaier, Claude, 'Analysis of military forces in the principality of Liège and the county of Looz from the twelfth to the fifteenth century', *Studies in Medieval and Renaissance History* (1965) 205–61

Gaier, Claude, *L'industrie et le commerce des armes dans les anciennes principautés belges du XIIIe siècle à la fin du XVe siècle* (Paris, 1973)

Gaier, Claude, 'Le commerce des armes en Europe au XVe siècle' (in *Armi . . . Bresciano*)

Gaier, Claude, 'Pauvreté et armement individuel en Europe occidentale au moyen âge', forthcoming in proceedings of Sedicesima Settimana di Studio, Istituto Datini, Prato, 7 May 1984

Gardot, André, 'Le droit de la guerre dans l'oeuvre des capitaines français du XVIe siècle', *Académie de droit international: Recueil des cours* (1948) 397–539

Gilbert, Felix, 'Machiavelli: the renaissance of the art of war', in *Makers of Modern Strategy*, ed. E. M. Earle (Princeton University Press, 1943)

Gilbert, Felix, *The pope, his banker and Venice* (Harvard University Press, 1980)

Gilbert, Felix, 'Venetian war finances during the war of the League of Cambrai' (typescript, 1983, kindly lent by the author)

Goodman, Anthony, *The Wars of the Roses. Military activity and English society, 1452–97* (London, 1981)

Gutmann, Myron P., *War and rural life in the early modern Low Countries* (Princeton University Press, 1980)

Hahlweg, W., *Die Heeresreform der Oranier und die Antike* (Berlin, 1941)

Hale, J. R., Chapters on war in *New Cambridge Modern History*, vols. 1, 2, 3 (Cambridge University Press, 1957, 1958, 1968)

Hale, J. R., *Renaissance war studies* (London, 1983)

Hale, J. R., see Mallett and Hale

Haliczer, Stephen, *The comuneros of Castile: the forging of a revolution, 1475–1521* (University of Wisconsin Press, 1981)

Harding, R. N., *Anatomy of a power-elite: the provincial governors of early modern France* (New Haven and London, 1978)

Hayes-McCoy, Gerald A., *Scots mercenary forces in Ireland, 1565–1603* (Dublin, 1954)

Heers, J., *Gênes au XVe siècle. Activité économique et problèmes sociaux* (Paris, 1961)

Herlihy, David, 'Vieillir à Florence au Quattrocento', *Annales* (1969) 1338–52

Herlihy, David, 'Some psychological and social roots of violence in the Tuscan cities', in Lauro Martines, ed., *Violence and disorder in Italian cities, 1240–1500* (University of California Press, 1972)

Hexter, J. H., *The vision of politics on the eve of the Reformation: More, Machiavelli and Seyssel* (New York, 1973)

Hillgarth, J. N., *The Spanish kingdoms*, vol. 2, *1410–1516: Castilian hegemony* (Oxford University Press, 1978)

Howard, Michael, *War in European history* (Oxford University Press, 1976)

Hoyer, Siegfried, *Das Militärwesen im deutschen Bauernkrieg 1524–1526* (East Berlin, 1975)

Hoyer, Siegfried, 'Arms and military organization in the German Peasant War', in Scribner, B. and Benecke, G., *The German Peasant War of 1525* (London, 1979)

Huppert, George, *Les bourgeois gentilshommes: an essay on the definition of elites in Renaissance France* (Chicago University Press, 1977)

Hurstfield, Joel, 'County government: Wiltshire *c.* 1530–*c.* 1650', in ib., *Freedom, corruption and government in Elizabethan England* (London, 1973)

Jähns, Max, *Handbuch einer Geschichte des Kriegswesens* (Leipzig, 1880)

James, Mervyn, *English politics and the concept of honour, 1485–1642*, Past and Present supplement no. 3 (1978)

January, Peter, *War, defence and society in the Venetian terraferma 1560–1630* (London, PhD thesis, 1983)

Jeannin, P., *Merchants of the sixteenth century* (New York, 1972)

Jesperson, Knud J. V., 'Social change and military revolution in early modern Europe', *Historical Journal* (1983) 1–14

Johnson, James Turner, *Ideology, reason and the limitation of war: religious and secular concepts 1200–1740* (Princeton University Press, 1975)

Jorgensen, Paul A., *Shakespeare's military world* (University of California Press, 1956)

Kamen, H., *The iron century. Social change in Europe 1550–1660* (London, 1971)

Keen, Maurice, 'Brotherhood in arms', *History* (February 1962) 1–17

Keen, Maurice, *Chivalry* (Yale University Press, 1984)

Kiernan, V. G., 'Foreign mercenaries and absolute monarchy', in *Crisis in Europe 1560–1660*, ed. Trevor Aston (London, 1965)

Kiernan, V. G., *State and society in Europe 1550–1650* (Oxford, 1980)

Kipling, G., *The triumph of honour: Burgundian origins of the English Renaissance* (Leiden, 1977)

Knecht, R. J., *Francis I* (Cambridge University Press, 1982)

Knecht, R. J., *French Renaissance monarchy: Francis I and Henry II* (London, 1984)

Koenigsberger, H. G., *The government of Sicily under Philip II of Spain* (London, 1951)

Koenigsberger, H. G., *The Habsburgs and Europe 1516–1660* (Cornell University Press, 1971)

Koenigsberger, H. G. and Mosse, George C., *Europe in the sixteenth century* (London, 1968)

La guerre et la paix, Actes du CIe Congrès national des sociétés savantes, Lille, 1976. Section de philologie et d'histoire jusqu'à 1610 (Paris, 1978)

Labande-Mailfert, Y., *Charles VIII et son milieu (1470–1498): la jeunesse au pouvoir* (Paris, 1975)

Lapeyre, H., 'L'art de la guerre au temps de Charles-Quint', in ib., *Charles-Quint et son temps* (Paris, 1959)

Le Roy Ladourie, E., *Les paysans de Languedoc*, 2 vols. (Paris, 1966)

Le Roy Ladourie, E., 'History that stands still', in ib., *The mind and method of the historian*, tr. S. and B. Reynolds (University of Chicago Press, 1981)

Le Roy Ladourie, E. and Morineau, M., *De 1450 à 1660: paysannerie et croissance*, vol. 1 part ii of *Histoire économique et sociale de la France*, ed. F. Braudel and E. Labrousse (Paris, 1977)

Lindley, K. J., 'Riot prevention and control in early Stuart London', *Transactions of the Royal Historical Society* (1983) 109–26

Livet, Georges, *Les guerres de religion (1559–1598)* (Paris, 1962)

Lloyd, Howell A., *The Rouen campaign, 1590–1592: politics, warfare and the early-modern state* (Oxford, 1973)

Lot, Ferdinand, *Recherches sur les effectifs des armées françaises des guerres d'Italie aux guerres de religion 1494–1562* (Paris, 1962)

Lovett, A. W., 'Francisco de Lixalde: a Spanish paymaster in the Netherlands (1567–77)', *Tijdschrift voor Geschiedenis* (1971) 14–23

Major, J. Russell, 'Noble income, inflation and the wars of religion in France', *American Historical Review* (1981) 21–48

Mallett, M. E., *Mercenaries and their masters: warfare in Renaissance Italy* (London, 1974)

Mallett, M. E., 'Preparations for war in Florence and Venice in the second half of the sixteenth century', in *Florence and Venice: comparisons and relations*, ed. Sergio Bertelli et al. (Florence, 1979)

Mallett, M. E., 'The military organization of Florence and Venice in the fifteenth century', forthcoming in proceedings of Sedicesima Settimana di Studio, Istituto Datini, Prato, 7 May, 1984

Mallett, M. E. and Hale, J. R., *The military organization of a Renaissance state: Venice c. 1400 to 1617* (Cambridge University Press, 1984)

Maltby, William S., *Alba, a biography of Fernando Alvarez de Toledo, third duke of Alba, 1507–1582* (University of California Press, 1983)

Mandrou, R., *Classes et luttes de classes en France au début du XVIIe siècle* (Florence, 1965)

Mariéjol, P. H., *The Spain of Ferdinand and Isabella*, tr. B. Keen (Rutgers University Press, 1961)

McFarlane, K. B., *The nobility of later medieval England* (Oxford, 1973)

McNeill, W. H., *The pursuit of power: technology, armed force and society since A.D. 1000* (University of Chicago Press, 1982)

Michaud, H., 'Aux origines du secrétariat d'état à la guerre: les règlements de 1617–1619', *Revue d'Histoire Moderne et Contemporaine* (1972) 389–413.

Michaud, H., 'Les institutions militaires des guerres d'Italie aux guerres de religion', *Revue Historique* (1977) 29–43

Millar, Gilbert John, *Mercenaries and auxiliaries: foreign soldiers in the armies of Henry VII and Henry VIII, with special reference to their origins, recruitment and employment in the French war of 1544–46*, 2 vols. (University Microfilms, 1982)

Miskimin, H. A., *The economy of later Renaissance Europe, 1460–1600* (Cambridge University Press, 1978)

Möller, Hans-Michael, *Das Regiment der Landsknechte: Untersuchungen zu Verfassung, Recht und Selbsverständnis in deutschen Söldnerheeren des 16. Jahrhunderts* (Wiesbaden, 1976)

Mousnier, Roland, *The institutions of France under the absolute monarchy 1598–1789* (University of Chicago Press, 1979)

Neale, Sir John, 'Elizabeth and the Netherlands, 1586–7', *English Historical Review* (1930) 373–96

Nef, J. U., *War and human progress: an essay on the rise of industrial civilization* (Harvard University Press, 1950)

Nef, J. U., *Industry and government in France and England, 1540–1640* (Ithaca, 1957)

Nickle, B. H., *The military reforms of Prince Maurice of Orange* (University Microfilms, Ann Arbor, 1975)

Oestreich, G., *Neostoicism and the early modern state* (Cambridge University Press, 1982)

Oman, Sir Charles, *A history of war in the sixteenth century* (London, 1937)

Outhwaite, R. B., *Inflation in Tudor and early Stuart England* (London, 1969)

Pablo, Jean de, 'Contribution a l'étude de l'histoire des institutions militaires huguenotes, ii, L'armée huguenote entre 1562 et 1573', *Archiv für Reformationsgeschichte* (1957) 192–216

Parker, Geoffrey, *The army of Flanders and the Spanish road 1567–1659* (Cambridge University Press, 1972)

Parker, Geoffrey, 'War and economic change: the economic costs of the Dutch revolt' (in Winter)

Parker, Geoffrey, 'The "Military Revolution", 1560–1660 – a myth?', in ib., *Spain and the Netherlands, 1559–1659* (London, 1979)

Parker, Geoffrey, 'Mutiny and discontent in the Spanish army of Flanders, 1572–1607', in ib., *Spain and the Netherlands, 1559–1659* (London, 1979)

Pearce, Brian, 'Elizabethan food policy and the armed forces', *Economic History Review* (1942) 39–46

Perry, M. A., *Crime and society in early modern Seville* (Hanover, USA, 1980)

Pieri, Piero, 'La scienza militare italiana nel rinascimento', *Rivista Storica Italiana* (1933) 262–81

Pieri, Piero, *Il rinascimento e la crisi militare italiana* (Turin, 1952)

Pieri, Piero, 'Sur les dimensions de l'histoire militaire', *Annales* (1963) 625–38

Pieri, Piero, 'L'evoluzione dell'arte militare nei secoli XV, XVI e XVII e la guerra del secolo XVIII', *Nuove Questioni di Storia Moderna*, vol. 2 (Milan, 1966) 1123–79

Postan, M. M., 'The costs of the Hundred Years War', in ib., *Essays in medieval agriculture and general problems of the medieval economy* (Cambridge University Press, 1973) 63–80

Pound, J. F., *Poverty and vagrancy in Tudor England* (London, 1971)

Puddu, Raffaele, *Il soldato gentiluomo: autoritratto d'una società guerriera: la Spagna del Cinquecento* (Bologna, 1982)

Quatrefages, René, *Los tercios españoles, 1567–1577* (Madrid, 1979)

Quatrefages, René, 'Les industries de la guerre en Espagne au XVIe siècle', forthcoming in proceedings of Sedicesima Settimana di Studio, Istituto Datini, Prato, 7 May 1984

Rabb, Theodore A., *The struggle for stability in modern Europe* (New York, 1975)

Read, Conyers, ed., *William Lambarde and local government* (Cornell University Press, 1962)

Redlich, Fritz, 'De praeda militari', *Vierteljahrschrift für Sozial- und Wirtschaftsgeschichte* (1956)

Redlich, Fritz, *The German military enterpriser and his work force*, vol. 1 (Wiesbaden, 1964)

Reichel, D., ed., *1476, essai d'approche pleuri-disciplinaire d'une action militaire du XVe siècle* (Lausanne, 1976)

Riccotti, E., *Storia delle compagnie di ventura in Italia*, 2 vols. (Turin, 2nd ed., 1893)

Richardson, Walter Cecil, *Stephen Vaughan, financial agent of Henry VIII: a study of financial relations with the Low Countries* (Louisiana University Press, 1953)

Roberts, Michael, *Gustavus Adolphus: a history of Sweden 1611–1632*, 2 vols. (London, 1953–8)

Roberts, Michael, *The military revolution, 1560–1660* (Belfast, 1956)

Rossiaud, Jeynes, 'Prostitution, youth, and society in the towns of Southeastern France in the fifteenth century', in Forster, R. and Ranum, O., eds., *Deviants and the abandoned in French society: selections from Annales* (Baltimore, 1978)

Russell, Conrad S. R., 'Monarchies, wars and estates in England, France, and Spain c. 1580–c. 1640', *Legislative Studies Quarterly* (May 1982) 205–20

Schwoerer, Lois G., *No standing armies! The antimilitary ideology in seventeenth-century England* (Baltimore, 1974)

Seguin, J.-P., *L'information en France de Louis XII à Henri II* (Geneva, 1961)

Sharp, Buchanan, *In contempt of all authority: rural artisans and riot in the West of England, 1586–1660* (University of California Press, 1980)

Silberner, E., *La guerre dans la pensée économique du XVIe au XVIIIe siècle* (Paris, 1939)

Smith, A. Hassall, *County and court. Government and politics in Norfolk, 1558–1603* (Oxford, 1974)

Smith, A. Hassall, 'Militia rates and militia statutes 1558–1662', in Clark, P., Smith, A. G. P. and Tyacke, N., eds., *The English Commonwealth 1547–1640* (London, 1979)

Solon, P. D., 'Popular response to standing military forces in fifteenth century France', *Studies in the Renaissance* (1972) 78–111

Stewart, Paul, 'The soldier, the bureaucrat and fiscal records in the army of Ferdinand and Isabella', *Hispanic American Historical Review* (1969) 281–92

Stewart, Paul, 'Military command and the development of the viceroyalty under Ferdinand and Isabella', *Journal of Medieval and Renaissance Studies* (1975) 223–42

Stone, Lawrence, *The crisis of the aristocracy, 1554–1641* (Oxford, 1965)

Taylor, Frederick L., *Art of war in Italy, 1494–1529* (Cambridge, 1921)

Thoen, E., 'Warfare and the countryside: social and economic aspects of military destruction in Flanders during the late middle ages and the early modern period', in *The Low Countries History Yearbook*, vol. 13 (1980)

Thompson, I. A. A., *War and government in Habsburg Spain, 1560–1620* (London, 1976)

Thompson, I. A. A., 'Taxation, military spending and the domestic economy in Castile in the later sixteenth century' (typescript, 1983, kindly lent me by the author)

Thompson, I. A. A., 'The impact of war: war in the 1590s' (typescript, 1983, kindly lent me by the author)

Tracy, James D., *The politics of Erasmus: a pacifist intellectual and his political milieu* (University of Toronto, 1978)

Vale, Malcolm, *War and chivalry. Warfare and aristocratic culture in England, France and Burgundy at the end of the Middle Ages* (London, 1981)

Van den Boogaar, E. et al., eds., *Johan Moritz van Nassau – Siegen 1604–1679. A humanist prince in Europe and Brazil* (The Hague, 1979)

Van Deursen, A. Th., 'Holland's experiences of war during the revolt of the Netherlands' (in Duke and Tamse)

Van Doren, Llewain Scott, 'War taxation, institutional change and social conflict in provincial France – the royal taille in Dauphiné, 1494–1559', *Proceedings of the American Philosophical Society* (February 1977) 70–95

Vaughan, R., *Valois Burgundy* (London, 1975)

Vaux de Foletier, F. de, *Galiot de Genouillac, maître de l'artillerie de France (1465–1546)* (Paris, 1925)

Vicens Vives, J., 'The administrative structure of the state in the sixteenth and seventeenth centuries', in Cohn, Henry J., ed., *Government in Reformation Europe 1520–1560* (London, 1971)

Vigón, Jorge, *El ejército de los reyes católicos* (Madrid, 1968)

Weisser, Michael R., *Crime and punishment in early modern Europe* (Brighton, 1982)

Wernham, R. B., 'Queen Elizabeth and the Portugal expedition of 1589', *English Historical Review* (1951) 1–26, 194–218

Wernham, R. B., 'Elizabethan war aims and strategy', in Bindoff, S. T. et al., eds., *Elizabethan government and society: essays presented to Sir John Neale* (London, 1961)

Wernham, R. B., *The making of Elizabethan foreign policy* (University of California Press, 1980)

Wernham, R. B., *After the Armada: Elizabethan England and the struggle for Western Europe 1588–1595* (London, 1983)

Williams, Penry, 'Rebellion and revolution in early modern England', in Foot, M. R. D., ed., *War and society: essays in memory of John Western* (London, 1973)

Williams, Penry, *The Tudor regime* (Oxford, 1979)

Winter, J. M., ed., *War and economic development* (Cambridge University Press, 1975)

Wolfe, Martin, *The fiscal system of Renaissance France* (New Haven, 1972)

Zeller, G., 'La vie aventureuse des classes supérieurs en France sous l'Ancien Régime: brigandage et piraterie', *Cahiers Internationaux de Sociologie* (1960) 13–22

Addenda to Bibliography

Abulafia, David, ed., *The French Descent into Renaissance Italy, 1494–95. Antecedents and Effects* (Aldershot, 1995)
Adams, Simon, 'Tactics or Politics? The Military Revolution and the Hapsburg Hegemony, 1525–1648' (in Lynn, 1990)
Anglo, Sydney, ed., *Chivalry in the Renaissance* (Woodbridge, 1990)

Baumgartner, Frederick J., 'The final Demise of the Medieval Knight in France', in Jerome Friedman, ed., *Regnum, Religio et Ratio: Essays presented to Robert M. Kingdom* (Kirksville MO, 1987) pp. 9–17
Baumgartner, Frederick J., *From Spear to Flintlock: A History of War in Europe and the Middle East to the French Revolution* (New York, 1991)
Black, Jeremy, *The Origins of War in Early Modern Europe* (Atlantic Highlands NJ and Edinburgh, 1989)
Black, Jeremy, *A Military Revolution? Military Change and European Society, 1500–1800* (Atlantic Highlands NJ and Basingstoke, 1991)

Chambers, David S., Clough, Cecil H., and Mallett, Michael E., eds., *War, Culture and Society in Renaissance Venice: Essays in Honour of John Hale* (London, 1993)
Contamine, Philippe, trans. M. Jones, *War in the Middle Ages* (Oxford, 1984)
Cook, Weston F., Jr., 'The Cannon Conquest of Nasrid Spain and the End of the Reconquista', *Journal of Military History*, 57, 1993, pp. 43–70
Corfis, I., and Wolfe, M., eds., *The Medieval City under Siege* (Woodbridge, 1995)
Cresti, C., Fara, A., and Lamerini, D., *Architettura militare nell'Europa del XVI secolo* (Siena, 1988)

DeVries, Kelly, *Medieval Military Technology* (Peterborough, Ontario, 1992)
DeVries, Kelly, 'Siegecraft in late medieval Italy' (in Corfis and Wolfe)
Downing, Brian M., *The Military Revolution and Political Change: Origins of Democracy and Autocracy in Early Modern Europe* (Princeton, 1992)

Eltis, David, 'Towns and Defense in Later Mediaeval Germany', *Nottingham Medieval Studies*, 33, 1989, pp. 91–103

Eltis, David, *The Military Revolution in Sixteenth-Century Europe* (London and New York, 1995)

Glete, J., *Navies and Nations. Warships, Navies and State Building in Europe and America, 1500–1860* (Stockholm, 1993)

Guillerm, A., *La pierre et le vent. Fortifications et marine en occident* (Paris, 1985)

Hale, J. R., 'A humanistic Visual Aid; the military Diagram in the Renaissance', *Renaissance Studies*, II, 1988, pp. 280–98

Hale, J. R., *Artists and Warfare in the Renaissance* (New Haven CT and London, 1990)

Hale, J. R., 'Venezia e la rivoluzione militare europea', in *Crisi e rinnovamenti nell'autunno del rinascimento a Venezia*, ed. V. Branca and C. Ossola (Florence, 1991)

Hale, J. R., *The Civilization of Europe in the Renaissance* (New York and London, 1993)

Hall, Bert S., 'The Changing Face of Siege Warfare: Technology and Tactics in Transition' (in Corfis and Wolfe)

Hall, Bert S., *Weapons and Warfare in Renaissance Europe. Gunpowder, Technology and Tactics* (Baltimore, 1997)

Heers, J., *Fortifications, portes de ville, places publiques dans le monde méditerranéan* (Paris, 1985)

Howard, Michael, Andreopolos, George J., and Shulman, Mark R., *The Laws of War. Constraints on Warfare in the Western World* (New Haven CT and London, 1994)

Kennedy, P., *The Rise and Fall of Great Powers: Economic Change and Military Conflict from 1500 to 2000* (New York, 1987)

Kingra, Mahinder S., 'The *Trace italienne* and the Military Revolution during the Eighty Years' War', *Journal of Military History*, 57, 1993, pp. 431–46

Knecht, R. J., *French Renaissance Monarchy: Francis I and Henry II* (London, 1996)

Knecht, R. J., *The French Wars of Religion* (2nd edn., London, 1996)

Lynn, John A., 'Tactical Evolution in the French Army, 1560–1660', *French Historical Studies*, 14, 1985, pp. 176–91

Lynn, John A., ed., *Tools of War: Instruments, Ideas and Institutions of Warfare, 1445–1871* (Urbana, 1990)

McNeill, W. H., *The Age of Gunpowder Empires* (Washington DC, 1989)

Mallett, Michael E., 'Venice in the War of Ferrara, 1482–84' (in Chambers, Clough and Mallett)

Mallett, Michael E., 'The changing face of Siege Warfare: Technology and Tactics in Transition' (in Corfis and Wolfe)

Needham, J., Ho Ping-Yu, Lu Gwei-Djen and Wang Ling, *Science and Civilization* vol. IV, Part VII, *Military Technology, the Gunpowder Epic* (Cambridge, 1986) n.b. on European firearms

Paret, Peter, *Imagined Battles: Reflections of War in European Art* (Chapel Hill NC and London, 1997)

Parker, Geoffrey, *The Military Revolution: Military Innovation and the Rise of the West, 1500–1800* (Cambridge, 1988; 2nd edn, Cambridge, 1996)

Pepper, Simon, and Adams, Nicholas, *Firearms and Fortifications. Military Architecture and Siege Warfare in Sixteenth-Century Siena* (Chicago, 1986)

Pepper, Simon, 'Fortress and Fleet: The Defence of Venice's Mainland Greek Colonies in the Late Fifteenth Century' (in Chambers, Clough and Mallett)

Pepper, Simon, 'Castles and Cannon in the Naples Campaign of 1494–95' (in Abulafia)

Potter, David, *War and Government in the French Provinces: Picardy, 1470–1560* (Cambridge, 1993)

Rogers, Clifford J., 'The Military Revolutions of the Hundred Years War', *Journal of Military History*, 57, 1993, pp. 241–79

Rogers, Clifford J., ed., *The Military Revolution Debate. Readings in the Military Transformations of Early Modern Europe* (Boulder, Colo., and Oxford, 1995)

Saunders, Andrew, *Fortress Britain: Artillery Fortification in the British Isles and Ireland* (Liphook, 1989)

Tallett, F., *War and Society in early Modern Europe, 1495–1715* (London, 1992)

Van Crefeld, Martin, *Technology and War: From 2000 BC to the Present* (New York, 1989)

Index

(Names and places are in Roman, subjects in italic type)